BEGINNING
WITH HEIDEGGER

D1570486

MICHAEL MILLERMAN

BEGINNING *WITH* HEIDEGGER

Strauss, Rorty, Derrida, Dugin &
the Philosophical Constitution of the Political

ARKTOS
LONDON 2020

ISBN	978-1-912975-79-2 (Paperback)
	978-1-912975-80-8 (Hardback)
	978-1-912975-81-5 (Ebook)
EDITING	John Sebastian Cumpston
COVER & LAYOUT	Tor Westman

⊕ Arktos.com   ￼ fb.com/Arktos   🐦 @arktosmedia   ⊙ arktosmedia

CONTENTS

CHAPTER ONE

CHAPTER TWO

Abstract

This book is based upon my doctoral dissertation. In it I examine how Leo Strauss, Richard Rorty, Jacques Derrida, and Alexander Dugin responded to Martin Heidegger's *inceptual* thought in defining and relating philosophy and the political. The *Introduction* discusses the general concepts, motivations, and aims of this study. Chapter One provides a précis of Heidegger's philosophy from *The History of the Concept of Time* to his middle-period writings. Chapter Two compares Strauss and Heidegger on the Idea of the Good in Plato. Chapter Three argues that Rorty is prevented from a philosophically serious reading of Heidegger by his *a priori* social-democratic commitments. Chapter Four distinguishes the spaces of Derridean and Heideggerian political philosophy. Chapter Five is an account of Dugin's embrace and extension of Heidegger's inceptual thought. The Conclusion analyses obstacles blocking access to Heidegger in political theory and argues for a new way forward.

For Ruth and Lola

Introduction

Since the beginning of the twentieth century, the rational foundations of liberal democracy have been attacked and undermined by anti-liberal philosophers. Foremost among them is Martin Heidegger. Heidegger and the philosophical revolution he initiated posed such a challenge to liberal democracy that more than a few of its defenders were faced with a dilemma once expressed by Leo Strauss: the crisis of rational liberalism needs to be solved with the help of great thinkers, but the only great thinker of the time, Heidegger, is a critic of rational liberalism.[1] Scholars have long studied responses to Heidegger's thought by political theorists partially sympathetic to his philosophy, yet completely opposed to his illiberal, Nazi politics. Wolin and Fleischacker, for instance, have both examined the strange fact that many of Heidegger's "children" or "followers," such as Hannah Arendt, Hans Jonas, Herbert Marcuse, Karl Löwith, Emmanuel Levinas, and Leo Strauss, were Jewish. Woessner, Janicaud, and Love most recently have focused on regional responses, producing works on Heidegger in America, France, Russia and Eastern Europe.[2]

---

1   Leo Strauss, "Existentialism," *Interpretation* 22, No. 3 (1995).

2   Richard Wolin, *Heidegger's Children: Hannah Arendt, Karl Löwith, Hans Jonas, and Herbert Marcuse* (Princeton: Princeton University Press, 2015); Samuel Fleischacker, ed. *Heidegger's Jewish Followers: Essays on Hannah Arendt, Leo Strauss, Hans Jonas, and Emmanuel Levinas* (Pittsburgh: Duquesne University Press, 2008). *Heidegger in Russia and Eastern Europe* ed. Jeff Love (Lanham: Rowman & Littlefield, 2017); Martin Woessner, *Heidegger in America* (New

However, despite work on Heidegger's philosophical challenge to liberalism that focuses on isolated geographical regions or political perspectives, scholars to date have done little to compare the philosophical and political significance of responses to Heidegger across a broader geographical and political spectrum. At the same time, Heidegger has become increasingly relevant to those who wish to attack liberalism, as well as to those who wish to defend it.[3] The result is that the political possibilities of Heideggerian philosophy have not been grasped as completely as can be done through a comparative approach. To fill the gap, the present work brings together four major responses from four regions — Germany, America, France, and Russia — encompassing political positions spanning far left to far right, to show how Leo Strauss, Richard Rorty, Jacques Derrida, and Alexander Dugin constitute their understanding of philosophy and the political, as well as the relationship between the two, in response to the challenge of Heidegger. This broad, comparative approach to encounters with Heidegger across a geographic and political spectrum will clarify the underlying self-understanding of the post-Heideggerian left and right as well as the liberal center and bring into relief the theoretical issue of competing philosophical constitutions of the political.

Heidegger wrote his best-known works in the 1920s and 1930s in Germany. In his lifetime he was widely renowned for his studies of ancient Greek philosophers and for his ideas about the nature of philosophy and man. He left an indelible impression on a generation of

York: Cambridge University Press, 2010); Dominique Janicaud, *Heidegger in France* (Bloomington: Indiana University Press, 2015).

3   Ronald Beiner, *Dangerous Minds: Nietzsche, Heidegger, and the Return of the Far Right* (Philadelphia: University of Pennsylvania Press, 2018), Matthew Sharpe, "In the Crosshairs of the Fourfold: Critical Thoughts on Aleksandr Dugin's Heidegger," *Critical Horizons* 21:2 (2020), Julian Göpffarth, "Rethinking the German nation as German *Dasein*: Intellectuals and Heidegger's philosophy in contemporary German New Right nationalism," *Journal of Political Ideologies* (2020).

students, many of whom, fleeing the Nazis, were later to make names for themselves in America or elsewhere. Through his students' works and his own texts, including books and lecture transcripts, he also influenced many political theorists outside of Germany who had never studied directly with him. It is widely acknowledged that Heidegger played a dominant role in shaping the intellectual landscape of the twentieth century.[4] It is certainly true that he has shaped the field of political theory.

One of Heidegger's main ideas is that the major concepts from the Western philosophical tradition are historically constituted, rather than universal or timelessly true. Today this appears trivial. But that is in part evidence of Heidegger's influence. Previously, concepts like "truth" and "right" were regarded as stable, universal, or eternal, and they served to an extent as foundational concepts used to justify social and political orders. Heidegger, however, showed how such concepts arise from finitude and history, and even from the inauthentic relationship of man to his own true self. For many among his politically minded readers, his philosophical ideas promised liberation from a set of conceptual constraints, and indeed from the constraining nature of concepts as such, a simultaneously philosophical and political liberation. Derrida's project of deconstruction, for instance, which emphasizes the exclusions that conceptual arrangements effect, owes much to Heidegger. Richard Rorty, an American neo-pragmatist, used Heidegger's ideas about history, finitude, and the instability of traditional concepts to support social-democratic politics, arguing that foundational master concepts tend to underpin reactionary politics, whereas a post-truth attitude can facilitate freedom and creativity.

---

4   "It is no exaggeration," writes Tom Rockmore, for instance, "to say that at present Heidegger and Heidegger alone is the dominant influence, the master thinker of French philosophy, and that his thought is the context in which it takes shape and which limits its extent." Tom Rockmore, *On Heidegger's Nazism and Philosophy* (Berkeley: University of California Press, 1997): 249.

Unlike Derrida and Rorty, each of whom embraces some of the consequences of Heidegger's argument—putting them into the service of more or less leftist political aims—Leo Strauss, a Jewish German émigré to America, was worried about the consequences for liberal democracy and Western civilization if their foundational concepts were to be regarded as historical, rather than as rational. His most famous book, *Natural Right and History*, therefore sought to critique the turn to history and to defend the possibility of natural right, i.e., of an ahistorical, stable foundation for a type of political order.[5] Strauss sought to avoid the historicism of both the left and right, seeing in Heidegger's support for the Nazis a concrete political expression of his philosophical categories.

Because of that support, almost no English-speaking political theorists have read Heidegger positively from the right. In Russia, however, Alexander Dugin fully embraced Heidegger's thought as the foundation for his own "fourth political theory," which aims to negate liberalism, communism and its variants, and third-way theories, like fascism and Nazism.[6] In Dugin's system, Heidegger provides the foundation for a political theory that, although rejecting liberalism, also rejects its historical-political alternatives. Dugin's Heideggerianism is anti-liberal, but also anti-fascist and anti-Nazi, and unlike Rorty and Derrida he is not on the left. Dugin's use of Heidegger is therefore of some significance to political theorists, particularly in its notions of *Volk als Dasein* and the existential plurality of Daseins: only Dugin adopted Heidegger's philosophical musings on *das Volk*. The present work examines these four confrontations with Heidegger to unearth the philosophical and political logic operative in each case.

There are many schools of political theory, including those represented by the authors in this study. The differences among them arguably stem from their differing sets of first principles. Rarely

5   Leo Strauss, *Natural Right and History* (Chicago: Chicago University Press, 1950).

6   Alexander Dugin, *The Fourth Political Theory* (London: Arktos, 2012).

made thematic, these first principles can be regarded as philosophical ideas, and assessed from the perspective not of political theory, but of philosophy. That is, to assess and compare political theories, one can trace them back to their underlying philosophical ideas. Often the basic philosophical differences arise from disputes over the meaning of a major philosophical figure. In many cases today, Heidegger is that figure.

Beginning with Heidegger

This project is called *Beginning with Heidegger*, a title with three meanings. First, it refers to Heidegger's notion of "inceptual thought," or "another beginning." Heidegger argues that the Western philosophical tradition has a beginning, an arc, and an end. It begins with the pre-Socratics and arcs toward its end in Nietzsche. In his middle-period writings especially, which are the focus of the present work, Heidegger explores the idea that original philosophical thought (i.e., the sort of which he was engaged in), no longer belongs completely to the philosophical tradition. Instead, having freed itself from the dominant structures of that tradition, namely from the traditional interpretation of being as that which is most common to beings, it prepares to inaugurate a new history of philosophy, another beginning, in which an original revelation of being would be granted.

Some readers of Heidegger have rejected his notion of the history of being in the philosophical tradition and his idea of another beginning in his own thought. But this project is motivated by the following question: how might the problem of the relationship of philosophical thought to political thought present itself to those who begin with a favorable philosophical predisposition toward Heidegger's philosophical claims about another beginning? The title therefore refers in the first place to beginning with Heidegger at the end of the philosophical tradition, through inceptual thinking, towards the inauguration of another beginning.

The second meaning of the title refers to the fact that all four of the theorists discussed in this work somehow begin their own activity as political theorists in response to the challenge of Heidegger. For some of them, Heidegger is the springboard for a more complete elaboration of the possibilities of existential politics (Dugin). For others, he is "the greatest thinker" who therefore becomes a priority resource for thinking about the problem of the rational foundations of liberalism (Strauss). In each case, Heidegger is of fundamental importance for the thinker and his respective school, whether negatively or positively. Each theorist's own act of beginning with Heidegger is the second meaning of the title.

To understand the third meaning of the title, it helps to remember that a major theme of this study concerns how different notions of philosophy give rise to, or constitute, different notions of the political in what may be called "the philosophical constitution of the political." The sometimes troubled relationship between philosophy and the political is one of the main themes of this work. The title refers to the fact that the case of Heidegger is perhaps the main case of that strange relationship, since Heidegger is not only acknowledged as a philosophical master, but has also been lambasted for his Nazism, which many think is inseparably bound to his ideas about history and man.[7] Taking all of these three meanings together, the title therefore means the following: from the standpoint of a prejudice in favor of inceptual

---

7   The literature on this issue is voluminous. The latest round of the dispute over the relationship of Heidegger's philosophy to his politics concerns the so-called "Black Notebooks." Martin Heidegger, *Ponderings II–VI: Black Notebooks 1931–1938, Volume I* (Bloomington: Indiana University Press, 2016); Martin Heidegger, *Ponderings VII–XI: Black Notebooks 1938–1939* (Bloomington: Indiana University Press, 2017); Martin Heidegger, *Ponderings XII–XV: Black Notebooks 1939–1941* (Bloomington: Indiana University Press, 2017); *Reading Heidegger's Black Notebooks 1931–1941*, edited by Ingo Farin and Jeff Malpas (Cambridge: MIT Press, 2016). For an older review and summary of the issue, see *The Heidegger Controversy*, edited by Richard Wolin (Cambridge: MIT Press, 1991).

thinking, four responses to Heidegger that begin from a recognition of his philosophical-political priority are considered, the better to grasp issues associated with the theme of the philosophical constitution of the political.

As the foregoing indicates, the idea of beginning looms large over this work. Any philosophical or political reflection must begin somewhere. Philosophical thought in particular is impelled to seek an absolute beginning, something lacking presuppositions, since the status of the presupposed threatens to undermine systematic, comprehensive, encyclopedic rationality, to state it in Hegelian terms.

Knowledge, wherever it begins, should thus come full circle to render its own presuppositions firm, on at least one plausible account. Political thought must also begin somewhere. Often it begins with the statement of a present problem or a desired outcome. But another sense of the beginning of political thinking is that it begins from the axioms of the regime, party, or ideology, without calling those very axioms into question. It is among the main contentions of this study that we ought to try to trace the axioms of political thought to their philosophical ground.

Are there such grounds? Is there, as in Plato's divided line, an "unhypothetical first principle of all things," or are philosophical and political thought both necessarily "hypothetical," based on indemonstrable, unstable suppositions?[8]

The question whether there is or is not a ground of thought, and what it means if there is or isn't, is a question concerning the status and constitution of the political arising from a movement in the philosophical domain. In other words, the philosophical question of beginnings and foundations has a political dimension and is part of the general theme of the philosophical constitution of the political.

Perhaps there is a ground of thought and as such it should ground an understanding of the political. Or perhaps there is a ground of

---

8   *Republic*, 510b6.

thought that should not ground an understanding of the political. Perhaps what grounds thought is an ultimate openness. In that case, openness might have the potential both to undermine a given political order, taken hypothetico-noetically, axiomatically, and, on the other hand, to destine or constitute political orders, if each thinker takes or receives from it only something partial and one-sided.

If we say, that "because politics demands standards of such and such a sort, therefore we need a foundationalist political ontology," or "because foundations give rise to hierarchies and discrimination, therefore, since we are committed egalitarians, we reject foundationalism," we are offering specific perspectives on the relationship between philosophical and political notions and aims. This project circumscribes and evaluates a select group of alternatives among the possible ways of defining and relating such notions and aims, rather than operating within the domain constituted by any one axiomatic commitment.

This study does begin, as indicated, with a commitment or prejudice, namely one in favor of Heidegger's inceptual thinking. However, this starting point provides more fundamental access to a broader spectrum of philosophical-political topographies than another starting point might. Although it begins, as it must, its beginning is not quite as constraining as an axiomatic commitment to natural rights or equality, for instance, for as argued in Chapter Two, it is possible to reconstruct an argument for natural right as a response to Heidegger, but comparatively difficult on the basis of natural right to make sense of inceptual thinking.

The Road to Heidegger

I should now like to describe some of the arguments and ideas that brought me to a prejudice in favor of Heidegger's inceptual thinking well before I knew what that was.[9] I cannot say just to what extent this is so, but it seems that a background understanding of this sort can be helpful to understanding the appeal Heidegger eventually had on me and the role he played in my coming to the idea of a philosophical constitution of the political.

Thinkers with other intellectual trajectories might have encountered Heidegger at such different moments in their own personal intellectual drama that, should we have adequate knowledge of these, the consequent points of departure and destinations might be altogether predictable. At any rate, it cannot hurt to know the route that led to Heidegger. Without being able to demonstrate it, I suspect that this background will throw some light on the present work as a whole.

First I was interested in beginnings. From there, I eventually fell under the sway of Heidegger's thinking of another beginning. Perhaps indicatively, a positive inclination toward theological thought preceded the prejudice in favor of inceptual thinking. This positive inclination was the unexpected result of a critical desire to refute the rationality of theological belief, which required considering arguments against that belief. The attempt at refutation backfired. The first major argumentative step on the way to inceptual thinking proved to be refutation not of the theological position, but rather of the atheistic one. It established a basic distinction between beings and being. In simple terms, the reasoning was as follows.

Suppose we ask about the origin of the universe and believe that to posit a creator, or God, of the universe is to answer the question of its origination. One problem with positing God as creator is that one inevitably is led to inquire into the origin of the creator himself. The religious mind might either claim that one cannot explain the origin of God or deny that God originated at all. But that means, to

---

9   Heidegger: "Thinking without presuppositions can itself be achieved only in a self-critique that is historically oriented in a factical manner." Quoted in Alexander S. Duff, *Heidegger and Politics: The Ontology of Radical Discontent* (Cambridge: Cambridge University Press, 2015).

the non-religious mind, that one can be satisfied with something having an origin that cannot be explained, or else, in the second case, with the notion of an un-originated "X." In either case, then, one need not explain the origin of the universe, for which God was to be the *explanans*: if we can say of God that he is un-originated or has an origin about which nothing can be known, why can we not say the same about the universe and save ourselves the trouble of positing God?[10]

A response to this objection is that the *kind* of being of the *explanandum* differs from that of the *explanans*: the latter is not manifold, material, or extended, like the former. Something about the nature of God, the kind of being God is, makes the question of God's origin or lack thereof an entirely different question from that of the origin or lack thereof of the universe: these are, roughly stated, different sorts of being. Consequently, it is no longer evident that the move in the argument from the level of the God-being to the level of the universe-being is warranted, and the conclusion that we can rest content with the idea that the universe has no origin no longer follows.[11]

Without delving any deeper into the issues with this argument, suffice it to say that this response to the atheist objection to God as the origin of the universe carries with it the idea of essentially different kinds or levels of being, which may help one as a prerequisite

10 George Smith, *Atheism: The Case Against God* (Amherst: Prometheus Books, 1979).

11 Martin Heidegger, *History of the Concept of Time: Prolegomena* (Bloomington: Indiana University Press, 1985), note on page 7. Heidegger sets out three "co-original or equiprimordial elements" of the phenomenological approach: reduction, construction, and destruction. The first refers to "the move away from beings and the ontic (for example, the empirical sciences) to their being (to their regional ontologies and then to fundamental ontology)." I would say that the argument against atheism was my first exposure or transposition into the experience of the reduction, from beings (the objects in the world) to regional ontology ("the universe" as all existing beings taken together) to something else (not yet fundamental ontology, but neither beings nor regional ontology). It was this experience, I think, that later made Husserl's phenomenological reduction relatively easily accessible.

to be open eventually to Heidegger's distinctions between being and beings, and between original being ("beyng") inceptually understood and later, "metaphysical" interpretations of being as "essence," "idea," "actuality," etc.

Also important on the way to Heidegger was the phenomenon of the mystic, of an "experience" — thus, incidentally, an empiricism of sorts — of vertical self-transcendence, as well as the contextualization or interpretation of that experience.[12] The mystic ascent can be regarded as leading towards the point of departure for religious traditions, all of which interpret the experience in terms available to them. *Shekhinah*,[13] the Mysterious light of Tabor,[14] the Rose on the Cross, the Divine Sophia,[15] and the whole world of occult or concealed reality,

---

12   William James, *Essays in Radical Empiricism* (Lincoln: University of Nebraska Press, 1996).

13   Aryeh Tepper, *Progressive Minds, Conservative Politics: Leo Strauss's Later Writings on Maimonides* (Albany: State University of New York, 2013): 72. According to Tepper, Strauss shows that Maimonides implicitly regarded the teaching of the Shekhinah as a sign of "the rabbis' exaggerated concern with Israel, their exaggerated love of their own." However, I am referring here to non-nationalistic, mystical interpretations of Shekhinah.

14   http://www.gutenberg.us/articles/Light_of_Tabor: "According   to   the Hesychast mystic tradition of Eastern Orthodox spirituality, a completely purified saint who has attained divine union experiences the vision of divine radiance that is the same 'light' that was manifested to Jesus' disciples on Mount Tabor at the Transfiguration. This experience is referred to as *theoria*." On *theoria*: "In Eastern Orthodox theology, *theoria* refers to a stage of illumination on the path to *theosis*, in which one beholds God. As rather than the term meaning to contemplate as to 'think of' the term here means to see or 'behold' and then by doing so to understand though this experience. *Theosis* is obtained by engaging in contemplative prayer resulting from the cultivation of watchfulness (Gk: *nepsis*). In its purest form, *theoria* is considered as the 'beholding,' 'seeing' or 'vision' of God." Whether or not this derivation and interpretation of *theoria* is correct, it has been my tendency to read theory as theosis, and hence political theory as mystical political theology. If that is in error, may it at least prove to be a fruitful one.

15   Vladimir Solovyov, *Lectures on Divine Humanity* (Lindisfarne Books, 1995). From the book description: "These lectures, given by Solovyov in St. Petersburg

as well as its meaning and effect, are bound up with an experience of self-transcendence and mystical initiation or illumination. If the previous argument had introduced the idea of distinctions among kinds of being, and thus something like the notion of the highest being, mystical literature introduced the idea of multiple interpretations of a single event of self-transcendence and direct, personal existential conversion through a divine encounter. It also introduced the figure of that which is beyond being and unsayable.

A shocking encounter with Hegel's *Preface* to the *Phenomenology of Spirit*, for its part, introduced the notion of a rational articulation of the whole, which, in light of previous events, was interpreted as a sort of rational mysticism distinct from the "night in which all cows are black," a phrase that crudely captures something of the non-rational, un-differentiated self-transcendence toward the Absolute.[16] Hegel's text occurred as an invitation to another sort of initiatory divine encounter, one characterized not by ineffability, but total rational articulation, where the rigorous conceptuality of encyclopedic or all-embracing circular speech becomes the voice of the spirit itself, working

---

in 1878, mark a seminal moment not only in Russian but also in world philosophy. Dostoyevsky, Tolstoy, and other luminaries were in the audience. It was recognized by everyone that something astonishing had occurred. The young philosopher, mystic, and visionary, Solovyov, had given unexpectedly concise, intellectual expression to the reality of the evolution of consciousness and religion. He had spoken movingly of the actualization of Divine Humanity in eternity and time, of the divine world and the fall of spiritual beings into sin, of the origin and meaning of the natural world, and the incarnation of Christ, leading to the redemption of the visible and invisible worlds in the full revelation of Divine Humanity. Sophia, whom Solovyov experienced three times in his life, inspires this great work. He conceives Sophia in a variety of ways: as the eternal ideal prototype of humanity, as the world soul actively engaged in actualizing this idea, and as the fully developed divine-human being. This Sophia is both the active principle in the process of creation and its realized goal: the kingdom of God."

16 Glenn Alexander Magee, *Hegel and the Hermetic Tradition* (Ithaca: Cornell University Press, 2001).

in you and through you as it brings itself to full self-consciousness. The question of how to begin and how to come full circle to give a satisfactory account of initial presuppositions arose precisely within this mystically charged context.

The next major moment of my intellectual history on the way to Heidegger was reading Strauss. I read Strauss in a specific context: not in a department of political science, but as a student of philosophy, and not because he was assigned—he wasn't—but from an inner need.[17] Only with Strauss did an initial interest in theology, mysticism, ontology, and phenomenology start to intersect with the political. The locus for the first moment of intersection is the essay *An Epilogue*, which includes such remarks as these: "The new [social and political] science rests on a dogmatic atheism which presents itself as merely methodological or hypothetical"; "…we cannot forever remain blind to the fact that what claims to be a purely scientific or theoretical enterprise has grave political consequences"; and, for the "weaker brethren" among those challenging the new political science, "the belief accepted by the empiricists, according to which science is in principle susceptible of infinite progress, is itself tantamount to the belief that being is irretrievably mysterious."[18]

---

17 I discovered Strauss by trying to solve the puzzle of what it was that made my first philosophy professor stand out so drastically from the other professors I met and studied with while earning my degrees. It seemed that *they* had been lost in a forest for so long that they could show you around the place: they were experts in being lost. But *he* seemed like a wise man who had found the way out. What I learned later, the clue that led me to Strauss, was that the translators of the books he assigned were all students of Strauss: Allan Bloom, Thomas Pangle, Harvey Mansfield. Strauss then became the center of my attention.

18 Leo Strauss, *Liberalism, Ancient and Modern* (Chicago: Chicago University Press, 1995): 315–22. Heidegger, *Being and Time*, 49: "The fact that positivistic investigation does not see these [ontological] foundations and considers them to be self-evident is no proof of the fact that they do not lie at the basis of any thesis of positive science and are problematic in a more radical sense than such science can ever be."

Now we come to Heidegger. I did not start reading Heidegger by reading *Being and Time*, which for many is the natural way to begin. Instead, before *Being and Time*, I first met Heidegger and his thinking of another beginning in Dugin.[19] That means that in my case, beginning with Heidegger happens together with Dugin. I meet Heidegger not directly, but through another's encounter with him, one differing markedly from others, and from Heidegger himself. Dugin begins his presentation of Heidegger, introducing him within the Russian language adequately for the first time, volume one, section one, with the distinction between the first and the other beginning, a distinction that I eventually came to think sets one Heidegger — previously, I have called him "Right-Heidegger" — apart from another, the French and Left Heidegger, where the end of metaphysics is embraced together with its political consequences, while the other beginning is rejected, because of its political consequences.[20]

Although this is merely a personal history, and although I have of course read and reread the texts and arguments anew to test them and myself again and again, it is a fact of my own noetic genealogy, and I suppose not an irrelevant one, that I meet Heidegger from the beginning as a point of departure for the philosophical constitution of various geopolitical readings: an inceptive reading in Russia, and a deconstructive reading, one that accepts the end of the first beginning, but not the beginning of the other beginning, in France, on the "noetic Left." Later I came to regard Strauss's Janus-faced reading as vital precisely for America, given his defense of natural right and constitutionalism. The theme of a "geopolitics of political ontology,"

19   Dugin, *Heidegger: The Philosophy of Another Beginning.*

20   Michael Millerman, "Heidegger, Left and Right: Differential Political Ontology and Fundamental Political Ontology Compared" *Journal of Eurasian Affairs* 2:1 (2014). Again: "It is no exaggeration," writes Tom Rockmore, "to say that at present Heidegger and Heidegger alone is the dominant influence, the master thinker of French philosophy, and that his thought is the context in which it takes shape and which limits its extent." Tom Rockmore, *On Heidegger's Nazism and Philosophy* (Berkeley: University of California Press, 1997): 249.

or something like that, thus imposed itself on my discoveries from the beginning of my interest in Heidegger.[21] This is the origin for me of the philosophical constitution of the noetic left (end of metaphysics, end of the first beginning) and the noetic right (beginning of another beginning).[22]

Sovereignty and Conversion

Because this study surveys a range of philosophical-political topographies, or philosophical constitutions of the political, or, in simple terms, a range of opinions about what philosophy is, what the political is, and how the two relate to one another, it is natural to ask how at the end it will be possible to adjudicate among the alternatives. What are the criteria for judgment? Are they somehow independent of the alternatives? If they are dependent on the alternatives, arising from some already constituted domain, it does not seem possible to judge among them neutrally, but only to beg the question in favor of one or the other.

In that case, a second question arises: what would it take to displace one from a commitment to or prejudice in favor of one approach into an alternative? Concretely, what, for instance, would it take to persuade someone sharing Strauss's perspective that Derrida's is better or more correct, or more in line with some criterion of judgment? What would it take to displace someone from a Derridean topography into, say, a Duginian one, or vice versa?

Let us take an example. Strauss has a point. As I argue below, Strauss thinks that Heidegger, or philosophical thought more generally, traverses a way beyond "natural right," calling it into question.

---

21 Peter Eli Gordon, *Continental Divide: Heidegger, Cassirer, Davos* (Cambridge: Harvard University Press, 2010).

22 That is, I call the "noetic left" those who accept the end of metaphysics but do not accept inceptual philosophy, and I call the "noetic right" those who accept both the end of metaphysics and inceptual philosophy.

But moderation demands that the way shall not pass beyond natural right toward history.[23] The philosophical traversal of the political is thus to be limited by a political virtue, moderation. But the limitation of the way of philosophy by the political means that to some extent in Strauss's thought the political has the upper hand, the guiding hand, the ruling hand. Strauss also recognizes the limitation of the political by the philosophical, but here "the philosophical" already means "philosophy-as-limited," such that Strauss intends to constrain the political by the guiding hand of a *political* philosophy of natural right, not history.

Leaving it in such preliminary terms for the time being, the question must be posed whether or not to depart from "history," from Heidegger, from the way of philosophical traversal, to the way of "natural right," of the political limitation of the philosophical. If so, on what grounds? "The political history of the 20th century," a critic might say: isn't Nazism proof enough of everything we need to know about whether to prefer historicism to natural right? And yet, what would have to be true in order for the shift from noetic history to political history to be the decisive argument in favor of abandoning Heidegger for Strauss?

We can imagine someone making the following argument: "You are not only a thinker, assuming you are even that: you are also political, and as such you know that thought thinks in a context, a political context, and you do your own task of thinking harm, rather than good, by removing the political ground on which it stands." But does this statement imply that the political is the priority because it stands prior to the philosophical, since the philosophical does not stand if it does not stand on the political? Is the political therefore the precondition for the philosophical? Does it then deserve philosophy's condescension, since it is a mere precondition? Or does the political only truly become what it is when it is constituted by and transposed

---

23   Leo Strauss, *Natural Right and History* (Chicago: Chicago University Press, 1950).

into the philosophical? If philosophy must be subservient to political considerations, do not those considerations ultimately stand above philosophy, which is not supposed to have anything above it?

Strauss wants to protect politics from both excess and lack of philosophy and to protect philosophy from political persecution and corrupting influences. But it begs the question in favor of a certain notion of philosophy, as well as of the political, to suppose (or to presuppose) this relation.²⁴ In short, on one hand Strauss may never have refuted Heidegger's way of thinking, yet he advanced criteria that are plausible and persuasive to distinguish his own way from Heidegger's. These are two ways, to be sure. But what is the point of departure between them, how do things stand with that point, and what would displace someone partial to either beginning onto the other's path? Finally, what happens to a thinker who grants the greatest significance, greatest importance, and greater desirability to the compelling sovereignty of the primordial?²⁵

We must speak of sovereignty and conversion.²⁶ First, what does the compelling sovereignty of the primordial, or of the sovereignty of philosophy, mean? Why should the language of sovereignty be used to describe the status of philosophy? In the writings that are the primary focus of this work, when Heidegger talks about philosophy he is referring to a profound, inceptual meditation on being, not as that which is most common to beings but as the concealed ground of our existence. Philosophical meditation or philosophical thought does not leave the thinker untouched. It is transformative. The transformation

---

24 A big problem for me — maybe the biggest — is that I share Strauss's wish but find that it is at odds with philosophy's essential nature to deprive it of its inherent sovereignty or sovereignties.

25 Martin Heidegger, *The History of Beyng* (Bloomington: Indiana University Press, 2015): 59 — "Sovereignty is the Χάρις of beyng as beyng, quiet worthiness of the gentle binding that never needs to calcify into the need for power."

26 Conversion is the topic of my next book. Here, I present some of its basic aspects as they relate to the main claims of the present work.

effected in the person, the transformation of the person, may be called
a philosophical conversion. It occurs, as it were, from two directions:
the person acts and is also acted upon. He does not merely turn himself around, nor does some higher authority merely turn him. The two
motions coincide in this "*Kehre*" or turning.[27] Philosophical conversion effects existential transformation. Philosophical conversion
effects existential transformation. The existence of the transformed
being, which Heidegger sometimes names "*Da-Seyn*" in these texts,
stands under a new star.

Philosophical conversion, philosophical transformation, existential conversion, existential transformation, the birth of a new star,
the constitution of *Da-Seyn*—what does all of this have to do with
sovereignty, a seemingly all-too-political concept? To be sovereign
is to have no law above oneself. The compelling sovereignty of the
primordial refers to the fact that one's star is one's highest law. In the
event of existential conversion there occurs the emergence, birth, or
inception of philosophy from the chaos of one's *Dasein*, as the introduction into one's existence of an authority to which all other aspects
of one's existence must answer. Phenomenologically, the authority is
no mere external authority, because the distinction between internal
and external itself becomes transformed in the act of conversion, or in
the constitution of *Da-Seyn*.

Heidegger's ways of speaking when discussing inceptual thinking
are strange, and it is understandable why they should be: inceptual
thinking is inseparable from existential conversion, and hence from
a sort of linguistic reconfiguration stemming from language's rooted-
ness in existence. All the derivative problems of the language of the
mystics, discussed in Chapter Four, occur here in their fundamental
configuration. The main point is that the philosophical experience is

---

27 Laurence Paul Hemming, "Speaking out of Turn: Martin Heidegger and *die
    Kehre*," *International Journal of Philosophical Studies* 6, No. 3 (1998): 393–423.
    In his own discussion of Heidegger's *Kehre*, Hemming speaks of "a return to the
    turn with the promise of conversion" (394).

not simply an accidental modification of essential existence, a new bit of knowledge added to a stable and knowing subject. It is rather a transformative experience resulting in a reconfiguration of the subject (into *Da-Seyn*) and its language, which introduces into its existence, as phenomenological matter of fact, a sovereign authority.

It would seem to be the destiny of this sovereign authority in the transfigured philosophical self not only to direct the questioning and to affect the mood of that self, but also, as *Da-Seyn*, to act constitutively, to constitute and ground fields. The compelling sovereignty of the primordial, then, should result in the reconfiguration or reconstitution of the field of the political. It is hard to say in advance precisely what that might look like in practice, particularly because Heidegger did not give many indications along these lines, instead directing his meditations to the inaugural stirrings of another beginning of philosophy.

Because almost no thinkers followed him into what he calls in the *Contributions* "the grounding," preferring instead either to resist the completion of philosophy or to meditate with steadfast patience in its end without inaugurating anything new, there is little hint in the post-Heideggerian literature about the possible shape of "*Da-Seyn* politics." Only Dugin has ventured this "experiment" as a result of applying his philosophical "experience" to this question.[28]

However, it is possible to regard the master thinkers of the Western tradition of philosophy and political philosophy as having each responded to their own existential conversion and thereby , constituting a field as a result. These master thinkers together form, for Heidegger, a great mountain range, as it were; they are the peaks of the mountains.[29] Each mountain of thought arises from a depth,

---

28 One of his books has a title that can mean both "experiments in existential politics" and "experiences in existential politics," and although the book is experimental, it also refers directly to undergoing the "experience" of philosophical transformation or existential conversion, as I've been calling it.

29 Heidegger, *Contributions*, 147.

reaching upward and configuring the land around it into what Derrida has called a "topolitology."[30] Using this image, it should be possible to trace geopolitical or politico-theoretical topographies to describe the philosophical heights and depths that configure them, and vice versa. Heidegger's intimation of another beginning seems to be comprised of the promise of the formation of a ground for a new mountain range, with new peaks and abodes gathered around itself.

Political Spiritualities

In his *Phenomenology of Spirit*, Hegel begins by already knowing the result of his inquiry.[31] He takes the reader with him along a philosophical journey from this preexistent beginning to that result, which is already there for him from the outset. Heidegger says the following about the fact that Hegel presupposes what he sets out to show:

> We ought not to bring this up as an objection to the work. For it pertains to the essential character of philosophy that wherever philosophy sets to work in terms of its basic question and becomes a work, it already anticipates precisely that which it says later. But that is not to be taken as a surreptitious proof or as a sham procedure; for philosophy is not concerned with proving anything in the usual sense of following a formal principle of proof in a logic which is not that of philosophy itself.[32]

Rather than objecting to the procedure, what is required is to "enter into philosophy," that is, to "yield to what is essential in philosophy, so that, in view of the tasks shown there, we may gain clarity *about ourselves* — whether we still have or can have essential tasks, and, if so, what kind of tasks." "This entering into what is essential" in philosophy "forms the core of a true confrontation," according to Heidegger,

---

30   See Chapter Four.

31   G.W.F. Hegel, *Phenomenology of Spirit* (Oxford: Clarendon Press, 1977).

32   Martin Heidegger, *Hegel's Phenomenology of Spirit* (Bloomington: Indiana University Press, 1994): 30.

"without which every interpretation remains a blind and pointless exercise."[33]

Applying Heidegger's outlook to the tasks of this project, it would be blind and pointless to approach the problems gathered together under the name "Beginning with Heidegger" with the sledgehammer of critique ready at hand. "Every thinker stands under the claim of an essence of truth," Heidegger says, "and we must first enter into this essence and must have entered into it in order then to correspond to it with equal essentiality." "The mere 'criticizing' from any arbitrary standpoint, the counting up of errors...on the 'basis' of a philosophy that is 'free of standpoint,'" he continues, "is not so much wrong as it is simply childish."[34] Thus, neither the criticisms of an arbitrary standpoint, nor the mere identification and enumeration of errors are required. Rather, the need is for an "essential correspondence" as "confrontation," that is, to test or to be tested by "the claim of an essence of truth" that a given thinker and we ourselves might stand under, thus to "gain clarity about ourselves," and our capacity for "essential tasks."

In order not to be arbitrary, a critical standpoint ought to undertake the task and bear the burden of the question as to where and how to begin. What indeed is the relationship between this task and burden, and clarity about oneself? There is no way for one not to be implicated in the transformations that may arise from and become enacted in the *being-who-I-am* out of a lingering questioning into, at, around, or out of the point of departure. Not every thinker discussed in the following pages acknowledges this fact. For example, Strauss does not describe the *becoming-philosopher of the philosopher* from the perspective of the philosopher: Heidegger, however, does.[35] [36]

---

33   Heidegger, *Hegel's Phenomenology*, 31.

34   Heidegger, *The Event*, 249.

35   Martin Heidegger, *The Essence of Truth: On Plato's Cave Allegory and Theatetus* (New York: Bloomsbury Academic, 2004).

36   Strauss does mention Judah Halevi's "conversion to philosophy" in an important passing comment in his essay on his conversion to Judaism of the Kuzari

This project operates within, invites one into, and is in itself subject to various becomings or conversions: not merely the *becoming-philosopher* (transversion) of the *being-a-theorist* (hypothetico-noetically), but also the *becoming-the-bearer-of-an-essential-claim* (from out of the philosophical) that is different from, and not reducible to, another claim (also from there).

Thought about the relationship between the philosophical and the political is therefore *not* static thinking, something stable, unchanged, pre-constituted, known, predictable, objective, and dogmatic about a *single thing*, called "the relationship," between two pre-constituted realms. Rather, what "thought," "thinking" "relationship," "the philosophical," and "the political," all are or mean varies as a function of the transformative potentials of inquiry.[37]

In Foucault's words, this project operates in the mode not of philosophy, but of spirituality. For Foucault, philosophy is the perspective according to which "truth is…given to the subject by a simple act of knowledge, which would be founded and justified simply by the fact that he is the subject and because he possesses this or that structure of subjectivity." Spirituality, by contrast, "postulates that for the subject to have right of access to truth he must be changed, transformed, shifted, and become, up to some extent and up to a certain point, other than himself." "It follows," he writes, "that from this point of view there can

---

king. Leo Strauss, *Persecution and the Art of Writing* (Chicago: University of Chicago Press, 1952): 109. As Laurence Lampert notes, "Strauss uses Plato's word from the *Republic* where Socrates's lesson after his cave image describes the genuine education of the cave dweller as a conversion." Laurence Lampert, *The Enduring Importance of Leo Strauss* (Chicago: University of Chicago Press, 2013): 45–46.

37 Thomas Sheehan, *Making Sense of Heidegger: A Paradigm Shift* (Lanham: Rowman and Littlefield, 2015): 155: Sheehan writes that the personally transformative potential of Heidegger's thinking was "the ultimate goal of his philosophical project, the reason why he taught and wrote at all." Heidegger, *Contributions* 13: "In philosophical knowledge…the very first step sets in motion a transformation of the one who understands."

be no truth without a conversion or a transformation of the subject."[38] The present work regards philosophy as a state of existence befalling a subject through a transformative act of conversion, and hence, it treats political theories as "political spiritualities."[39]

As for the political, it would not be enough to say that it is known to every "man from Missouri."[40] Such a person sees what there is to be seen within what can be termed simple "pre-scientific" experience: that is, that there are rulers and ruled, political parties, partisans, cowards, generals, financiers, and the like. He knows that his country has enemies, debts, strengths and weaknesses. He knows that his country is a country with a history, and perhaps even surmises that the history is *its* history, that the country has an identity, that its identity changes over time, remaining, within limits, its own self, like Theseus's Ship. But how well does he know this self, these limits? If the political is philosophically constituted, the "man from Missouri" does not know the political if he does not know philosophy, and he cannot know what politics is through and through without knowing the nature of the political.

The nature or domain of the political is neither obvious nor given. It is not unproblematic (indeed, in Stanley Rosen's terms, it is "elusive").[41] Its only proper establishment arises from the philosophical. But the philosophical is a profound inquiry into, a questioning lingering in and around, into and from out of, what is most questionworthy in its obscurity and reticence, an act rooted in existential conversion. Questioning lingering receives that which is granted by what is most question-worthy: it becomes the bearer of an essential

---

38 Michael Foucault, *The Hermeneutics of the Subject* (New York: Palgrave, 2005): 15.

39 Ruth Marshall, *Political Spiritualities: The Pentacostal Revolution in Nigeria* (Chicago: University of Chicago Press, 2009).

40 Strauss, *Liberalism, Ancient and Modern*, 211.

41 Stanley Rosen, *The Elusiveness of the Ordinary* (New Haven: Yale University Press, 2008).

claim, the carrier of a compelling sovereignty. Regimes of political life and regimes of political thought and theory can be traced back to the "shelterings," or existential embodiments and elaborations, of these "grantings," or conversion-encounters.

The preceding pages have approached the theme of the philosophical constitution of the political through its more esoteric aspects, such as conversion, configuration, and the sovereignty of the philosophical. The theoretical elaboration of these aspects is not the purpose of the present work.

In the remainder of this introduction I shall discuss the issue of Heidegger and the relation between philosophy and the political among his readers from a different perspective, that is, in terms of theory, practice, and the various responses to Heidegger's "historicism." In conclusion I shall demonstrate that both approaches are needed to fulfill the intentions of this project.

Heidegger's Gordian Knot

Heidegger was not the first philosopher whose writings and life questioned the relationship between theory and practice.[42] Plato's *Republic* most famously presents the figure of the philosopher-king, for whom wisdom secures a title to rule, crowning practical wisdom with the crown of theoretical knowledge.[43] Within his own life, too, Plato's infamous attempt to educate the tyrant of Syracuse has long served

---

42 As the remainder of this work shall show, I disagree with Michalski's judgment that, "Philosophy — thought as Heidegger understands it — serves neither theory nor practice," as well as with his characterizations of theory and practice, "to master the world or to discover unchangeable laws which govern this world." However, I agree with his observation that "Heidegger's thought in a mysterious way describes the spiritual life of our [20th] century." Krzysztof Michalski, "Heidegger," in *Heidegger in Russia and Eastern Europe*, ed. Jeff Love (Lanham: Rowman & Littlefield, 2017): 200; 182.

43 Christopher Ingraham, "What Ivy League students are reading that you aren't," *Washington Post*, February 3, 2016.

as a case study of the temptation to attain practical power through an assumed command of theoretical knowledge.

Heidegger never wrote a *Republic*. Nor for that matter does he have a *Laws*. His writings do not question the relationship between theory and practice in the manner of presenting *ad oculos*, as Plato does, by way of dialogical form, the promise and pitfalls of philosophical statesmanship or the limits and liabilities of non-philosophical rule. Unlike Plato, Heidegger does not write dialogues where characters adumbrate the facets of such complex problems and personify particular responses to them.[44] Instead, he presents his profound meditations on being and truth directly, in interpretations of other philosophical writings and in his own original, prophetic articulations. These theoretical meditations do not leave the practical realm unaffected, however. Heidegger's philosophy of resoluteness and German rebirth, demands, in the minds of many, to be interpreted in light of his involvement with NSDAP.

The problem for every reader, admirer, and detractor of his writings, the Gordian knot of theory and practice confronting everyone who approaches it, consists in the fact that Heidegger, whose oeuvre lacks an *Apology* also, was both nearly a god in the realm of thought and in deed a member of the demonic Nazi party. Some modern Alexanders cut the knot and salvage select scraps of theory, leaving Heidegger's aside, paying it no more mind while conquering new lands with the help of just those bits of his theory that preclude the politics of *Blut und Boden*. Others leave both theory and the politics in a heap, becoming the rulers of a new expanse wherein both Heideggerian thinking and Nazi practice are relics. All agree that the Nazism must go and inquire whether and to what extent the theory must go with it.

---

44 He did write the occasional dialogue, however. Martin Heidegger, "Dialogue on Language between a Japanese and an Inquirer," in *On The Way to Language* (San Francisco: Harper & Row, 1982); Martin Heidegger, *Country Path Conversations* (Bloomington: Indiana University Press, 2010).

Old Masters and New

Heidegger first earned his philosophical reputation as an expositor of philosophical texts, who in interpreting them redirected students' attention to such fundamental matters as seemed, by all reports, to involve the serious student entirely in his or her full being, not merely incidentally, accidentally, or derivatively.[45] Unlike other professors who treated the writings of Plato and Aristotle as dead material to be dissected using the cutting edges of historical or dogmatic scholarship, Heidegger brought those and other authors to life. In their revived shadows, historical and dogmatic scholarship acquired a macabre, even murderous hue: "The philosophers are dead: we have killed them" was the implicit truth of such scholarship. The revolution Heidegger effected set the proportions straight. Once more, after many centuries, students were able to fall under the direct spell of the old masters. Many fell concomitantly under the spell of their new master, Martin Heidegger.

The 1927 publication of *Being and Time* extended Heidegger's burgeoning fame. His inquiries no longer only impressed themselves upon a small classroom of listeners but now acquired a much wider audience of readers in both his native Germany and abroad. The neologisms and new twists on old words required by Heidegger's phenomenological project launched "Dasein," "the existential analytic," "being-in-the-world," "authenticity," and a whole host of new philosophemes into circulation in an "initial public offering" into Weimar's marketplace of ideas. Before long, Heidegger's ideas had become nearly a monopoly.

The work gained such circulation that Heidegger could soon afterward lament the fact that its contents were being dragged around in the very inauthenticity he had diagnosed, instead of being received as

---

45 John van Buren, *The Young Heidegger: Rumor of the Hidden King* (Bloomington: Indiana University Press, 1994).

a way to the question of the meaning of being.[46] *Being and Time* had become the cheap talk of the town.

While its reception had proceeded in accordance with the strange logic of the time, Heidegger's questioning was proceeding, too, in accordance with the even stranger logic of a sustained meditation on the meaning of being and truth. Eventually, that strange logic, which estranges a thinker for a time, brought Heidegger towards his "middle-period," writings, including the *Contributions to Philosophy (of the Event)*, his "second masterpiece."[47]

Though he stuck with his initial inquiries, Heidegger now abandoned the academic formalism of *Being and Time* and devoted himself more completely to being's transformational disclosures and concealment. It was no longer the preliminary and transitional existential analytic of Dasein that promised phenomenological access to the meaning of being as temporality. Instead, it was an even more fundamental experience of being itself, hard won through the earlier approach, that claimed Heidegger and gave rise to the direct expression of another beginning of philosophy, one beyond and before Aristotle and Plato, and the entire philosophical tradition stemming from them and their predecessors.

The beyng-historical (*seynsgeschichtlich*) writings no longer talk of any customary concept of being, for Heidegger had left such concepts behind, marking that transgressive movement with an archaic spelling, *Seyn*, "beyng." These texts are no longer a phenomenological analysis of the ways in which Dasein, the being that we are, is, with the hope that such an analysis will provide access to being as temporality. Instead, they arise from the ground of the experience of "beyng" as the original source for the first beginning of philosophy, as the

---

46 Heidegger, *Contributions*, 222–24.

47 I take the term "second masterpiece" from Lukacher's review on the publisher's website. See http://www.iupress.indiana.edu/product_info. php?products_id=19919 [Accessed June 20, 2018].

self-occluding "x" that unfolds in the history of philosophy through the garb of such concepts as idea, energy, subject, and will.

Heidegger's middle-period writings are beyng-historical because in them history is the history not of things, nor of men and their deeds, nor of states, countries, empires, or whatever else, but of beyng, which is not in a time given non-problematically, but which *is* time, eventuating historically, giving rise to history, to histories, to epochs.

Because Heidegger apparently experiences himself as more completely open to beyng than anyone but the German poet Hölderlin, he understands himself in these writings as having been transposed or transported into beyng as the ground of his existence. "I am crucified with Christ," says Paul, "nevertheless I live. Yet not I but Christ liveth in me."[48] It is somewhat similar with Heidegger and beyng, which, so to speak, crucifies Heidegger's "I" or individual subjectivity yet lives "in" him, or, more precisely, appropriates him, as Da-seyn (as we shall see, Heidegger warns against a misleading interpretation of what "being in" means when it comes to Dasein). In these writings, Heidegger has become dislodged into Da-seyn, the localization (Da) of the temporalization of the self-concealing revelation of beyng (Seyn).

Three Responses to Heidegger's "Historicism"

Heidegger's notion of history (*Geschichte*, as opposed to *Historie*) is an unusual one. It is crucial to his thinking and appears among the fallen scraps of the Gordian knot mentioned above. For many of his critics and even for some of his supporters, it is the crux of the matter. Heidegger's emphasis on the historical character of being as he understands it has led some, like Leo Strauss, to call him an historicist.

According to one version of the critique of Heidegger's historicism, Heidegger thinks that all truth is relative to a time. There are no eternal, everlasting, timeless truths. Context bars every age from the possibility of self-transcendence. What is worse, the thesis of the

---

48 Galatians 2:20.

relativism of truth to time shuts the door on sound, rational judgment of political orders, as Heidegger's involvement with the Nazi party proves.

Against Heidegger's dangerous, immoderate historicism, rational political life requires steady, rational principles, an idea of human nature, right and wrong, good and bad, just and unjust. Strauss's school especially championed "natural right" in response to "history," defending political moderation against the tyrannical potential of an obsession with resolution that fails to give rational criteria for what is to be resolved upon.

In a defense of Lincoln's natural right philosophy, Strauss's student, protégé, and admirer Harry Jaffa summed up what he and others regard as Strauss's knock-out punch against historicism: if all truth is relative to a time, the statement that says so is in the best case but a truth relative only to a time and not for all time: it is therefore not the case that truth is relative to a time (if truth is relative to a time, the truth that truth is relative to a time is relative to a time, and hence not simply true, and there may have been a time when truth was not relative to a time, and such a truth ought to be true now, too). But though such an argument may be enough to problematize the notion that all truth is relative to a time, it fails to deal with Heidegger's more complicated *seynsgeschichtliche* notion of being *as* time.

Such criticism of Heidegger's historicism thus sometimes employs notions of history, truth, and time that do not take sufficient account of what those words mean in Heidegger's writings. Even so, wanting among other things to defend the noble cause of political moderation, such critics do recognize that contestations about history, truth, and time, however abstract and theoretical they might otherwise seem, can yet give rise to such practical political consequences as must interest not only every political philosopher, but a great many ordinary citizens, as well.

Naturally, those who might err by giving Heidegger's historicism too much credence at the expense of political moderation are on the

xxxviii   BEGINNING WITH HEIDEGGER

opposite side of the equation. The first group sacrifices the claims of theory to the exigencies of practice. The second transfigures practice in theory's all-consuming fire. Proponents of this latter approach could not rest content with a doctrine of natural right after having become convinced of the merits of the (beyng)-historical critique of natural right.

Heidegger's historicism teaches them that key concepts of the philosophical tradition have been destabilized and uprooted in Heidegger's writings, revealing them as inauthentic incrustations formed over a long-forgotten original experience. These readers of Heidegger can either stop short of his project of *another* beginning of philosophy (Derrida) or throw themselves into it (Dugin). Both go further than those who cautiously reject Heidegger's historicism.

Those who stop short of the new beginning nevertheless embrace the critical potential of the historicist position, but either ignore the incipient moment or redeploy the uprooting operation against it before it can even get off the ground. Every other beginning is for them cursed, as it were, with an original sin. It is "always-already" undermined. The theoretical belief that traditional philosophical concepts are baseless engenders among such theorists in varying degrees of intensity a practical critical thrust against institutions and practices buttressed by those concepts. Heidegger temporarily shared the desire to reconfigure practices in the light of that theoretical belief, but his position included, to repeat, the additional element of another beginning, which these critical theorists omit in their attempt to disentangle good theory from bad Nazism. Those who throw themselves headlong into the new beginning believe in the possibility of a Heideggerian reconfiguration of the political that is distinct from Nazism, as we shall soon see.

A third group of readers seem to have learned a different lesson from Heidegger's historicism. Heidegger had shown that traditional philosophical concepts were not to be regarded as eternal, stable verities. Such concepts could occasionally exert a political influence; for instance, truths about human nature are often reflected in moral and legal theory. But once their historical provenance had been demonstrated, they no longer commanded authoritatively, similarly to the way that today one cannot necessarily be expected to believe in the divine right of kings. As the first group disputed the demonstration and fought for a reauthorization of such concepts as natural right, and the second group half-accepted the demonstration on philosophical grounds, ignoring the other, incipient half and aiming to bring practices in line with theory, the third group reasoned as follows. "If the conceptual throne is now empty," they said "we should acclaim neither being and truth, as Heidegger does, nor theory itself, as these others do. Heidegger has given us the tools to freely re-describe concepts, and this free redescription best accords with who we say we are: free people in free societies. Let us be done with the gods of being, truth, and theory, with all gods except those of our making, and let us make the gods that best serve us and our purposes, so that it is we who become the demiurges of our world — a world of our free making." Led by Rorty, this group turns Heidegger's historicism against theory itself, but accepts the main theoretical results of that historicism as expressed in the thesis that traditional concepts have lost their philosophical authority.

Here it would be helpful to briefly examine Heidegger's so-called beyng-historical historicism before saying an additional word about Dugin's approach, which despite being the least well known adopts Heidegger's perspective more completely than any other approach.

Beyng-Historical Historicism

Heidegger's historicism in *Being and Time* stems from an analysis of Dasein, the being for whom being is, or can become, a question. That analysis is itself motivated by the question of the meaning of being. It culminates, however incompletely, in the thesis that being "is" temporality. Heidegger's analysis includes a phenomenological explication of Dasein as always structurally "ahead of itself," drawing possibilities of being from its past and projecting them into a future in the authentic moment constituted by resolute anticipation of its own finitude, which Heidegger terms "being-towards-death." Past, present, and future are structural, existential aspects, to be thought from being itself, that is, as fundamental ontology, and not from out of the history (*Historie*) of the merely "ontic," thing-like-being, which can be subjected to calculation, measurement, and quantitative analyses. There can only be history in the latter, derivative sense because Dasein is historical in the former, authentic, existential sense. Derivative history not rooted in the authentic recognition of Dasein's historicity lacks philosophical validity.[49]

Heidegger extends his insights into historicity in his middle-period writings, where not Dasein but "beyng itself" becomes the center of attention. It is true that being had been the target of the inquiry in *Being and Time* — a fact that was not well understood, to Heidegger's dismay.[50] It is all the more true that being (beyng) stands more explicitly as the center of attention later. The heart of these works is not the analysis of Dasein's existentials, but an account of the history of beyng.

The account of the history of beyng may be outlined briefly as follows. The first thinkers of the first beginning of philosophy underwent a fundamental experience of being as emergence and concealment. However, starting mainly with Plato, concealment was never thoroughly thematized and emergence (interpreted as *physis* and *idea*) was encrusted in the notion of being as presence. In Plato, for instance — setting aside the question whether this interpretation is correct or not — the ideas are the most beingful beings, present to the mind's eye, whereas the briefly mentioned notion of that which

---

49 Heidegger criticizes also the unphilosophical claptrap of "blood and race" when skewering historiology (*Historie*) for being unhistorical. Martin Heidegger, *Contributions to Philosophy (of the Event)* (Bloomington: Indiana University Press, 2012): 388.

50 Heidegger, *Contributions*, 28, 68.

is beyond being in the *Republic*, that which is concealed and beyond presence, never receives the sustained meditation that Heidegger thinks is its due.

The congealment and encrustation that occur after the first "forgetting" of being are embodied in what we know as the traditional concepts of philosophy, each of which marks an era within the great epoch of the first beginning. What gradually increases at each stage is the forgetting of being, or the abandonment by being. Being withdraws itself from constant presence into concealment. It is as though we have turned on a light to illuminate a room and eventually focus our attention only on what has been thereby illuminated (beings), all the while losing sight of the dark (self-concealing) origin of the light that lighted up a space for beings to appear in the first place (Dasein). This process of forgetting the "clearing-concealing" dimension of being culminates in the apparent *beinglessness* or nihilism of modern technological culture, marked by calculation, speed, and "the massive."[51]

Heidegger often uses the term "machination" when describing the mode of being of the era of nihilism. Machination, he writes, "does not [in this context] name a kind of human conduct but a mode of the essential occurrence of being."[52] Consistent with the view that philosophical-historical eras, however marked by forgetting they might be, are nevertheless eras of beyng (i.e. beyng-historical), even the age of machination should not be "depreciated," despite the fact that it "[promotes] the distorted essence of being," for "this *distorted* essence itself…is essential to the essence."[53] If, grasping the "plight of the lack of a sense of plight," or in other words, if having become genuinely troubled by the fact that we are not troubled by being's having abandoned us, a thinker performs the "leap" into another beginning,

51 Heidegger, *Contributions*, 96–7.

52 Heidegger, *Contributions*, 99.

53 Heidegger, *Contributions*, 99.

as Heidegger puts it, then nihilism might be followed by another inception of philosophy from out of its most original and concealed wellsprings.[54] In this case, beyng will no longer be forgotten nor will man any longer be abandoned by it. Rather, the human being will be transformed into Da-Seyn and will ground and shelter the truth of beyng amidst beings.[55]

All that is rather more than is said by the facile statement that, "all truth is relative," uttered in order to demonstrate its own self-refutation (Strauss). Furthermore, in "grounding" another beginning, Heidegger's historicism clearly exceeds both the merely critical, deconstructive tendencies of the group of critics who stop short of another beginning (Derrida) and the a-theoretical, openly machinational attitude of the third group (Rorty), which embraces machination for having destabilized traditional concepts without hope for the kindling or flaring up of beyng.[56] The most faithful to Heidegger's vision are those who leap into another beginning (Dugin).

A Fourth Response

Dugin's way fully embraces Heidegger's historicism. It agrees that traditional philosophical concepts have been destabilized without lament. Acknowledging the end of the first beginning, it leaps together with Heidegger into the other beginning, aiming to witness the kindling and flaring up of beyng and endeavoring to be the appropriated custodian of beyng.

From an outsider's perspective, dangers arising from the relationship between theory and practice threaten this way more than any other; for the theoretical embrace of another beginning seems to entail Heidegger's practical commitment to the discredited politics of National Socialism. And as stated above, those who cut the Gordian

---

54 Heidegger, *Contributions*, 79–80.

55 Heidegger, *Contributions*, 179–257.

56 See Chapter Three.

knot of theory and practice in Heidegger unanimously agree to let Heidegger's Nazism, whatever it may have been, lie on the ground, salvaging scraps of his theory, not of his practice.

Yet the outsider, in this case, can learn from the insider (in this case, in all cases, and vice versa). For the proponent of the fourth way, the political practice corresponding to an embrace of another beginning cannot be merely reduced to Hitlerism. Everything depends on generating basic political concepts from out of the semantic matrix and fundamental-ontological well-spring of inceptual thinking.

In this regard, Heidegger's project may be extended further into the realm of the political than had been done by Heidegger himself. It is true that Heidegger's meditations on machination and nihilism touch upon "political concepts," or concepts with political import, such as calculation, culture, religion (the gods), Americanism, Bolshevism, and peoplehood. But Heidegger never elaborated a "political theory" out of the grounds of inceptual thinking. Despite a few remarks on Germany, Russia, and America, he never constructed a comprehensive "theory of international relations." And although he relates the questioning of being to the question of "who" a people are, his writings are without extended thematic construction of something like an "existential theory of society." By contrast, Dugin extends Heidegger in precisely these directions.[57] Importantly, Dugin extends his criticisms of Nazi "metaphysics," too. The proponents of a political philosophy that leaps into another beginning criticize Nazism as incompatible with inceptual thinking, following Heidegger's own muted theoretical criticisms of Nazism.

---

57 Alexander Dugin, "The Existential Theory of Society," in *Political Platonism* (London: Arktos, 2019); Alexander Dugin, *The Fourth Political Theory* (London: Arktos, 2012); Alexander Dugin, "Theory of a Multipolar World," (London: Arktos, forthcoming). Heidegger, *Contributions*, 34–7, 252, 316. Michael Millerman, "Alexander Dugin's Neo-Eurasianism and the Eurasian Union Project: A Critique of Recent Scholarship and an Attempt at a New Beginning and Reorientation," *Journal of Eurasian Affairs* 1, No. 2 (2014).

Heidegger's criticisms *were* muted. They can be found in his writings, to be sure, and perhaps deduced therefrom, and by stretching the principle of charity to its breaking point, from a handful of his actions. But what screams out loudest to critics most of the time is precisely the absence of criticism and opposition, that is, the absent apology. Heidegger, in short, was too much of a sycophant to philosophically object or politically oppose Nazism at its height, and regrettably too great a coward to meaningfully reject or critique it after the fact. His failure to repent of ever having supported an annihilationist regime and maniacal leader, contend critics, seemingly lent monstrous crimes the semblance of philosophical cover.

In the present context, however, the question is whether the outsiders' castigation of Heidegger's all-too-quiet "critique" of Nazism is applicable to those who extend his historicism more expressly into field of political concepts than he himself had. Are Dugin and his lot also blameworthy for a practical failure to distance themselves from Nazi politics?

Here, let "Nazi politics" refer primarily to a doctrine of racial superiority coupled with an attitude of genocidal hatred towards those perceived as threats to the community – Jews, especially – and to an embodied radical opposition to liberalism (i.e., Americanism) on the one hand and Bolshevism (or egalitarianism, more broadly) on the other. We can add that for its critics, it amounts to a fascistic orientation characterized by a pseudo- or quasi-scientific or seemingly irrational and magical ideological worldview, featuring total Führer worship, as well as demonstrated and utter disregard for the concept of the individual as such and for individual rights, in favor of racial politics.

Dugin's extended Heideggerianism does not espouse or imply racial superiority. Rather, he explicitly rejects both the principle of race and the idea of racial superiority as such. If for Heidegger the Germans and the Greeks alone were or could be the people of beyng, for Dugin, distinctly, every people ought to be understood in light of their actual or potential appropriation by and custodianship of beyng, giving rise to the doctrine of the existential plurality of Dasein(s) and manifesting a fundamental-ontological multi-polarity.

Liberalism and Bolshevism come under devastating meta-political scrutiny, and in this respect Dugin faithfully follows Heidegger and may seem to espouse Nazi politics. Yet, in his extension of Heideggerianism into the political domain, Dugin has marked Heideggerian political theory as a "fourth political theory," standing in opposition to liberalism, yes, and communism (Bolshevism, etc.), too, but also and explicitly Nazism, fascism, racism, and nationalism (i.e. representatives of the so-called "third political theory," on this model).

Dugin's Heideggerian political theory is opposed to egalitarianism in favor of hierarchy. And it does have a "magical" or non-rational dimensiondimension, for instance with the theme of the return of myths and the archaic in the period of the collapse of modernity. But it is self-consciously explicit about the relationship between the philosophical and the ideological, which it constitutes on Heideggerian grounds as the relationship between the ortho-*aletheaic* and the ortho-*doxic*, the latter looking to the former for its justification. In other words, it is not at all *irrational*, which does not imply that it must be rationalistic, and although it has an ideological dimension, that dimension is itself understood to be a function of a genuine philosophical outlook, quite unlike what is the case with Nazi politics. As Heideggerian, Dugin's political theory is based on a phenomenological approach that aims to situate our self-understanding on a level that precedes the division between rationality and irrationality. Stated differently, it is not content to take for granted "reason" as a faculty of the "rational animal," precisely because it is involved in the project of transforming the human essence from that of rational animal to Dasein, which transforms our understanding of reason, too.

There is a disregard for the individual in it, but not necessarily for the "self." The concept of the individual is attacked as inauthentic, "metaphysical," and wrongheaded, and the human is defined as "anything but an individual."[58] Yet, as reconstituted in light of inceptual thinking, people are neither reduced to their race, nor are they deprived of their dignity. Admittedly, nothing like "human rights" can be found here. But that is not in order to make humans slaves, but rather because the philosophical presuppositions of human rights blocks access to a genuine grasp of our authentic existence as Dasein.

As this brief overview suggests, those theorists who leap into another beginning do not see the need to cut Heidegger's Gordian knot, for to them, even though the result is far from liberal, the relationship between beyng-historical theory and beyng-historical practice does not entail Hitlerism or Nazism, but instead entails their rejection in the name of beyng. It is a separate and obviously important question whether sound political judgment is hindered or not by this approach, regardless of the fact that it escapes the accusation, or suspicion, that it might, in its open embrace of Heidegger, reproduce the worst excesses of a commitment to Nazism.

Philosophy and Worldview

When faced with the question of theory and practice, a non-philosopher must request clarification and further specification of the question. She likely does not think about it in the same way as a philosopher does. The issue for political philosophers is whether the person who claims to have philosophical insight into profundities unavailable to both ordinary observation and technical-scientific apparatuses acquires by virtue of that supposed insight something along the lines of a title to rule, wisdom making her a natural ruler more so than strength, experience, or a high birth could ever do.

The "title to rule" need not mean that the philosopher sits upon the throne or wields the scepter. But it does mean that those who sit upon the throne and wield the scepter, or do whatever is appropriate to their own political order, receive, from however great a distance,

---

58   Alexander Dugin, *The Fourth Political Theory* (London: Arktos, 2012).

the impress of the philosopher's revelations, as embodied in the concepts of the constitution, for instance, and in the founded customs and institutions of the land (philosophers as "hidden legislators of the world.")

The philosopher may rule by virtue of a successful reconstitution of preexisting semantic fields and by the new creation of such fields. A reinterpretation of what justice calls for, of the character of national aims, of the meaning of political history — all such acts of hermeneutic ingenuity comprise some of the potential political aspects of the philosopher's secret rule. The ways of encountering Heidegger described above are more concerned with understanding and responding to that kind of claim than they are in disputing whether Heidegger or any other philosopher would make a good president or prime minister within a real political order.

The ordinary non-philosopher, for his part, must think of theory and practice rather differently. If something happens in practice that should not have happened in theory, the theory should be reviewed and reassessed, so that it can incorporate, predict, and in the best case explain such outcomes as it might have missed in a given case. There can be no question in a situation like the one described that theory responds to practice. He who clings to the theory despite what happens in practice, without somehow accounting for the unexpected outcome, is rightly rebuked. The question for the ordinary understanding in the best case is primarily: does the theory predict the outcomes as well as can be expected on the basis of good evidence? If not, does another theory do so, or — an extreme, misological position — are all theories and theorists simply blameworthy for failing to understand what happens in practice?[59]

---

59 The discipline of political science dealt with these and related matters after Donald Trump's election victory. One result of that victory was that confidence increased among those who repudiate "elites" and intellectualism (theory) as completely detached from an understanding of the people (practice), as out of touch (unrelated to practice).

Sophisticates, of whom there are many, may take the additional step of asking whether what happened in practice makes itself quite as available to our grasp as it seems to do at first pass. Do we really know what happened? Was it terrorism or the courageous acts of freedom fighters? Was it the military-industrial deep state complex lashing out against lovers of truth, humanity's last great hope, or was it a treasonous undermining of national security by non-state hostile intelligence agents? When "what happened" does not present itself immediately, when it is thought to depend on a worldview, ideology, position, or perspective, the relationship between theory and practice may take its own forms. Sophisticates may not want Professor X to be President, but they will vote for Politician Y, the practitioner seen to most approximate the former's theory.

The sophisticates, like the sophists, resemble philosophers in the best case, and the question of theory and practice among them eventually acquires a quasi-philosophical character, too. Yet the differences are decisive. They are those described by Heidegger when he distinguishes between philosophy and worldview, "so incommensurable that no image could possible depict the distinction between them. Every image would necessarily bring them too close together."[60]

"A 'worldview,'" Heidegger writes, "sets experience on a definite path and within a determinate range, and this in such a broad way that it does not allow the worldview itself to come into question; the worldview thereby narrows and thwarts genuine experience." Similarly, although apparently resembling philosophy in their privileging of theory, the ideological positions of sophisticates have a ready-made interpretative semantic matrix ready to cast as a net over whatever happens. Their ideological positions precisely "narrow and thwart genuine experience." Their matrix "must forgo new possibilities in order to remain one with itself." And in erecting their worldview as master of experience, they "seek to set [themselves] *above* philosophy," and "must ultimately *resist* philosophy."⁶¹ For worldview is total. It "claims for itself the determination and regulation of every kind of acting and thinking," and "[closes] itself off from the opening of its ground."⁶²

Philosophy, on the other hand, is primarily *questioning*. It does not narrow experience; it "*opens* experience." It bypasses the apologetics, propaganda, and bustle of worldview, instead elevating "[only] questioning and the decision in favor of question-worthiness." And although in the history of its first beginning philosophy may have congealed into something "total," the new beginning "[reveals] what is abyssal in philosophy, which must turn back to what is inceptual in order to bring into the free domain of its meditation the fissure and the 'beyond itself', the strange and the perpetually unusual."⁶³ Ultimately, worldview is not, and philosophy is, "immediately useless." Philosophy though is "nevertheless sovereign," and there, of course, is the rub.⁶⁴

A Strange Axiom

As we shall see in a later chapter, Derrida wonders whether what Heidegger calls sovereign is not so far removed from every theological, political, or theologico-political understanding of sovereignty as to be beyond this realm altogether. The sovereignty of philosophy is unlike the sovereignty of a monotheistic god-ruler-creator: the latter is still bound to the metaphysics of the first beginning. Nor is philosophy sovereign in the sense of Hobbes' or Bodin's sovereign. So what is the sovereignty of philosophy, and what does it mean for politics and the political?

---

61 Heidegger, *Contributions*, 31–2.

62 Heidegger, *Contributions*, 33.

63 Heidegger, *Contributions*, 30–34.

64 Heidegger, *Contributions*, 35.

For Heidegger, philosophy is sovereign in the sense that all fields of thought and action presuppose an understanding of and relationship towards being, whereas only philosophical questioning makes being its theme and brings the human being into authentic correspondence with being. Furthermore, no fields have the capacity to transfigure philosophy essentially, whereas philosophy has it in its nature to be able to reconfigure other fields essentially. It is our task here to explore some of the ways in which his philosophical reflections configure or threaten to reconfigure the constitution of the political.

Although some theorists have disputed the sovereignty of philosophy by subsuming it under the sovereignty of another instance, as we shall see most clearly in the case of Rorty, Heidegger has good reasons for insisting on the primacy of the question of the meaning of being. As Horujy has observed, Heidegger's account is thoroughly ontologized: even in the deepest recesses of the forgetting of being and abandonment by being, "being remains," and it remains a matter of principal importance to recollect it, entering into the process of sheltering it and being appropriated by it.

Yet, there is justice in criticisms of Heidegger's single-mindedness. More so than the theorists studied in the present work, Horujy indicates a promising line of critique.[65] Unlike the theorists who *avoid* some part of Heidegger for whatever reason, and whose positions therefore remain dialectically bound to his in the act of avoidance, Horujy includes Heidegger in a higher-order account that may be able to comprehend both Heidegger and some vital alternatives to the Heideggerian outlook unaccounted for adequately by him alone. Specifically, he distinguishes between the ontological, de-ontologized (ontic), and virtual paradigms. Whereas Heidegger's view is thoroughly being-bound, such that in every case, even the most extreme, "being remains," Horujy's "synergic anthropology" includes in its purvey

---

65   Sergey Horujy, "Synergic Anthropology and the Problem of Anthropological Pluralism," in *Heidegger in Russia and Eastern Europe*, ed. Jeff Love (Lanham: Rowman & Littlefield, 2017), chapter 14.

the possibilities of de-ontologized and virtual humanity. Without depriving Heidegger of his authority on the question of being, Horujy's approach promises to expand our philosophical vocabulary to include varieties of political experience that no adequate account can ignore. The key to the potential utility of his approach, given the central thrust of the present study, is that, whereas the theorists now under consideration never quite do justice to the full scope of Heidegger's thinking, Horujy's broader spectrum can go beyond Heidegger by including, rather than excising or refashioning him. Moreover, Horujy's spectrum expansion differs from the one example of Heideggerian extension featured in this study, Dugin's.

Although Dugin provides a legitimate extension of Heideggerian themes into new political theses while remaining true to Heidegger, he is less successful in articulating the character of non-Heideggerian political alternatives, even though he is acutely aware of the problem of virtual post-humanity and both formally indicates it in his *Ethnosociology* and presents it as a foil to authentic existence in his *Fourth Political Theory*, with some success, where he argues that post-humanity is the logical outcome of post-liberalism.

Political philosophy should have a broad enough vocabulary and set of methods and approaches to account for *as much as possible* of political-philosophical phenomena. Political-theoretic operations that are constrained by worldviews have their own technical warrant. Party theorists need to work out party policies. Defenders of a constitution must theorize as cases arise that relate to the constitutional order in whatever manner. There is always a need within a system to defend, maintain, and elaborate it. All such operations work with a given set of axioms (the party, the constitution) and it is not their business to undertake higher-order reflection on the provenance of those axioms — that is, their limitations and alternatives to the axioms. But these operations fall short of the goal of a comprehensive account of political things.

Comparatively speaking, philosophical political theory projects do better. At a minimum they must call their own axioms into question. They must be aware of competing axiomatic sets and be able to reconstruct their logic charitably. The philosophical political theorist is not a party hack, because the philosophical spirit is inherently transgressive, that is, transgressing a given order (party, constitution, etc.). The philosophical political theorist is less likely to be satisfied with the merely given, which he feels obliged to transform through reflection into the earned or constituted. But philosophical political theory is itself variegated. The more we distinguish the varieties and present them in a broad array that preserves them without becoming limited to any one of them, the better.

By the conclusion of this study, it will become clear that Heidegger alone is not enough. It makes sense to "begin with Heidegger." Yet we must move beyond Heidegger — without leaving him behind or making him into something he is not. In our tarot deck of political philosophy, we cannot rest content with any one Arcana, whether Fool, Magus, or Emperor. Only the entire deck permuted will do. "Strauss," "Rorty," "Derrida," "Dugin," and even "Heidegger," are cards in this deck, spokes in the "wheel of tarot" that "speaks" both "law" and "love." *Rota Taro Orat Tora Ator*: thus the strange axiom of this study, which now turns to Heidegger.

CHAPTER ONE

Heidegger

This chapter is a précis of some of the most important of Martin Heidegger's philosophical arguments and discoveries. Each of the thinkers this study examines was well acquainted with them and often wrote in direct response to them, whether expressly, as in the case of Rorty, Derrida, and Dugin, or with reserve, as in the case of Strauss. Each tended to emphasize one or another aspect of Heidegger's oeuvre, one or another set of consequences that might seem to follow from his way of thinking, as will become clear in subsequent chapters.

Although not strictly necessary to comprehend those chapters, which can be read by themselves, a background understanding of Heidegger's philosophy is indispensable for eventually judging the adequacy of individual responses to Heidegger, as well as for formulating and evaluating the fundamental questions discussed in the preface. For instance, scholars studying Strauss often recognize the great importance of Heidegger for Strauss. However, they sometimes present inadequate accounts of Heidegger, making it impossible for their readers to judge the dispute between Strauss and Heidegger appropriately, unless those readers have first done the necessary groundwork of studying Heidegger's thought.[1]

Heidegger is best known for his 1927 book *Being and Time.* However, we may begin an overview of his work not with that book, but with a lecture course he gave in 1925, called *History of the Concept of Time: A Prolegomena to a Phenomenology of History [Geschichte] and Nature.*[2] Gadamer called the written copy of that course the *Urform* or "original form" of *Being and Time.*[3] Because of the clarity of its presentation and the background it gives on Heidegger's relation to the phenomenological tradition, it is a good place to start on the way that leads to inceptual thinking. Next, I examine *Being and Time,* before finally outlining the *Contributions to Philosophy (of the Event).* My aim is to elucidate the basic trajectory of Heidegger's thought in a way that preserves it in its continuity as arising from a single-minded focus on the theme of being.

Phenomenology and the Constitution of the Sciences

A science, Heidegger writes, investigates a domain of objects. The natural sciences investigate the domain of nature; the human sciences investigate the domain of history. Each of these, nature and history, tends to be understood "by way of the sciences which investigate

---

1 See for instance Michael P. Zuckert and Catherine H. Zuckert's excellent *Leo Strauss and the Problem of Political Philosophy* (Chicago: University of Chicago Press, 2014): pp. 50–1 and 67 for a wanting account of Heidegger. The mistake on p. 67 is that they are too quick to collapse Heidegger's thoughts on philosophy into his argument on the genesis of the theoretical attitude in *Being and Time.*

2 That is the name of the course, which was published in German and English under a shorter title. For the English, see Martin Heidegger, *History of the Concept of Time: Prolegomena* (Bloomington: Indiana University Press, 1985).

3 Heidegger, *History of the Concept of Time,* xiv.

them."[4] This means that they are "accessible only insofar as they are objects thematized in these sciences." But there is no guarantee that the thematized domains provide access to "the actual area of subject matter out of which the thematic of the sciences is first carved." Heidegger continues,

> To say that the science of history deals with history does not necessarily mean that history as this science understands it is as such also the authentic reality of history. Above all, no claim is made as to whether historiological knowledge of historical reality ever enables us to see history in its historicity. It might well be that something essential necessarily remains closed to the potentially scientific way of disclosing a particular field of subject matter; indeed, must remain closed if the science wishes to perform its proper function.[5]

The problem of points of departure is already contained in this preliminary formulation of the basic program of the occlusion of authentic reality by the constitution of sciences and their respective domains, both in relation to the constitution of the domain, and in relation to the fact of the multiplicity of sciences-domains. Thus, Heidegger continues by remarking that, "the separation of the two domains [of nature and history] may well indicate that an original and undivided context of subject matter remains hidden."[6]

The phenomenology of the "authentic reality" of history and nature is not same as a phenomenology of the natural or historical sciences and their objects. It aims at a "phenomenological disclosure of the original kind of being and constitution of both," thus providing "the basis for a philosophy of these sciences."[7] By showing "their genesis from pretheoretical experience," "the kind of access they have to the pregiven reality," and "the kind of concept formation" at work

---

4   Heidegger, *History of the Concept of Time*, 1.

5   Heidegger, *History of the Concept of Time*, 1.

6   Heidegger, *History of the Concept of Time*, 2.

7   Heidegger, *History of the Concept of Time*, 2.

in each science, this phenomenology "becomes…an anticipatory dis-closure and conceptual penetration of potential domains of objects for the sciences." It "leaps ahead into the primary field of subject matter of a potential science and first makes available the basic structure of the possible object of the science by disclosing the constitution of the being of that field."[8]

When a science's "basic relationship to the subject matter" it investigates becomes "insecure" or "questionable," the science is in "crisis," and "reflection…to dispel the insecurity over the fundamental concepts of the science in question or to secure those concepts in a more original understanding of its subject matter" becomes the task.[9] In undertaking this task, "scientific research assumes a philosophical cast," inasmuch as the sciences "say that they are in need of an original interpretation, which they themselves are incapable of carrying out." Now, "sciences themselves" Heidegger says," are nothing but concrete possibilities of human Dasein[10] speaking out about the world in which it exists and about itself."[11] Consequently,

> If the sciences are not to be regarded as a spurious enterprise, founding their justification merely by invoking the prevailing currents of the tradi-tion, but instead are to receive the possibility of their being from their meaning in human Dasein, then the decisive question, and the place where an answer to the crisis is to be found, is in bringing the subject matters under investigation to an original experience, before their concealment by a particular scientific inquiry.[12]

The philosophical turn from the constituted sciences to the authentic reality of their subject matter and to original experience leads us, Heidegger says, to human Dasein. In the lecture course, Heidegger

8   Heidegger, *History of the Concept of Time*, 2.

9   Heidegger, *History of the Concept of Time*, 3.

10 More about "Dasein" below.

11 Heidegger, *History of the Concept of Time*, 4.

12 Heidegger, *History of the Concept of Time*, 4–5.

does not move directly to human Dasein. First, he argues that, "to exhibit history and nature" phenomenologically, it is necessary, "to arrive at a *horizon*" — a "*field of constituents* against which history and nature stand out in relief" — "from which history and nature can be originally contrasted."[13] Heidegger accesses this field through the concept of time — specifically, through "the *history of the discovery of time* and the *history of its conceptual interpretation*," which he regards as "the *history of the question of the being of entities*."[14]

To investigate "the history of the concept of time" requires that we not understand "history" on the basis of an everyday notion of "time."[15] Heidegger distinguishes between *Historie* ["historiology"] — the study that proceeds on the basis of an assumed and unoriginal notion of time — and *Geschichte*, "original history," so to speak, which emerges from a fundamental ground, where what "time" is is not yet presupposed or taken for granted.[16] Heidegger limns the difference as follows:

> [T]he historiology of the time concept could be carried out as a gathering of opinions about time and a summary of its conceptual formulations. Through such a doxographical survey of the concept of time, one might expect to obtain an understanding of time itself... But even the most meticulous collections of opinions remain blind so long as one does not first have a clear idea of just what is constantly being sought in gathering such information. The understanding of time itself will never be obtained from the historiology of the time concept. Instead, it is precisely the understanding of the phenomenon of time, worked out in advance, which permits us to understand earlier concepts of time.[17]

In this lecture course, Heidegger develops the history of the concept of time phenomenologically from an analysis of "the fundamental

---

13 Heidegger, *History of the Concept of Time*, 5.

14 Heidegger, *History of the Concept of Time*, 6.

15 Heidegger, *History of the Concept of Time*, 6.

16 Heidegger, *History of the Concept of Time*, 6.

17 Heidegger, *History of the Concept of Time*, 6.

structures of the basic constitution of Dasein."[18] Thus, beginning from the crises of the constituted sciences vis-à-vis their subject matter, he lays bare a pre-scientific horizon ("the concept of time") and grounds it in an analysis of that being for whom the meaning of being is or can become a question, namely Dasein. The "authentic reality" of nature and history is made accessible through the being through whose being those sciences are originally constituted

Phenomenology: Its Basic Discoveries

The first major discovery of phenomenology is *intentionality*. Intentionality is a "structure of lived experience," according to which "the very being of comporting is a directing-itself-toward."[19] Edmund Husserl had discovered the intentional structure of perception, and Heinrich John Rickert, a leading Neo-Kantian philosopher of the time, extended this to apply to "other forms of comportment" besides perception. But Rickert failed to go far enough, or so Husserl thought.[20] He was impeded by "dogmas." For instance, Rickert denies that representation has an intentional structure, because he denies that representation is a directing-itself-toward something outside consciousness (knowing). Thus, Rickert "lays claim to intentionality in his own starting point to the extent that it fits his theory but casts it aside when it contravenes his theory that representing is not knowing."[21] [22]

---

18 Heidegger, *History of the Concept of Time*, 151 and following.

19 Heidegger, *History of the Concept of Time*, 31.

20 Edmund Gustav Albrecht Husserl, (German of Jewish descent) (8 April 1859–27 April 1938) was a philosopher who established the school of phenomenology. He was also Heidegger's philosophical mentor. Heinrich John Rickert (German) (25 May 1863–25 July 1936) was a philosopher, one of the leading neo-Kantians. (Ed.)

21 Heidegger, *History of the Concept of Time*, 32.

22 These distinctions between knowing consciousness and representation emerged from Kant's *Critique of Pure Reason*, the discussion of which led to the

Heidegger faults Rickert for his failure to admit "matters of fact as they are given," a failure that makes his thinking "groundless."[23] Rickert thinks what he thinks "not from a study of the matters themselves but by an unfounded deduction fraught with dogmatic judgments."[24] He "presupposes a mythical concept of representing from the philosophy of natural science," which leads him astray. The simple experience is as follows: "In the case of a representation on the level of simple perception a representation is not represented; I simply see a chair…When I look, I am not intent upon seeing a representation of something, but the chair…what is represented is not a representation, not a content of consciousness, but the matter itself." Thus, "the most primitive matters of fact which are in the structures themselves are overlooked simply for the sake of a theory."[25] For Heidegger, by contrast, the task is to uncover the structure of comportments generally, without obstructive, dogmatic blinders.

When we attend to the intentional structure of comportment without limiting our discoveries by the presupposition of epistemological and metaphysical dogmas, we begin to discover some interesting things. Heidegger starts by focusing on the "toward-which" of intentionality, rather than on the "directing itself" thereof.[26] What, he asks, is "the perceived of perception?" "If I answer without prejudice," he continues, "I say the chair itself. I see no 'representations' of the chair, register no image of the chair, sense no sensations of the chair I simply see *it* — it itself."[27] More specifically, "it is not just any chair but a

---

emergence of the various forms of idealism propounded by Schelling, Fichte and Hegel. Hegel was especially instrumental in dismissing Neo-Kantianism in his *Phenomenology of Spirit*, which in turn influenced Husserl's and Heidegger's "phenomenological" theory of perception during this early period. (Ed.)

23 Heidegger, *History of the Concept of Time*, 32.

24 Heidegger, *History of the Concept of Time*, 33.

25 Heidegger, *History of the Concept of Time*, 35.

26 Heidegger, *History of the Concept of Time*, 37.

27 Heidegger, *History of the Concept of Time*, 37.

very particular one, the desk chair in Room 24 at Marburg University, perhaps somewhat worse for wear and poorly painted in the factory from which it evidently came."[28]

Heidegger designates the naturally (as opposed to the scientifically or dogmatically) perceived thing "the environmental thing."[29] This chair can also be perceived not as an environmental thing (as such and such a chair), but as a natural thing (as something that falls if lifted and otherwise shares matters in common with other wooden things).[30] Thirdly, it can be taken neither as an environmental thing nor as a natural thing (neither this particular chair nor this wooden thing), but in its very "thingness," the structures of which concern "materiality, extension, coloration, local mobility, and other determinations of this kind which do not belong to the chair as this peculiar chair but to any natural thing whatsoever," to the extent that these structures "can be read out from the given itself."[31] These perceptions are not scientific; rather they are "naïve." "The field of what is found in [such] simple cognizance," however, "is in principle much broader than what any particular epistemology or psychology could establish on the basis of a theory of perception."[32]

In addition to the structures of the entity, there are also structures that belong to the entity *as perceived*.[33] Accordingly, Heidegger writes

> We can distinguish along the following lines: *the entity itself*: the environmental thing, the natural thing, or the thingness; and *the entity in the manner of its being intended*: its being-perceived, being-represented, being-judged, being-loved, being-hated, being-thought in the broadest sense.[34]

---

28 Heidegger, *History of the Concept of Time*, 37–8.

29 Heidegger, *History of the Concept of Time*, 38.

30 Heidegger, *History of the Concept of Time*, 38.

31 Heidegger, *History of the Concept of Time*, 39.

32 Heidegger, *History of the Concept of Time*, 39.

33 Heidegger, *History of the Concept of Time*, 40.

34 Heidegger, *History of the Concept of Time*, 40.

One distinction in the structures of intentionality concerns the *given-ness* of the perceived thing. The thing itself, a bridge, for instance, can be envisioned: "I place myself before it, as it were. Thus the bridge is itself given. I intend the bridge itself and not an image of it, no fantasy, but it itself."[35] Yet, this givenness is not "bodily": "It would be bodily given if I go down the hill and place myself before the bridge itself."[36] Givenness can be present, but not bodily: it can also be "empty": "Empty intending is the mode of representing something in the manner of thinking of something, of recalling it, which for example can take place in a conversation about the bridge. I intend the bridge itself without thereby seeing it simply in its outward appearance, but I intend it in an empty intending…without any intuitive fulfillment."[37] Another "totally different structure" concerns "the perception of a picture," for example a postcard of a bridge. "In perceiving a picture," Heidegger writes,

> I do not thematically apprehend the picture-thing. Rather, when I see a picture postcard, I see — in the natural attitude — what is pictured on it, the bridge, [which is now seen as] what is pictured on the card. In this case, the bridge is not emptily presumed or merely envisaged or originarily perceived, but apprehended in this characteristic layered structure of the portrayal of something.[38]

This recognition undermines the theoretical dogma that takes "the apprehension of a picture as the paradigm by means of which…any perception of any object can be illuminated."[39] Perceiving is "totally distinct from the consciousness of a picture," and the theory that

---

35   Heidegger, *History of the Concept of Time*, 41.

36   Heidegger, *History of the Concept of Time*, 41.

37   Heidegger, *History of the Concept of Time*, 41. "*Intuition* means: simple apprehension of what is itself bodily found just as it shows itself." 47.

38   Heidegger, *History of the Concept of Time*, 42.

39   Heidegger, *History of the Concept of Time*, 42.

says otherwise is "a theory without phenomenology."[40] To proceed, by contrast, on the basis of a phenomenology without a theory is to be in a much better position "to see…in intentionality itself and through it directly into the heart of the matter, that of which it is the structure and how it is that structure."[41] The first major discovery of phenomenology, then, concerns the intentional structures of a range of comportments, a discovery that should not be hastily subsumed under a theoretical framework.

The second major discovery of phenomenology, according to Heidegger, is "categorial intuition." Categorial intuition means that "in the most everyday of perceptions and in every experience," "there is an apprehension of the *categorial*."[42] Heidegger develops this notion by first phenomenologically establishing three concepts of truth. In a basic sense, truth is a state in which there is "demonstrative fulfillment" of what is intentionally presumed. For example, there can at first be an empty intending, as discussed above, of a bridge. This empty intention "can in a certain sense be fulfilled in intuitive envisaging," when a bridge is intended, though not given bodily. A greater degree of fulfillment is reached with direct sense perception. But even that is only partial since, "the perceived entity always shows itself only in a particular adumbration."[43] Heidegger calls "*a definitive and thoroughgoing fulfillment* when on the side of presuming *all the partial intentions are fulfilled* and, on the side of the intuition which bestows fulfillment, that intuition presents the *whole matter in its totality*."[44] The fulfilling of the empty intention is a "bringing-into-coincidence," an "act of identification."[45] The same thing is intended at the beginning and the end; only the degree of fulfillment changes. This "identifying

---

40   Heidegger, *History of the Concept of Time*, 43.

41   Heidegger, *History of the Concept of Time*, 47.

42   Heidegger, *History of the Concept of Time*, 48.

43   Heidegger, *History of the Concept of Time*, 49.

44   Heidegger, *History of the Concept of Time*, 49.

45   Heidegger, *History of the Concept of Time*, 49.

fulfillment" is a "universal function" of all acts, which all have an intentional structure and thus share the structure described.

Truth can be regarded as (1) the "being-identical of presumed and intuited," which Heidegger says is a sort of "living *in* the truth," rather than "thematically studying" it, (2) the account or thematic study of this structure of being-identical, and (3) "the very object which is," which "*makes* knowledge *true,*" "*being, being-real.*"[46] Take the sentence, "The chair is yellow." This states, Heidegger says, the "being-yellow" of the chair. We can stress "being" or "yellow" in this formulation.[47] In the former case, we mean that, "the chair is *really* and *truly* yellow." "Being here means something like the *subsistence* of truth, of the *truth-relation,* subsistence of identity."[48] In the latter case, "the concept of being does not refer to the subsistence of the truth-relation...but to a structural moment of the state of affairs itself" — the chair is *yellow* (predication).[49] These two senses of truth have long been confused with one another and can be clarified in their distinction and relatedness through phenomenological analysis. On this view, not only judgments, but also simple perceptions can be true.[50] Heidegger recognizes, however, that even "simple perception"[51] occurs in a context of interpretation and assertion: "we do not say what we see, but rather the reverse, we see what *one says* about the matter."[52]

---

46 Heidegger, *History of the Concept of Time,* 51–3.

47 Heidegger, *History of the Concept of Time,* 53.

48 Heidegger, *History of the Concept of Time,* 54.

49 Heidegger, *History of the Concept of Time,* 54.

50 Heidegger, *History of the Concept of Time.*

51 Defined as the level of a perception where "every phase of the perceptual sequence is a full perception." Heidegger, *History of the Concept of Time,* 61. That means that even though you only see the chair from a certain perspective, there is a level at which "every single phase of perception in the whole of the continuous sequence [of adumbration] is in itself a full perception of the thing."

52 Heidegger, *History of the Concept of Time,* 56.

So for instance, we make a statement with the form: "this S is P and Q": "this chair is yellow and upholstered."[53] "Our question," Heidegger explains, "is whether this assertion finds its complete fulfillment in what is perceived." More specifically, "Are the 'this,' the 'is,' the 'and' perceptually demonstrable in the subject matter?"[54] No, they are not. Instead, "there is in the full perceptual assertion a *surplus of intentions* whose demonstration cannot be borne by the simple perception of the subject matter."[55] The "true sense of the discovery of categorial intuition" is the demonstration that, "the non-sensory and ideal," i.e. this surplus, "cannot without further ado be identified with the immanent, conscious, subjective."[56]

Categorial intuition is "non-sensory perception." It is a "founded act" erected on the "founding act" of simple perception. Simple perception refers to the act that phenomenologically gives the "real object," the full perception. For instance, although I perceive the lamp at an angle and see one of its sides, there is a phenomenological level at which the lamp itself, "the entity itself in the present" is given in each act of perception. "The parts, moments, portions of what is at first simply perceived, by contrast, are there implicitly, unsilhouetted — but still given so that they can be made explicit."[57] Categorial intuition builds on the founding act of simple perception. "Categorial acts make the objectivity upon which they build — the simply given — accessible in a new kind of object." These acts "*disclose* the simply given objects *anew*, such that these objects come to explicit apprehension precisely in what they are."[58] Categorial acts do not change the given reality — the chair, for instance. However, in this case, "the chair becomes expressly visible precisely in what it is... [such that its]

53 Heidegger, *History of the Concept of Time*, 57.

54 Heidegger, *History of the Concept of Time*, 57.

55 Heidegger, *History of the Concept of Time*, 57–8.

56 Heidegger, *History of the Concept of Time*, 58.

57 Heidegger, *History of the Concept of Time*, 61–2.

58 Heidegger, *History of the Concept of Time*, 62.

presence, its being present, becomes more authentic through [the assertion that articulates the 'state of affairs' of the simply given chair, for instance its being-yellow]."[59]

The upshot of all of this is that, "the objectivity of an entity is really not exhausted by [a] narrow definition of reality, that objectivity in its broadest sense is much richer than the reality of a thing, and what is more, that the reality of a thing is comprehensible in its structure only on the basis of the full objectivity of the simply experienced entity."[60]

The acts that disclose the entity in its full objectivity on the basis of the simple perception of it are called acts of synthesis. Acts of ideation, on the basis of simple perception, bring out not the fullness of the object in its objectivity, but rather "what is called an idea" or species.[61] In earlier examples, it was "this chair" that was given in perception. Now, Heidegger is dealing with the presence in perception of the "chair-as-such." Whereas acts of synthesis co-intend the object of simple perception, acts of ideation do not, for the latter intend something that can be isolated from any particular, individual objects of perception. These and other categorial acts reveal categorial forms, which are "not something made by the subject and even less something added to the real objects, such that the real entity is itself modified by this forming." "Rather," Heidegger clarifies, "they actually present the entity more truly in its 'being-in-itself.'"[62] This means that phenomenology "arrives at the form of research sought by ancient ontology" and that, in short, "*scientific ontology is nothing but phenomenology.*"[63]

The third major discovery of phenomenology — the other two, to repeat, are intentionality and categorial intuition — concerns the *a priori*, which, Heidegger notes, had been taken since Descartes to refer to structures of knowing in a subject that do not depend on the

---

59 Heidegger, *History of the Concept of Time*, 63.

60 Heidegger, *History of the Concept of Time*, 66.

61 Heidegger, *History of the Concept of Time*, 66–7.

62 Heidegger, *History of the Concept of Time*, 70.

63 Heidegger, *History of the Concept of Time*, 72.

givenness of anything sensual or empirical.[64] It follows from the previous discussion of categorial intuition that for phenomenology, the *a priori* is not necessarily subjective: ideational acts can read ideational structures off of the perceived thing that have not been constructed or imposed by a subject.

Radicalizing Phenomenology: From Consciousness to the Question of Being

For phenomenology, "the apriori is *a feature of the structural sequence in the being of entities, in the ontological structure of being.*"[65] Heidegger aims to show in his lecture course that "the discovery of the apriori is really connected or actually identical with the discovery of the concept of being in Parmenides or in Plato."[66] This means, however, that a sense of being is presupposed in the notion of the apriori. Accordingly:

> Phenomenological questioning in its innermost tendency itself leads to the question of the being of the intentional and before anything else to the question of the sense of being as such. Phenomenology radicalized in its ownmost possibility is nothing but the questioning of Plato and Aristotle brought back to life: *the repetition, the retaking of the beginning of our scientific philosophy.*[67]

Heidegger's, "more radical conception of being" entails a modification of both the sense of the apriori in phenomenology, as well as the method of its apprehension.[68] To focus on the question of being is not dogmatically to exclude other themes, Heidegger notes:

---

64 Heidegger, *History of the Concept of Time*, 74.

65 Heidegger, *History of the Concept of Time*, 74.

66 Heidegger, *History of the Concept of Time*, 75.

67 Heidegger, *History of the Concept of Time*, 136.

68 Heidegger, *History of the Concept of Time*, 140.

A question is a prejudgment when it at the same time already contains a definite answer to the issue under question, or when it is a blind question aimed at something which cannot be so questioned. But now, entities are familiar to us and being is in a certain sense understood. The question of being as such, however, when it is put in a sufficiently formal manner, is the *most universal* and *emptiest*, but perhaps also the *most concrete* question, which a scientific inquiry can ever raise. *This question can be attained in any entity*; it need not be intentionality [that is interrogated in its being]. It does not even have to be an entity taken as a theme of a science. But we come to the question of being as such only if our inquiry is guided by the drive to *question to the very end* or *to inquire into the beginning*, that is, if it is determined by the sense of the phenomenological principle radically understood — *to allow entities to be seen as entities in their being…*But this at the same time implies what was already said about 'setting out to do the most radical research in philosophy.' It is 'in philosophy' and not in an already given theory laden with definite problem-horizons, disciplines and conceptual schemata that philosophy, under the guidance of the phenomenological principle, is to be restored to itself.[69]

Phenomenology is opposed to "construction and free-floating questioning in traditional concepts."[70] Instead of construction and groundless questioning, it aims "to do research that is autochthonously demonstrative, to provide demonstrations rooted in the native ground [and] to arrive at and to secure this ground…[i.e.] to lay [open] the foundation."[71] Phenomenology lays open the foundation through an "*accentuating articulation*" or "*analysis*" — an "*analytic description*" — of the "*intentionality in its apriori*," by way of categorial intuition.[72] In carrying this task out fully, Heidegger discloses that the traditionally thematic field of phenomenology, "pure consciousness," is "*not derived phenomenologically by going back to the matters themselves*" but by going back to a traditional idea of philosophy [namely,

69 Heidegger, *History of the Concept of Time*, 137.

70 Heidegger, *History of the Concept of Time*, 76.

71 Heidegger, *History of the Concept of Time*, 76.

72 Heidegger, *History of the Concept of Time*, 77–80.

Descartes' idea that *"consciousness is to be the region of an absolute science]."*[73] That is, Heidegger discovers that phenomenology is *"un-phenomenological"* with respect to "the basic task of determining its ownmost field."[74] A long passage captures Heidegger's exasperation at this state of affairs:

> What shows itself in the neglect of the primary question of being as such is rather the force and weight of the tradition to a degree which cannot be easily overestimated. Whenever the being of entities is treated without the explicit question of it [...] then those determinations of being and categories whose basic traits were discovered by Plato and Aristotle come into play. But the results of these [traditional] reflections are in command to some extent *without* maintaining the ground from which they were drawn in the expressly interrogative experience or without first of all bringing them to such an experience. These results prevail without the initial vitality of the articulating question, that is, without the full force of the interrogative experience and its explication from which these categories originated.
>
> The question posed by Plato in the *Sophist* [...] 'What then do you mean when you use (the word) "being"?' In short, what does 'being' mean? — this question is so vigorously posed, so full of life. But ever since Aristotle it has grown mute, so mute in fact that we are no longer aware that it is muted, because from then on we have continually dealt with being in the determinations and perspectives handed down by the Greeks. So muted is this question that we think we are raising it without actually coming within its reach at all, without seeing that the mere application of old concepts, whether these be the expressly conscious and most traditional concepts or even the more abundant unconscious and self-evident concepts, does not yet and does not really include the question of being.[75]

What is the meaning of this "neglect of the primary question of being"?[76] According to Heidegger, it is no accident. Instead, the omission "[serves] to manifest *the history of our very own Dasein* — history

---

73 Heidegger, *History of the Concept of Time*, 107.

74 Heidegger, *History of the Concept of Time*, 128.

75 Heidegger, *History of the Concept of Time*, 129.

76 Heidegger, *History of the Concept of Time*, 129.

understood not as the totality of public events but as the *mode of happening of this Dasein*."[77]

It becomes necessary to look to Dasein when elaborating the question of the meaning of being, because Dasein, "*the* entity which we ourselves are," is the entity "of which we say that it questions, looks upon, considers as, relates" — and so on.[78]

> To work out the articulation of the question of the sense of being [...] means to exhibit the questioning, that is, the Dasein itself, as an entity; for only in this way does what is sought become something sought in its most proper sense. The questioning is here itself co-affected by what it asks for, because the questioning is after being and questioning is itself an entity. This affectedness of the questioning entity by what is asked for belongs to the ownmost sense of the question of being itself. [...] The actual elaboration of the articulation of the question is accordingly a *phenomenology of Dasein* [...] Only the phenomenological tendency — to clarify and to understand being as such — bears within itself the task of an explication of the entity which is the questioning itself — the *Dasein* which we, the very questioners, are.[79]

The task at hand is this: "the explication of Dasein as the entity whose way of being is questioning itself."[80] As previously indicated, a phenomenology of Dasein means an "analytic" of Dasein, a description of its apriori. Accordingly, the next section of the *History of the Concept of Time* is an existential analytic of Dasein, which asks after the question of the meaning of being.

Let us now transition to *Being and Time* (1927), a better-known source for Heidegger's existential analytic of Dasein.[81] As in his 1925 lecture, in *Being and Time* Heidegger draws attention to the

---

77 Heidegger, *History of the Concept of Time*, 129.

78 Heidegger, *History of the Concept of Time*, 143–150, 148.

79 Heidegger, *History of the Concept of Time*, 148–9.

80 Heidegger, *History of the Concept of Time*, 150.

81 Martin Heidegger, *Being and Time* (Albany: State University of New York Press, 2010).

constitution of the sciences out of basic concepts, "determinations in which the area of knowledge underlying all the thematic objects of a science attains an understanding that precedes and guides all positive investigation."[82] The "preliminary research that creates the fundamental concepts" — phenomenological research — "amounts," Heidegger says, summarizing his earlier presentation of the radicalization of phenomenology, "to nothing else than interpreting these beings in terms of the basic constitution of their being."[83] Because the meaning of being is not clear, but obscure, the clarification of the meaning of being is the "fundamental task" of the most fundamental research.[84] What is more, clarification of the meaning of being becomes possible through the interrogation of the privileged being, Dasein, that is "in its being…concerned *about* its very being."[85]

Heidegger distinguishes between two levels of analysis, the *ontic* and *existentiell*, on one hand, and the *ontological* and *existential*, on the other. The former pair concerns the particular case, such as whether this or that person decides upon this or that course of action, for instance. The latter pair, by contrast, refers to the analysis of constitutive structures.[86] Dasein is "privileged" with regard to the question of being both ontically and ontologically.[87] It is privileged ontically, because it is that being whose "essence lies…in the fact that in each instance it has to be its being as its own."[88] But this very "definition" also shows that Dasein is ontologically privileged: it is not defined by its substantiality, but by its relation to being.[89] In other words, it is "the

---

82   Heidegger, *Being and Time* 9.

83   Heidegger, *Being and Time*, 9.

84   Heidegger, *Being and Time*, 10.

85   Heidegger, *Being and Time*, 11.

86   Heidegger, *Being and Time*, 11.

87   Heidegger, *Being and Time*, 12.

88   Heidegger, *Being and Time*, 11.

89   Heidegger, *Being and Time*, 41.

being that always already in its being is related to *what is sought* in this question [of being]."[90]

Dasein thus has "ontic-ontological priority."[91] The analytic of Dasein will concern itself with the Dasein's ontological structures or existentials, but all the while the "roots of the existential analysis… are ultimately *existentiell*," i.e. they are rooted in "[possibilities] of being of each existing Dasein."[92] Thus, "the question of being is nothing else than the radicalization of an essential tendency of being that belongs to Dasein itself, namely, of the pre-ontological understanding of being."[93] Because "ontically" we have some "presupposed" (vague) understanding of being, we have the possibility of making being a theme in our questioning. Once this has been established, "the problem of gaining and securing the kind of access that leads to Dasein truly becomes crucial."[94]

In accordance with the dictates of phenomenology, the task is to ensure that Dasein, "can show itself to itself on its own terms," such that its essential structures are revealed.[95] But Dasein's essential structures are typically obscured, for at least two reasons. First, "Dasein… has the inclination to be entangled in the world in which it is and to interpret itself in terms of that world by its reflected light"; and second, "Dasein is also entangled in a tradition" that "bars access to

---

90 Heidegger, *Being and Time*, 13.

91 Heidegger, *Being and Time*, 12.

92 Heidegger, *Being and Time*, 12, 44: "All explications arising from an analytic of Dasein are gained with a view toward its structure of existence. Because these explications are defined in terms of existentiality, we shall call the characteristics of being of Dasein *existentials*. They are to be sharply delimited from the determinations of being of those beings unlike Dasein which we call *categories*."

93 Heidegger, *Being and Time*, 13.

94 Heidegger, *Being and Time*, 16.

95 Heidegger, *Being and Time*, 16–7.

the original 'wellsprings' out of which the traditional categories and concepts were in part genuinely drawn."[96]

So, for instance, phenomenological research, as we saw, was hampered by a tradition according to which it took "consciousness" for granted. It took Heidegger's radicalization of that tradition to uncover the "wellsprings" of the question of being. The philosophical tradition "uproots the historicity of Dasein [i.e. the structures in accordance with which something like 'history' and tradition are possible at all] to such an extent that it only takes an interest in the manifold forms of possible types, directions, and standpoints of philosophizing in the most remote and strangest cultures, and with this interest tries to veil its own groundlessness."[97]

Far from being proof of Dasein's abiding interest in the question of the meaning of being, the tradition of ontology specifically is, as a tradition, rather evidence that the question of being has in its genuine sense been forgotten.[98] Whatever "advances" the tradition might evince, and whatever "distinctive domains of being" it reveals, a "thorough neglect of the question of being" is decisive. Consequently, Heidegger calls for the "destruction" of this tradition. He characterizes the task of this destruction as the "demonstration of the provenance of the fundamental ontological concepts."[99] Destruction amounts neither to the relativization of standpoints nor to "disburdening ourselves of the ontological tradition":[100]

> On the contrary, it should stake out the positive possibilities in that tradi-
> tion, and that always means to stake out its *limits*. These are factually given
> with a specific formulation of the question and the prescribed demarcation

---

96 Heidegger, *Being and Time*, 20, 42: "The possibility of understanding the being of this being stands and falls with the secure accomplishment of the correct presentation of this being."

97 Heidegger, *Being and Time*, 22.

98 Heidegger, *Being and Time*, 21.

99 Heidegger, *Being and Time*, 22.

100 Heidegger, *Being and Time*, 22.

of the possible field of investigation. Destruction does not relate itself in a negative way to the past: its critique concerns 'today' and the dominant way we treat the history of ontology, whether it is conceived as the history of opinions, ideas, or problems. Destruction does not wish to bury the past in nullity; it has a *positive* intent. Its negative function remains tacit and indirect.[101]

Heidegger's plan for *Being and Time*, which he did not explicitly fulfill, was to undertake this destruction through readings of Kant, Descartes, and Aristotle. His later lecture courses and remarks on these and other thinkers, however, did carry out the task of destruction.

As for the obstruction posed not by tradition but by our everydayness, the analytic of Dasein aims to uncover the existential structures of everydayness and their impact.

The structures of everydayness are for the most part covered up, not given.[102] Moreover, in their operation, they can cover up other phenomena.[103] They "[constitute] the ontic immediate of this being."[104]

Dasein is to be explicated or described, and this is called "interpretation," an act by which "the proper meaning of being and the basic structures of the very being of Dasein are *made known* to the understanding of being that belongs to Dasein itself."[105]

Heidegger's plan for *Being and Time* was to proceed in two steps: (1) a "preparatory analytic" whose "aim…is to expose the horizon for the most primordial interpretation of being" (namely, "temporality") followed by (2) an existential analytic properly founded on that horizon.[106] The second part would have included the destruction of the history of ontology. The first part was also not completed as planned. According to the outline, it was to consist of three sections: (i) "The preparatory fundamental analysis of Dasein," (ii) "Dasein and

---

101 Heidegger, *Being and Time*, 22.

102 Heidegger, *Being and Time*, 33–4.

103 Heidegger, *Being and Time*, 122, 161–174.

104 Heidegger, *Being and Time*, 43.

105 Heidegger, *Being and Time*, 35.

106 Heidegger, *Being and Time*, 17.

temporality," (iii) "Time and Being." Only the first two sections were
completed.

The following offers a brief synopsis of some principal discoveries of Part 1, sections one and two, before turning to discuss the
move from the "transcendental" approach of *Being and Time* to the
"beyng-historical thinking" period starting with the *Contributions
to Philosophy (of the Event)*. The exposition highlights fundamental
continuities in Heidegger's thought. This basic overview will help the
reader grasp what Strauss, Rorty, Derrida, and Dugin encountered in
reading Heidegger.

Heidegger names the first main structure to which he draws attention, "being-in-the-world."[107] "This compound expression," he explains, "indicates, in the very way we have coined it, that it stands for
a *unified* phenomenon."[108] There is not a subject "in here" that I am,
and a world "out there" that I encounter, but rather a unified structure,
comprising a "multiplicity of constitutive structural factors."[109] These
factors are the "in-the-world," the "being which always has being-in-
the-world as the way it is," and "being-in ['in-ness'] as such."[110]

"World" means primarily for Heidegger neither:

1. An ontic totality of objectively present beings, nor
2. The region that embraces those beings ("the 'world' of the mathematician" as "the region of all possible mathematical objects," for
   instance), but rather:
3. That in which Dasein lives ("world can mean the 'public' world
   of the we or one's 'own' and nearest (domestic) surrounding
   world").[111]

---

107 Heidegger, *Being and Time*, 53.

108 Heidegger, *Being and Time*, 53.

109 "Subject and object" are "so little" the same as "Dasein and world" that "even
    putting them together in order to reject this is already fatal." Heidegger, *Being
    and Time*, 60.

110 Heidegger, *Being and Time*, 53–4.

111 Heidegger, *Being and Time*, 64–5.

What characterizes beings in the world most of all, for Heidegger, is that they are useful items. These items are not first pre-determined as mere "objects" or "things," upon which further constructions add layers of significance. Rather, they are always already encountered as meaningful in a network of signification.[112] Their pre-conceptual meaning (which Heidegger calls "handiness," *Zuhandenheit*)[113] is not added after the fact of encounter; it is *"the ontological categorial definition of beings as they are 'in themselves.'"*[114] "World" itself, then, comes to be discovered structurally as that referential system, and thus as something that Dasein "always already *was*."[115]

Because of this structure, beings are "relevant," i.e. they are "referred to something," or "together with something else," not as lying next to it, but as meaningfully related to it, as having a "wherefore" and a "what-for."[116] "*Which* relevance things at hand have," Heidegger emphasizes, "is prefigured in terms of the total relevance."[117] Eventually, structures of relevance can be traced back "to a what-for which *no longer* has relevance, which itself is not a being of the kind of being of things at hand within a world, but is a being whose being is defined as being-in-the-world" — Dasein.[118]

Dasein lets beings be relevant with respect to a purpose or "for-the-sake-of-which" that is a possible way of being for Dasein.[119] The complex structure of the world component of being-in-the-world concerns a "relational totality of significance," where the relevance of innerworldly beings is referred back ontologically to Dasein's

---

112 Heidegger, *Being and Time*, 68–71.

113 Or "Ready at hand." (Ed.)

114 Heidegger, *Being and Time*, 71.

115 Heidegger, *Being and Time*, 75.

116 Heidegger, *Being and Time*, 82.

117 Heidegger, *Being and Time*, 82.

118 Heidegger, *Being and Time*, 83.

119 Heidegger, *Being and Time*, 84.

self-understanding.[120] Dasein is the being that can "discover" inner-worldly beings (useful and meaningful) through the "world," a referential system and ontological structure or "existential" of Dasein.

Thus far, the discussion has characterized beings in the world and the definition and character of the "world." In addition, Heidegger also discusses "who" Dasein is within the everyday mode. This question arises with the revelation of being-in-the-world as Dasein's structure, because it is no longer accurate to speak of the self as mere "subject." "And thus," Heidegger writes, "an isolated I without the others is in the end just as far from being given initially [as an isolated subject is]."[121] Dasein is, by contrast, always "*Mitdasein,*" though, as in the case of its other existentials, this fact needs to be brought to phenomenological awareness correctly and rigorously. Reference to others is included in the referential totality of the world of useful items:

> The field, for example, along which we walk 'outside' shows itself as belonging to such and such a person who keeps it in good order…The boat anchored at the shore refers in its being-in-itself to an acquaintance who undertakes his voyage with it…The others who are at hand are not somehow added on in thought to an initially merely objective present thing, but these 'things are encountered from the world in which they are at hand for the others.[122]

In disclosing a world, then, Dasein discloses not only useful items, but also other beings that "*are like* the very Dasein which finds them," that are "*there, too, and there with it.*"[123] These "others" are not set over and against an "I," at least initially. "Others are," Heidegger explains, "rather, those from whom one mostly does *not* distinguish oneself, those among whom one also is."[124] Dasein is "with" the others, not in the

---

120 Heidegger, *Being and Time*, 85.

121 Heidegger, *Being and Time*, 113.

122 Heidegger, *Being and Time*, 115.

123 Heidegger, *Being and Time*, 115.

124 Heidegger, *Being and Time*, 115.

way that innerworldly beings are with one another. The "with-ness" pertaining to the kind of being Dasein is differs from that appropriate to whatever is not Dasein.

As world, Dasein is with others: "Dasein is essentially being-with."[125] The experience of being alone does not refute that fact: "The being-alone of Dasein, too, is a being-with in the world. The other can be *lacking* only *in* and *for* a being-with. Being-alone is a deficient mode of being-with, its possibility is a proof for the latter."[126] Conversely, actually being among a multitude, Dasein can be alone.[127] In this case, "Their Dasein-with is encountered in the mode of indifference and being alien."[128] Indeed, Heidegger asserts that deficient modes of being-with, such as "passing-one-another-by" and "not-mattering-to-one-another," are average, everyday modes of being.[129]

Besides modes of indifference, being-with in its everydayness is characterized by what Heidegger calls distantiality, averageness, and leveling down, as well as "disburdening" and accommodating.[130] Distantiality refers to Dasein's "constant care as to the way one differs" from others.[131] "The others" that are a point of reference for Dasein in

---

125   Heidegger, *Being and Time*, 117.

126   Heidegger, *Being and Time*, 117.

127   Heidegger, *Being and Time*, 117.

128   Heidegger, *Being and Time*, 117. Also 122: "Being-with-one-another cannot be understood as an accumulative result of the occurrence of multiple 'subjects.' Encountering a number of 'subjects' itself is possible only by treating the others to be encountered in their Dasein-with merely as 'numbers.' Such numbers are discovered only by a distinctive being-with and being-toward-one-another."

129   Heidegger, *Being and Time*, 118. Positive modes of demonstrating "concern" for another include the two extremes of stepping in to do something for another so that "he can take it over as something finished and available or disburden himself of it completely," on one hand, and, on the other, helping one to return "authentically" to an awareness of one's proper existential constitution. Heidegger, *Being and Time*, 119.

130   Heidegger, *Being and Time*, 123–4.

131   Heidegger, *Being and Time*, 122.

its deficient and everyday modes "are not *definite others*," but rather the general "they" (*das Man*). "In utilizing public transportation," Heidegger writes, by way of clarification, "in the use of information services such as the newspaper, every other is like the next. This being-with-one-another dissolves one's own Dasein completely into the kind of being of 'the others' in such a way that the others, as distinguishable and explicit, disappear more and more."[132]

The "they," which is a mode of being of Dasein's being-with existential, is a "true dictatorship," Heidegger says, in which "every priority is noiselessly squashed...[and] everything that is original is flattened down as something long since known."[133] Under the influence of the they as a mode of being-with, "[e]verything won through struggle becomes something manageable...[and] every mystery loses its power."[134] No outstanding possibilities of being are welcome under the dictatorship of the they.

The dictatorship of the they robs Dasein of its responsibility for itself. It "disburdens" Dasein of the task of being authentic — i.e., of acting in accordance with a proper grasp of its existentiality and possibilities — and "accommodates [it] in its tendency to take things easily and make them easy."[135] As Dugin might say, the they commands us to "relax."[136]

Although Pierre Bourdieu regarded Heidegger's presentation of the *they* as based on the cultural malaise of the Weimar Republic as seen through the eyes of conservative revolutionaries, Heidegger himself insists that the they is an ontological structure (or existential) of Dasein as being-in-the-world and hence also as being-with.[137] For

---

132 Heidegger, *Being and Time*, 123.

133 Heidegger, *Being and Time*, 123.

134 Heidegger, *Being and Time*, 123.

135 Heidegger, *Being and Time*, 124.

136 Dugin, *The Fourth Political Theory*, 22.

137 Pierre Bourdieu, *The Political Ontology of Martin Heidegger* (Stanford: Stanford University Press, 1991). Bourdieu also traced Heidegger's analysis of Dasein's

Heidegger, a public "they" of leveling averageness is possible as a "cultural" fact only because ontologically Dasein is what it is. Bourdieu and those like him have put the cart before the horse, confusing orders of priority and possibility in a very un-Heideggerian (meaning in this context: un-phenomenological) manner.

The third constituent of being-in-the-world, besides world and the who of Dasein, is Being-in. As noted, Dasein is not "in" a world the way that innerworldly objects are. Therefore, its "spatiality" is not that of an object like a table, such that it would make sense to think of your extension as similar to that of all "bodies in space." Rather, "Dasein itself has its own 'being-in-space,' which in its turn is possible only *on the basis of being-in-the-world in general.*"[138] Dasein also does not "enter in" after initially being "a sort of a being which is free from being-in": it is always-already being-in.[139] Dasein exhibits "existential spatiality."[140] Indeed, Dasein is the clearing, Heidegger says, because of which there can be a here and a there at all. In a passage prefiguring important notions in later writings, Heidegger asserts the following:

> When we talk in an ontically figurative way about the *lumen natural* in human being, we mean nothing other than the existential-ontological structure of this being, the fact that it *is* in such a way as to be its there [*sein*

"entanglement," "idle-talk," and other existentials and modes of its being to the "culture" and "politics" of Weimar-period anti-liberal conservatism, despite such statements from Heidegger as the following: "Our existential, ontological interpretation...does not make any ontic statement about the 'corruption of human nature'...because its problematic is *prior to* any statement about corruption or incorruption" (173). He writes of a "homology between the structure of the philosophical stances and the structure of overtly political stances," which "demarcates the very restricted range of philosophical stances compatible with the politico-moral options of any given thinker" (42). So for Bourdieu, Heidegger is a phenomenologist of such and such a kind *because* he has such and such a "political stance."

138 Heidegger, *Being and Time*, 56.

139 Heidegger, *Being and Time*, 57.

140 Heidegger, *Being and Time*, 56. Italicized in original. See also 102–110.

Da zu sein]. To say that it is 'illuminated' means that it is cleared in itself *as* being-in-the-world, not by another being, but in such a way that it *is* itself the clearing. Only for a being thus cleared existentially do objective present things become accessible in the light or concealed in darkness. By its very nature, Dasein brings its there [*Da*] along with it. If it lacks its there, it is not only factically not, but is in no sense, the being which is essentially Dasein. *Dasein is its disclosedness.*[141]

For Heidegger, to explicate Dasein's being-in means to explicate "the existential constitution of the there [Da]."[142] That constitution has two principal ways of being, attunement [*Befindlichkeit*] and understanding [*Verstehen*]. They are "determined by discourse [*Rede*]."[143] Let's take them one at a time.

Attunement and Mood

Being is always already disclosed to Dasein in non-cognitive states familiar to us ontically though unfamiliar to us ontologically as moods.[144] "Mood," Heidegger writes, "makes manifest 'how one is and is coming along.' In this 'how one is' being in a mood brings being to its 'there.'"[145] In its everyday modes, Dasein does not know "where" the being of these moods comes from. It "does not pursue what they disclose and does not allow itself to confront what has been disclosed."[146] Heidegger's name for Dasein's being-disclosed without knowing the "whence and whither" of its being is "thrownness," "the *thrownness* of this being into its there...in such a way that it is the there as *being-in-the-world*."[147] We shall see in later writings such as the *Contributions*

---

141 Heidegger, *Being and Time*, 129.

142 Heidegger, *Being and Time*, 130.

143 Heidegger, *Being and Time*, 130.

144 Heidegger, *Being and Time*, 131.

145 Heidegger, *Being and Time*, 131.

146 Heidegger, *Being and Time*, 131.

147 Heidegger, *Being and Time*, 131.

that this analysis continues to play an important role in Heidegger's thought, for instance when he distinguishes the predominant attunement of the first beginning of philosophy (wonder) from that of the other beginning (shock, etc.). Mood is "a primordial kind of being of Dasein in which it is disclosed to itself *before* all cognition and willing and *beyond* their scope of disclosure."[148]

From what has been said, it should be clear that it would be inappropriate to regard mood as a psychic phenomenon, since Dasein is not the subject but rather being-in-the-world, and since Heidegger does not think about Dasein in terms of psychological beings but in terms of being. Attunement, like understanding but not reducible to it, discloses "world, Dasein-with and existence because this disclosure itself is essentially *being-in-the-world*."[149] Heidegger adduces the example of theoretical looking in order to show that mood is "always-already" co-determinative: that is, even in theoretical looking, Dasein is determined by "*tranquil* lingering." In other words, to show that Dasein is co-constituted by attunement and understanding, and to indicate that attunement discloses beyond the scope of understanding, is not "to surrender science ontically to 'feeling.'"[150]

Understanding

Like attunement, understanding is a "fundamental existential" of Dasein. That is, it is an original mode of disclosure characterizing Dasein as *being-in-the-world*. More specialized and derivative modes of cognition are possible only because Dasein is originally always-already constituted in its being by understanding.[151] That Dasein is constituted by understanding means that it is disclosed (in positive and deficient modes) to itself in terms of the being it is, a

---

148 Heidegger, *Being and Time*, 132.

149 Heidegger, *Being and Time*, 133.

150 Heidegger, *Being and Time*, 134.

151 Heidegger, *Being and Time*, 138.

"being-possible."¹⁵² "As disclosing, understanding always concerns the whole fundamental constitution of being-in-the-world. As a potentiality of being, being-in is always a potentiality of being-in-the-world."¹⁵³ Understanding discloses Dasein in its being as being-possible, because "understanding in itself has the existential structure which we call *project [Entwurf]*."¹⁵⁴ Dasein is always being-projected, and "[disclosing]…its there as the there of a potentiality of being."¹⁵⁵ Accordingly, how the unity and multiplicity of "being-in-the-world" considered earlier are disclosed to it depends in part on the projected possibilities of being which are determining that disclosure. Incidentally, this allows us to ask about political constitutions as Dasein's projections, as Dugin does.¹⁵⁶

The intimate relation of these remarks to the project of *Being and Time* resides principally in the link between the question of the meaning of being, on one hand, and existential access to meaning and questioning through the existential of understanding, on the other.¹⁵⁷ The very ground for a potential elaboration of the question of being lies in Dasein as understanding:

> In the projectedness of its being upon the for-the-sake-of-which [of relevance], together with the projectedness of its own being upon significance

152 Heidegger, *Being and Time*, 139.

153 Heidegger, *Being and Time*, 139–141.

154 Heidegger, *Being and Time*, 140.

155 Heidegger, *Being and Time*, 141.

156 See Chapter Five.

157 Heidegger, *Being and Time*, 147: "Meaning is an existential of Dasein… Only Dasein 'has' meaning in that the disclosedness of being-in-the-world can be 'fulfilled' through the beings discoverable in it. *Thus only Dasein can be meaningful or meaningless.* This means: its own being and the beings disclosed with that being can be appropriated in an understanding or they can be confined to incomprehensibility…And when we ask about the meaning of being, our inquiry does not become profound and does not brood on anything which stands behind being, but questions being itself in so far as it stands within the intelligibility of Dasein." Italics in original.

(world), lies the disclosedness of being in general. An understanding of being is already anticipated in the projecting upon possibilities. Being is understood in the project, but not ontologically grasped.[158]

Because Dasein is understanding, Dasein can thematize its understanding through what Heidegger calls interpretation, "not the acknowledgement of what has been understood, but rather the development of possibilities projected in understanding."[159] Interpretation of innerworldly beings delineates their "as-what" or "what for" (the coffee "as" something to drink before it gets cold).[160] From what we saw in our earlier discussion of the character of beings disclosed in the world, we can easily follow what Heidegger means when he asserts that, "[i]nterpretation does not, so to speak, throw a 'significance' over what is nakedly objectively present and does not stick a value on it, but what is encountered in the world is always already in a relevance which is disclosed in the understanding of world, a relevance which is made explicit by interpretation."[161]

As discourse, interpretation expresses the intelligibility of Dasein as being-in-the-world.[162] Discourse is not only speech, but also silence and listening. Listening, Heidegger writes, "is the existential being-open of Dasein as being-with for the other."[163] Silence discloses understanding, in the following sense, for example: "In talking with one another the person who is silent can 'let something be understood,' that is, one can develop an understanding more authentically than the

158 Heidegger, *Being and Time*, 143.

159 Heidegger, *Being and Time*, 144, 35: "The *logos* of the phenomenology of Dasein has the character of *hermeneuein,* through which the proper meaning of being and the basic structures of the very being of Dasein are *made known* to the understanding of being that belongs to Dasein itself." "Λόγος " and "ἑρμηνεύειν" in the original Greek. (Ed.)

160 Heidegger, *Being and Time*, 144.

161 Heidegger, *Being and Time*, 145.

162 Heidegger, *Being and Time*, 156.

163 Heidegger, *Being and Time*, 158.

person who never runs out of words."[164] The existential importance of discourse for Heidegger [*Rede, logos*] in determining the being that we are allows us to grasp the importance for him of the fact that the Greek characterization of man as *zoon* logon *echon* was translated into Latin as *animal rationale*: the latter formulation "covers over the phenomenal basis" of the original definition.[165] In his *Contributions to Philosophy (of the Event)*, Heidegger will write that philosophy as he conceives of it "is equivalent to an essential transformation of the human being: from 'rational animal' (*animal rationale*) to Da-Sein," but we will come to that later.[166]

The last principle notion in the first half of *Being and Time* is this: not only is Dasein being-in-the-world, it is always ahead of itself as such. As a neologism, Heidegger calls this "being-ahead-of-oneself-already-being-in-the-world."[167] The shorter name for this unitary, yet articulated structure is "care."[168] Dasein can "take care" of things in the world only because it "is" care in this technical, existential sense.[169] It is also this structure that allows Dasein to "be free for" its possibilities of being, whether willingly and authentically, or unwillingly and inauthentically.[170]

By the second division of *Being and Time*, Heidegger admits that although the analytic has discovered the principle structures of the being in question (Dasein), it has not yet done so "primordially" enough

---

164 Heidegger, *Being and Time*, 159.

165 Heidegger, *Being and Time*, 149.

166 Heidegger, *Contributions*, 5.

167 Heidegger, *Being and Time*, 186.

168 Or *Sorge* in the German, which also means "worry." See footnote #234, however.

169 Heidegger, *Being and Time*, 186. As he reiterates elsewhere, "care — it must be said over and again — does not mean melancholy, preoccupation, or tormenting worry over something or other. All that is simply the distorted essence of care insofar as additionally it is placed into another misunderstanding according to which care is one 'disposition' or 'attitude' among others." (Heidegger, *Contributions*, 29).

170 Heidegger, *Being and Time*, 186–87.

for "radical clarification" concerning Dasein's understanding of being to be fully accessible.[171] With everyday, inauthentic modes of being at the forefront of the analysis, "the existential structure of authentic potentiality-of-being" has not been elucidated.

Primordiality, Heidegger argues, requires that we grasp the wholeness of Dasein, which it would seem the structure of care as always-being-ahead would prohibit us from doing.[172] The need arises, then, to clarify whether and to what extent Dasein is limited. Heidegger does this by analyzing the existential structure of death as end.[173] "Death," he writes, "is a possibility of being that Dasein always has to take upon itself [since it belongs to Dasein's very existence that it is constantly a being-toward-the-end]." He continues as follows:

> With death, Dasein stands before itself in its *ownmost* potentiality-of-being. In this possibility, Dasein is concerned about its being-in-the-world absolutely. Its death is the possibility of no-longer-being-able-to-be-there. When Dasein is imminent to itself as this possibility, it is *completely* thrown back upon its ownmost potentiality-of-being.[174]

Can Dasein disclose itself in attuned understanding through this possibility? Heidegger shows that *it can do so*, without actualizing the possibility and thus no longer being there to be disclosed.[175] It can do so through the anticipation of death as possibility.

"Anticipation" means "being toward possibility," without "realizing" it.[176] Anticipation brings the possible near, and "the nearest near-

---

171 Heidegger, *Being and Time*, 221–22.

172 Heidegger, *Being and Time*, 223–27.

173 Heidegger, *Being and Time*, 231–33. This does not exclude recognition of "birth," for: "Factical Dasein exists as being born, and in being born it is already dying in the sense of being-toward-death. Both 'ends' and their 'between' *are* as long as Dasein factically exists" (Heidegger, *Being and Time*, 357).

174 Heidegger, *Being and Time*, 241.

175 Heidegger, *Being and Time*, 249–55.

176 Heidegger, *Being and Time*, 251.

ness of being-toward-death as possibility is as far removed as possible from anything real."[177] It is in its anticipation of death as its ownmost and insuperable possibility that Dasein is disclosed to itself in its authentic existence, i.e. not as fleeing from itself and its possibilities in the everydayness of entanglement and the they.[178]

Heidegger says that in this anticipation, Dasein is also "individualized down to itself," revealing that "any being-together with what is taken care of and any being-with others fails when one's ownmost potentiality-of-being is at stake."[179] This does not mean that Dasein is ultimately and finally an individual, however, since its "authentic being a self" is nevertheless constituted as being-in-a-world (and hence also being-with).[180] It is just that there is a moment of individuation that occurs in authentically anticipating one's death that then "forces the being that anticipates into the possibility of taking over its ownmost being from itself of its own accord."[181]

Dasein can be truly "free for possibilities" only when it has first seized itself in anticipating the possibility of its death and thus disclosing itself in its wholeness.[182] Heidegger calls this act "resoluteness" [*Entschlossenheit*], and he devotes several sections to an elucidation of its characteristics, including its primary attunement, understanding, and mode of discourse.[183] (Heidegger's notion of resoluteness was criticized by some for failing to guide Dasein in the content of the possibilities it seizes. "Upon what," Heidegger asks, "does Dasein resolve itself in its resoluteness? To what should it resolve itself? Only

177 Heidegger, *Being and Time*, 251, emphasis in original.
178 Heidegger, *Being and Time*, 252.
179 Heidegger, *Being and Time*, 252.
180 Heidegger, *Being and Time*, 252.
181 Heidegger, *Being and Time*, 252.
182 Heidegger, *Being and Time*, 253.
183 Heidegger, *Being and Time*, 257–284.

the resolution itself can answer this."[184] It does so in a concrete "situation," in which it finds itself when it resolves).[185]

After showing why resoluteness as authentic disclosure of Dasein as a whole is ontologically possible, Heidegger asks whether Dasein ever actually ("ontically," "factically") demands of itself this utmost possibility of being.[186] Because anticipation describes an existential structure, and resoluteness an existentiell act, Heidegger inquires as to the relation of the two: "What if resoluteness, as the *authentic* truth of Dasein, reached the *certainty authentically belonging to it*, only on the anticipation of death? What if all the factical '*anticipatoriness*' of resolve were authentically understood, that is, existentielly *caught up with* only in the *anticipation* of death?"[187] Heidegger names this possible connection between the two "anticipatory resoluteness."[188] Because resoluteness is concerned with Dasein's fully embracing its character as thrown (i.e. with "nullity" at its ground), and because this nullity is the limit end for Dasein, which had been earlier characterized as being-toward-death, resoluteness "harbours in itself authentic

---

184 Heidegger, *Being and Time*, 285. Moreover, "To portray the factical existentiell possibilities in their general features and connections, and to interpret them according to their existential structure belongs to the scope of a thematic existential anthropology." Heidegger, *Being and Time*, 288, with note 16, where Heidegger refers to Jasper's *Psychologie der Weltanschauungen* as the first work along these lines.

185 Heidegger, *Being and Time*, 286. The situation "is disclosed only in a free act of resolve that has not been determined beforehand, but is open to the possibility of such determination" (Heidegger, *Being and Time*, 294).

186 Heidegger, *Being and Time*, 255.

187 Heidegger, *Being and Time*, 290.

188 Heidegger, *Being and Time*. This phrase and theme is the focus of Johannes Fritsche's study, *Historical Destiny and National Socialism in Heidegger's Being and Time* (Berkeley: University of California Press, 1989).

being-toward-death as the possible existentiell modality of its own authenticity."[189]

Here, Heidegger shifts his emphasis to the ways in which "temporality" is constitutive of Dasein's being as care, as disclosed by anticipatory resoluteness. In anticipation, Dasein is futural: "Anticipation makes Dasein *authentically* futural in such a way that anticipation itself is possible only in that Dasein, *as existing*, always already comes toward itself, that is, is futural in its being in general."[190] In seizing its null ground, Dasein seizes that which it has always been, and "only because Dasein in general *is* as I *am*-having-been can it come futurally toward itself in such a way that it comes-*back*."[191] Finally, in its authentic existence, Dasein discloses a situation. "Resolute being," Heidegger writes, "together with what is at hand in the situation, that is, letting *what presences* in the surrounding world be encountered in action, is possible only in a *making* that being *present*. Only as the *present*, in the sense of making present, can resoluteness be what it is."[192] Of course, here the terms past, present, and future are not meant simply in the ordinary sense. Rather, the ordinary sense of time is possible only as a modification of the temporality that Dasein is and can authentically or inauthentically *be*.[193] Heidegger continues his presentation and elaboration of the temporality of Dasein's fundamental structures for many sections that I shall pass over, in order to come to Chapter Five, on "temporality and historicity."

---

189 Heidegger, *Being and Time*, 292, italicized in original; 296: "The question of the wholeness of Dasein, initially discussed only with regard to the ontological method, has its justification, but only because the ground for that justification goes back to an ontic possibility of Dasein." For an interesting account of an "ontic" context that might might have informed Heidegger's thinking in these passages, see William H. F. Altman, *Martin Heidegger and the First World War: Being and Time as Funeral Oration* (Lanham: Lexington Books, 2012).

190 Heidegger, *Being and Time*, 311.

191 Heidegger, *Being and Time*, 311.

192 Heidegger, *Being and Time*, 311.

193 Heidegger, *Being and Time*, 312.

Dasein, as we have seen, is constitutionally being-toward-death. But it also always exists as being-born.[194] Dasein *is* the "between" of these two "ends."[195] That is to say, Dasein — characterized by care, whose meaning is temporality — is always "stretched out [and] stretching itself along."[196] Heidegger's name for this is Dasein's "occurrence" or *Geschehen,* a word connected with *Geschichte,* history, and *Geschichtlichkeit,* historicity. Something like the study of history ordinarily conceived of (*Historie*) is possible only because Dasein is already existentially historical. The former has its "ontological provenance [in] the historicity of Dasein."[197]

In considering the everyday notion of history, Heidegger asks what it is about certain items presently existing, those called "antiques," for instance, that imparts to them a historical character. It is not that they are no longer useable or in use. Rather, in use or not, "they are no longer what they were."[198] Why not? According to Heidegger's analysis, it is because the world of significance in which they had their relevance as useful things no longer is.[199] World, in turn, as we saw, "*is* only in the mode of *existing* Dasein."[200] And Dasein, as we say, is not only historical in the sense of having been and being no more, but as stretched out in the synchronous temporal "ecstases" of past, present, and future.[201] Thus,

beings do not become 'more historical' as we go on to a past ever farther away, so that what is most ancient would be the most authentically

---

194 Heidegger, *Being and Time,* 357.

195 Heidegger, *Being and Time,* 357. cf. Footnote #238.

196 Heidegger, *Being and Time,* 358, emphasis in original.

197 Heidegger, *Being and Time,* 359.

198 Heidegger, *Being and Time,* 362.

199 Heidegger, *Being and Time,* 362.

200 Heidegger, *Being and Time,* 362.

201 Heidegger, *Being and Time,* 319–363. cf. ἔκστασις (ékstasis, "displacement, cession, trance") (Ed.)

historical, [but rather] the 'temporal' distance from now and today has no
primarily constitutive significance for the historicity of authentically historical beings, not because they are not 'in time' or are timeless, but rather
because they *primordially* exist *temporally in a way that* nothing objective
present 'in time,' whether passing away or coming into being, could ever,
by its ontological essence, be temporal in such a way.[202]

The discussion of Dasein's historicity helps explain in general from
where authentic Dasein, in anticipatory resoluteness, draws its possibilities, namely from "the heritage [that] resoluteness takes over
as thrown."[203] Dasein authentically resolves for a possibility "that it
inherited and yet has chosen" — its "fate" [*Schicksal*].[204] It chooses its
fate, and not the "endless multiplicity of closest possibilities offering
themselves — those of comfort, shirking and taking things easy."[205]
But because Dasein is, as we saw, always being-with, authentic fate
or occurrence is always "an occurrence-with," which Heidegger calls
"destiny" [*Geschick*]. Since the possibility comes as an inheritance
from the temporal ecstasy of having-been, Heidegger can say that the
resolve for it amounts to a "repetition" of sorts.[206] And yet,

> the repetition of what is possible neither brings back 'what is past,' nor does
> it bind the 'present' back to what is 'outdated.' Arising from a resolute self-
> projection, repetition is not convinced by 'something past,' in just letting
> it come back as what was once real. Rather, repetition *responds* to [that]
> possibility... Repetition neither abandons itself to the past, nor does it aim
> at progress. In the Moment, authentic existence is indifferent to both of
> these alternatives.[207]

---

202 Heidegger, *Being and Time*, 363–4.

203 Heidegger, *Being and Time*, 364–5, emphasis in original.

204 Heidegger, *Being and Time*, 366.

205 Heidegger, *Being and Time*, 365.

206 For instance, the repetition of the original question of the meaning of being as
     it is recovered through the destruction of ontology.

207 Heidegger, *Being and Time*, 367.

As previously noted, *Being and Time* is not complete according to the plan Heidegger had for it. Instead, the last line of the book leaves open the following question: "Does *time* itself reveal itself as the horizon of *being*"?[208] Recall that the very analytic of Dasein, the unveiling of its structures, and inquiry into its modes of being were all in the service of clarifying the fundamental question of the meaning of being.[209] Despite the great importance of the analytic of Dasein, Heidegger nevertheless proclaims that the entire discussion remains "*underway*" toward proper preparation for the conflict over interpretations of the meaning of being.[210] "We must," he writes, "look for a *way* to illuminate the fundamental ontological question and *follow* it."[211]

Let us now turn from *Being and Time* to the other ways Heidegger pursued out of continuing to ask and to inquire into the question of being, found in his middle-period writings like the *Contributions to Philosophy (of the Event)*, *The Event*, and *The History of Beyng*.[212] For now, we can characterize this transition in Heidegger's own words as one that "shifts from the problematic of the meaning of being to the question of the truth of being, a truth whose disclosure is to be won through a confrontation with the history of being itself, instead of the existential analyses of Dasein."[213]

---

208 Heidegger, *Being and Time*, 415.

209 Heidegger, *Being and Time*, 414.

210 Heidegger, *Being and Time*, 414.

211 Heidegger, *Being and Time*, 414, emphasis in original.

212 Martin Heidegger, *Contributions to Philosophy (of the Event)*, (Bloomington: Indiana University Press, 2012); Martin Heidegger, *The Event* (Bloomington: Indiana University Press, 2013); Martin Heidegger, *The History of Beyng* (Bloomington: Indiana University Press, 2015).

213 Martin Heidegger, *Basic Concepts* (Bloomington: Indiana University Press, 1998): xi.

Beyond *Being and Time*

Let us first jump over the writings of the late 1930s for a moment to the 1941 lecture *Basic Concepts*, in order to indicate continuities between the questions and discoveries of *Being and Time* and those of later works. This brief excursus is meant to provide evidence not of "historical development" in Heidegger's thought, but rather of his continuing to ask "the *one* question" (of being) as preparation for grounding Dasein.[214]

For Heidegger, Dasein is historical either in an essential and authentic way, or else in an inauthentic, everyday mode. Heidegger muses over this distinction regularly, in order to approach and to unpack the meaning of essential historicity. For instance, just as in *Being and Time* he denied the historical [*geschichtlich*] importance of what is merely furthest away from us in the direction of the past as vulgarly understood [*Historie*], in *Basic Concepts* he writes of a "condition in which everything is gauged according to whether it is new or old," and in which "the old is...the antiquated."[215] What is regarded as old and new, antiquated or progressive, is here a function of an inauthentic regard for time. By contrast, "the essential has its own history [*Geschichte*] and is not calculable according to the ciphers 'new' and 'old.'"[216] The following passage relates directly to the discoveries of *Being and Time* and casts a light on the nature of the so-called beyng-historical thinking of the *Contributions* and other writings (see below for a discussion of the term "beyng"):

> According to the historiological [vulgar, inauthentic, derivative, everyday] reckoning of time the earliest is indeed the oldest, and, in the estimation of ordinary understanding, also the most antiquated. The earliest, however, can also be the first according to rank and wealth, according to originality and bindingness for our history [*Geschichte*] and impending historical

---

214 Heidegger, *Contributions*, 68.

215 Heidegger, *Basic Concepts*, 5–6.

216 Heidegger, *Basic Concepts*, 6.

[*geschichtliche*] decisions. The first in this essential sense *for us* is *the Greeks* [as we saw even in the discussion of the lecture course on the *History of the Concept of Time*, where phenomenology provides access to the original ontological inquiries of the Greeks]. We name this 'earliest' *the incipient* [*das Anfängliche*]. From it comes an exhortation [which Heidegger called the 'Call' in *Being and Time*], in relation to which the opining of the individual and the many fails to hear, and misconstrues its essential power, unaware of the unique opportunity: that remembrance of the inception can transport us into the essential.[217]

The "earliest" is accessible to us when we are "transported into the essential" by being called back to our ownmost relation to being, out of our everyday falling prey to beings in the world. When we do so, we are face to face with the question of being (the essential) authentically raised, and no longer reckon with time in the everyday ways that Heidegger so magisterially described in *Being and Time*.

To return to the inception, it is necessary to shift our understanding of time towards the view of Dasein's temporality and authentic historicity. Inceptual thinking is the "repetition" of a "heritage," whose provenance is not "in time" but "out of" existential temporality. On the basis of the previous discussions of authentic temporality and vulgar time, it becomes entirely comprehensible why Heidegger writes that "[t]he measure of whether remembrance of the inception is genuine can never be determined from an interest in reviving classical antiquity, but only from a resolve to attain an essential knowledge that holds for what is to come."[218] The rejection of everyday modes in favor of authentic resolve, where future (the yet to come), past (the heritage), and present (the resolve) are co-extensive reminds us of the essential proximity between the discoveries of the analytic of Dasein and the shift toward beyng-historical or inceptual thinking. Again: "The inception is certainly something that has been but not something past. What is past is always a no-longer-being, but what has been is being

217 Heidegger, *Basic Concepts,* 6.
218 Heidegger, *Basic Concepts,* 8.

that still presences but is concealed in its incipience."[219] As I discuss
in Chapter Five, Dugin employs Heidegger's notion of temporality to
define the essence of philosophically grounded conservatism, rein-
terpreting in a Heideggerian spirit van den Bruck's comment that the
conservative values the eternal.[220]

In the *Contributions*, Heidegger calls the great philosophies "tow-
ering mountains" in a mountain range.[221] In *Basic Concepts*, he writes
that "the bedrock in the mountain range of history" is "the knowing"
that comes with "being-embraced-into the 'essence' of the ground."[222]
This knowing is granted by inceptual thinking, which transports
Dasein into that which clears the Da.[223] To be historical is to think out
of that embracing ground. Becoming-historical is not granted to man
when determined as rational animal or subject. Rather, the questioning must "bring only this into experience as his sole determination:
that he stands in an abode laid out by being itself."[224]

Indeed, the last word of the first chapter of the *Contributions*
says that the decisive task is "to rethink…the whole essence of the
human being as soon as it is grounded in Da-Sein."[225] In *Being and
Time*, Dasein was the being for whom being is a question, and hence
has privilege as the being to be questioned when inquiring into the
meaning of being. From the perspective of a more primordial leap
into the grounding of Dasein, (which Heidegger here starts to write

---

219 Heidegger, *Basic Concepts*, 73.

220 Arthur Moeller van den Bruck, *Germany's Third Empire* (London: Arktos,
      2012).

221 Heidegger, *Contributions*, 147.

222 Heidegger, *Basic Concepts*, 18.

223 "Is not being that which opens, that which first unlocks the Openness of a
      'there,' [and thus] liberates so that we are free 'before' beings and in their midst,
      free 'toward' beings, 'free' from them, 'free' for them, and thus we have the pos-
      sibility to be ourselves." Heidegger, *Basic Concepts*, 57.

224 Heidegger, *Basic Concepts*, 71, 77.

225 Heidegger, *Contributions*, 81.

as Da-Sein or even Da-Seyn in order to mark that it is being thought more primordially), Heidegger refers to *Being and Time* as, "a first [i.e. preliminary] meditation," which attempted, "to set into relief at all, utterly with respect to extreme modes of being of the human being, the difference in kind between Dasein and all 'lived' experience and 'consciousness.'"[226] The *Contributions* should not, he says, be seen "historiologically" as a "development" of *Being and Time* or as "already… enclosed" therein.[227] Instead, "the 'changes' are so essential that their scale can be determined only if in each case the *one* question is pervasively asked out of its own site of questioning."[228]

The foregoing has shown how out of the question of the meaning of being that results from the radicalization of consciousness-based phenomenology, the analytic of Dasein arises, preparing the question of being more primordially, through discovering the primary ways in which the question has been occluded by inauthenticity, expressed in both everydayness and in tradition. I now turn to consider the readings that articulate an attempt to think and speak being inceptively, beyond all traditional metaphysics and ontology. In these works, Heidegger introduces a variety of new terms, important to know for the project at hand. For instance, he writes "beyng," rather than "being," to indicate that he is no longer thinking "being" metaphysically as the beingness of beings or in any of the ways in which it was thought during the history of Western philosophy, but "inceptively," out of its own ground. He also hyphenates Dasein as "Da-Sein" or "Da-Seyn" to mark that he is no longer dealing with an analytic of the given Dasein, but rather with something to be earned in a fundamental-ontological transformation.

As the attempt in *Being and Time* to disclose these phenomena adequately necessitated certain neologisms, so the inceptive speaking of

---

226 Heidegger, *Contributions*, 55.

227 Heidegger, *Contributions*, 67.

228 Heidegger, *Contributions*, 68.

the truth of beyng also necessitates certain unfamiliar formulations. The reader is asked to bear with the difficulties presented by these unfamiliar formulations, of which Heidegger writes the following:

> In ordinary language, which is ever more comprehensively used up today and degraded through idle chatter, the truth of beyng cannot be said. Can this truth be said immediately in the least, if all language is indeed the language of beings? Or can a new language be devised for beyng? No. Even if it could, and perhaps without artificially formulated words, such language would not be one that speaks. All saying must allow the co-emergence of a capacity to hear it. Both saying and hearing must be of the same origin. Thus all that matters is this one thing: to say the most nobly emerged language in its simplicity and essential force, to say the language of beings as the language of beyng. This transformation presses into realms which are still closed to us because we do not know the truth of beyng. Therefore something is said of the 'renunciation of pursuance,' of the 'clearing of the concealment,' of the 'appropriating event,' of 'Da-Sein'; and this is not a mere plucking of truths out of words but is the opening of the truth of beyng in this sort of transformed saying.[229]

We must be willing to explore the possibility that these unfamiliar words and formulations can attune our hearing to something profound and forgotten in our traditions, to which Heidegger's way of thinking provides access.

The bulk of the *Contributions* consists of six "junctures" in a "conjuncture" that is not a system.[230] Each of them, according to Heidegger, says "the same about the same, but in each case out of a different essential domain."[231] It is difficult to think of each juncture as whole and complete in itself, since Heidegger refers, for instance, to the first two of them as "soil and field for the first run-up of inceptual thinking to the *leap* into the essential occurrence of beyng."[232] This way of stating things leaves the strong impression that the first two junctures are prerequisites for proper entry into the latter ones. Without deciding here and now just how each of these junctures "stand[s] for themselves," they may be taken in order, since whatever their essential and synchronous relation might be, they do link into each other fittingly and comprehensibly.

Resonating

The first juncture is "the resonating." What resonates is that beyng has abandoned beings, such that they "are now taken only in their objectivity and come under human domination."[233] For Heidegger, it is beyng itself that conceals itself. So the age in which humans dominate beings as objects, which he calls "machination," is no accident, but rather "the first history of beyng itself, the history of the first beginning and of what stands in the lineage of that beginning, as well as the history of what is thereby necessarily left behind."[234]

The age of machination is destined by beyng. It is "beyng-historical." Indeed, Heidegger sees the moment of the withdrawal of beyng from beings in Plato's allegory of the cave, where attention quickly shifts to the *idea* from that which makes the *idea* possible.[235] It thus becomes a task to grasp the refusal of beyng "in the entire history of metaphysics," precisely as "the basic occurrence of our history."[236] "Through a disclosure of the abandonment by being," Heidegger writes, "the resonating of beyng seeks to bring back beyng in its *full essential occurrence*."[237] How this can be done is discussed in other junctures. Here, just bringing the abandonment of beings by beyng to thought already prepares the way.

---

233 Heidegger, *Contributions*, 88.

234 Heidegger, *Contributions*, 88.

235 Heidegger, *Contributions*, 88.

236 Heidegger, *Contributions*, 89.

237 Heidegger, *Contributions*, 92.

Reflection on modern science helps disclose the abandonment of beings. It does so if science is taken as "normative knowledge." Why? Science is "machinational" to the extent to which it "suppresses" or pays no attention to the concealment that lets beings be and instead treats beings "as represented objects" to be known by a "self-conscious certainty."[238] Heidegger understands representation, objectness, the self of self-consciousness, and the epistemological goal of certainty as derivative from the first beginning of philosophy, and therefore as no longer properly inceptual or historical. Science is so enmeshed in metaphysical concepts that on the one hand it becomes an obstacle to genuine thinking, and on the other hand it offers itself up as something to be reflected on in the transition to genuine thinking.[239]

"'Science' itself," Heidegger writes, "is not knowledge in the sense of a grounding and preserving of an essential truth." Rather it "is a derived instituting of knowledge, i.e. a machinational showcasing of a domain of correct findings within an otherwise concealed region of truth (about 'nature,' 'history,' 'law,' etc.), a region for which science is by no means worthy of question."[240] Science is always "positive," because the beings it studies are always pre-given (*positum*) to it as a region.[241] Because the regions vary, it is also always specialized. Every science "explains" something on the basis of "something known and already understood," e.g. "the explanation of a painting from a physical-chemical viewpoint."[242] Science's essence is "the instituting of correct findings within the domination and regulation of all objects." Heidegger says that this essence precludes essential discoveries. For instance, the science of history "could never recognize that historical beings might possess a completely different mode of being (one grounded on Da-Sein), because [then it] would have to renounce

---

238 Heidegger, *Contributions,* 111.

239 Heidegger, *Contributions,* 111.

240 Heidegger, *Contributions,* 114.

241 Heidegger, *Contributions,* 114.

242 Heidegger, *Contributions,* 114.

itself [since] *as science* [it] possesses for its pre-established operational domain that which is obvious" — i.e., certainly not the historicity of Dasein or Da-Sein.[243]

Science thus understood becomes a business establishment. It has a "craving to find profit in securing ever more efficiently and quickly ever more useful results," thereby "anchoring ever more firmly the dependence of needs and wants in the respective result and in its surpassing."[244] Yet, there is nothing here for philosophy to oppose.[245] "Philosophy is neither for nor against science."[246] Unlike science, which makes a home for itself in the universities, which Heidegger also regards as "business establishments," lacking any concern with the truth, philosophy "does not have a place in 'universities.'" Indeed, "nowhere at all does philosophy 'have' a place, unless it is the place it itself founds, to which indeed no path could lead immediately, starting from any established institution."[247] These remarks are not insignificant for an understanding of the fields of political philosophy and political science.

Interplay

The interplay refers to thinking about the history of metaphysics, the history of the first beginning, as a transition into another beginning.[248] The transition is not effected through opposition to metaphysics. Instead, "the task is an overcoming of metaphysics out of its ground."[249] Metaphysics is overcome out of its ground when instead of

---

243 Heidegger, *Contributions*, 115–16.

244 Heidegger, *Contributions*, 122.

245 It bears repeating: Heidegger the philosopher does not "oppose" science. He recognizes its metaphysical constitution as occasion for thoughtful meditation in transition to another beginning.

246 Heidegger, *Contributions*, 122.

247 Heidegger, *Contributions*, 122.

248 Heidegger, *Contributions*, 135.

249 Heidegger, *Contributions*, 136, 146–47.

asking about beingness on the basis of beings, such that beingness is what is common to beings, the question of the truth of beyng is asked. Raising the question of the truth of beyng first grounds the human being as Da-Sein.[250] That is, the human is here determined from a primordial sense of being, and not metaphysically on the basis of beings and beingness. Metaphysical determinations of the human include the definition of man as a rational animal. This is metaphysical because of the implied definitions of both rationality and animality. This point is familiar to us from our previous discussion of *Being and Time*.

The privileged point of access to overcoming metaphysics resides in confronting and passing beyond Platonism.[251] As argued in Chapter Two, this will prove to be the main bone of contention between Strauss and Heidegger. To confront and pass beyond Platonism "is a historical decision of the greatest proportions."[252] Overcoming Platonism allows us to be transposed into the "unadulterated greatness and uniqueness" of the first beginning, since "there is more in the first beginning than in the [decisive] Platonic interpretation."[253]

Platonism (together with its Aristotelian modifications) therefore comprises "the *first* end…of the first beginning," whose final end is Nietzsche.[254] It is an end that "necessarily forecloses to the entire history of Western philosophy" the question of the truth of beyng. "Not only do Christianity and its 'world'-interpretation," Heidegger writes, "have here [in Platonism] their framework and the predelineation of their constitution, but so do all post-Christian, anti-Christian, and non-Christian Western interpretations of beings, human beings included."[255]

---

250 Heidegger, *Contributions,* 145.

251 Heidegger, *Contributions,* 165–72.

252 Heidegger, *Contributions,* 173.

253 Heidegger, *Contributions,* 173.

254 Heidegger, *Contributions,* 165.

255 Heidegger, *Contributions,* 165.

Platonism means primarily the interpretation of beings in terms of ἰδέα: ἰδέα is the "constant presence" that makes a thing a thing. Moreover, it is "that *to which* the changing, many things are referred back, the *unifying One.*"²⁵⁶ It is thus what is shared in common by many things. Heidegger notes that in Plato this commonness "remarkably becomes the first and ultimate determination of beingness (or of being)."²⁵⁷ As what is common to and stable in what is changing, the ἰδέα is itself a being.

Indeed, it is the most beingful being, that which "*is* most eminently."²⁵⁸

Focusing on the peak of the cave allegory in the *Republic*, Heidegger continues his brief synopsis of Platonism with reference to the idea of the good, which is said there to be beyond being interpreted as the beingness of beings. "Because," Heidegger indicates, "this questioning asks only about beings and their beingness…it can never detach itself from beings and strike up against beyng itself. The [beyond] can therefore be determined only as something that henceforth characterizes beingness in terms of its relation to the human being," i.e. as the good.

Platonism does not reach the primordial reticent opening (or "clearing-concealing,") of the truth of beyng. Instead, starting from beings it comes to beingness as ἰδέα, and in moving "beyond" being(ness) it fails to reach beyng and circles back on the human being instead. This interpretation decides the history of Western philosophy fundamentally, becoming, as Heidegger writes,

> the prototype for all interpretation of beings and of their determination and configuration in the framework of a 'culture,'…the prototype for reckoning in accord with cultural values, for the interpretation of 'reality' in terms of its 'meaning,' for the appraisal of 'ideas' and the measuring up to

---

256 Heidegger, *Contributions*, 163.

257 Heidegger, *Contributions*, 163.

258 Heidegger, *Contributions*, 164.

'*ideals*,'...the prototype for the forming of an ἰδέα, for a view of beings as a whole, a view of 'the world,' i.e....the prototype for worldview.[259]

In short, if all Western philosophy consists, as Whitehead said, of footnotes to Plato, the possibility of another beginning consists, to repeat, of an overcoming of Platonism as "a historical decision of the greatest proportions."[260]

The interplay prepares the decision as leap.

The Leap

Heidegger calls the leap the "most daring venture in the course of inceptual thinking."[261] In the resonating, one begins to become aware of the abandonment of beings by beyng. Sensing the potential of another beginning, one follows Heidegger in the second "step," reflecting on and thinking through the first beginning and the history of metaphysics. Now, something occurs to transpose one into the domain of the other beginning.[262]

Heidegger indicates that *Being and Time* serves as a sort of preparatory dash before the leap, writing as follows: "The meditation of 'fundamental ontology' (laying of the foundation of onto*logy* as its overcoming) constitutes the *transition* from the end of the first beginning to the other beginning. This transition, however, is at the same time the run-up to the leap which alone can initiate a beginning and especially the other beginning."[263] The leap "originate[s] in and

259 Heidegger, *Contributions*, 165.

260 Heidegger, *Contributions*, 173. The quote is from Alfred North Whitehead, *Process and Reality* (New York: Free Press, 1979): 39.

261 Heidegger, *Contributions*, 179.

262 It is possible to categorize all four thinkers in terms of the junctures. All four experience the resonating and the interplay. Only Dugin and Derrida experience the leap. Only Dugin experiences the grounding onward.

263 Heidegger, *Contributions*, 180.

spring[s] from the confrontation (interplay) with the first beginning and with its history."[264]

In the first beginning, being always is for beings — for instance, as their cause. In the other beginning, beings are for beyng — for instance, as the clearing that shelters beyng in a configured work.[265] In the other beginning, the human becomes, as Da-Sein, the site for the grounding, preservation, and stewardship of beyng.[266] Heidegger again refers to *Being and Time* in this context. That work "does not present an 'ideal' or a 'program,'" but rather,

> it is the self-preparing beginning of the essential occurrence of beyng itself — not what *we* think up but what compels *us* (supposing we have become mature enough for it) into a thinking which neither teaches a doctrine, nor calls forth 'moral' action, nor secures 'existence,' but which 'merely' grounds truth as the temporal-spatial playing field wherein beings can again be beings, i.e. can be for the sake of the presentation of beyng.[267]

Heidegger repeatedly cautions against misreadings of *Being and Time* that fail to regard it in relation to the question of being. For instance, Heidegger emphasizes that the anticipation of death discussed in the relevant passages of *Being and Time* is intended "so that the openness for beyng might be disclosed," and not for any other reason that might suggest itself to those who still think anthropologically or in other ways inappropriate to Heidegger's task.[268]

"How pathetic and cheap it is," he writes,

> to latch onto the term 'being-toward-death' and explain it as a crude 'worldview,' one which is then laid to the charge of *Being and Time*. It seems that this reckoning works especially well, since the 'book' indeed

---

264 Heidegger, *Contributions*. A bit later, he is more explicit, writing that, "*Being and Time* is the *transition* to the leap." Heidegger, *Contributions*, 18.

265 Heidegger, *Contributions*, 181.

266 Heidegger, *Contributions*, 191.

267 Heidegger, *Contributions*, 191.

268 Heidegger, *Contributions*, 223.

also speaks of 'nothingness' in many other places. Hence the facile conclusion: being-toward-death, i.e., being-toward-nothingness, and this as the
[nihilistic] essence of Da-sein…

Crude readings provide fertile soil for utter misunderstandings. "But
the issue," Heidegger clarifies, "is surely not to dissolve being human
in death and to declare being human an utter nullity. On the contrary, the task is to draw death into Da-sein so that Da-sein might be
mastered in its abyssal breadth and thus the ground of the possibility
of the truth of beyng might be fully measured." No anthropological
reading or reading that desires to see the ideological as decisive can
penetrate to that level of the question. Then again, Heidegger writes,
this question, as a task, is not for everyone. "The carrying out of
being-toward-death is a duty incumbent only on thinkers of the other
beginning." Heidegger was well aware then, as we are now, that being-
toward-death and other such matters "give scholars in philosophy an
occasion for tasteless scoffing and journalists the right to know everything better," and yet here nothing is "touched in its essentiality" by
these scribblers.[269]

The leap is, in short, a leap beyond the problematic of beings and
beingness into the truth of beyng. Beyng essentially occurs (*das Seyn
west*). "The essential occurrence: that which we must enter *into*,"
Heidegger indicates. Moreover, "entrance into the essential occurrence, so as to stand in it and withstand it, happens as Da-sein and as
its grounding."[270] Accordingly, the next "joining" of the *Contributions*
is entitled "The Grounding." It begins with Da-sein, to which we now
turn. The next two sections following — "The Future Ones" and "The
Last God" — though rich, are comparatively brief and will be discussed together with "The Grounding."

---

269 Heidegger, *Contributions*, 224.

270 Heidegger, *Contributions*, 227.

The Grounding, The Future Ones, The Last God

Da-Sein is not the human being.[271] It is "the mode of *being* that is distinctive of humans *in their [highest] possibility*…namely the possibility of grounding and preserving truth itself."[272] In another formulation, Heidegger writes that "Da-sein is the enduring of the truth of beyng," and that in general is the sort of formulation he keeps to when articulating the grounding.[273] There occurs a leap, as we saw, which is towards and "into" Da-sein and which grounds it.[274] As in *Being and Time*, there occurs here a "thrown projection of beyng." A projection of beyng takes place: something is said of beyng that "cannot be read off from any particular being or from all known beings taken together" (projection).[275] And yet, the projection is already beyng-appropriated (thrown).[276] Beyng occurs as ground in and through Da-sein, which it needs and appropriates.[277]

In this section, Heidegger discusses various aspects of the grounding. He offers reflections on the origin of time and space in the grounding, as well as on the essence of truth and on what it means to shelter that essence. Let us pass over these specifics here. The question of the essence of truth will receive treatment in the chapter on Strauss's disagreement with Heidegger. It is possible to include the next joining in this section, for it is the briefest section of the *Contributions* and amounts to the following claim: not the many, but the few, the future ones, are to perform the leap and to ground Da-Sein. All inceptual thinking at this point is, Heidegger says, preparing the space for these few, rare futural thinkers, who linger in what is most question-worthy.

271 Heidegger, *Contributions*, 227.

272 Heidegger, *Contributions*, 227.

273 Heidegger, *Contributions*, 238.

274 Heidegger, *Contributions*, 240.

275 Heidegger, *Contributions*, 241.

276 Heidegger, *Contributions*, 240.

277 Heidegger, *Contributions*, 252.

The final of the six sections or joinings is called "The Last God."
Consistent with his attempt to think beyond computational and
machinational thinking, Heidegger cautions the reader not to regard
the term "last" "in the sense of sheer stoppage and endage, rather
than in the sense of the most extreme and most compendious decision about what is [incalculably] highest."[278] "The last god," Heidegger
writes, "has his own most unique uniqueness and stands outside of
the calculative determination expressed in the labels 'mono-theism,'
'pan-theism,' and 'a-theism.'" He continues as follows:

> There has been 'monotheism' and every other sort of 'theism,' only since
> the emergence of Judeo-Christian 'apologetics,' whose thinking presup-
> poses 'metaphysics.' With the death of this God, all theisms whither away.
> The multiplicity of gods is not subject to enumeration but, instead, to the
> inner richness of the grounds and abysses in the site of the moment for the
> lightening up and concealment of the intimation of the last god. The last
> god is not the end; the last god is the other beginning of the immeasurable
> possibilities of our history.

The god "awaits the grounding of the truth of beyng and thus awaits
the leap of the human being into Da-sein."[279]

In another section, which is not properly a joining but rather a
commentary of sorts on what has preceded and a sustained meditation on beyng, Heidegger writes that one way to think about beyng
is on the basis of the gods (as distinct from thinking about beyng
on the basis of reflecting on the question of what it is to be human,
for instance). As we have just seen, this is the farthest thing from
"polytheism." "To speak of the 'gods' does not mean that a decision
has been made here affirming the existence of many gods instead of
one," Heidegger reiterates; "rather, it is meant to indicate the undecidability of the being of gods, whether one or many. This undecidability
carries within it the question of whether something like being can be

---

278 Heidegger, *Contributions*, 322.

279 Heidegger, *Contributions*, 330.

attributed to gods at all without destroying everything divine."²⁸⁰ Let
us leave the figure of the last god with the comment that it arises in
conjunction with the leap into Da-sein and grounding of the truth of
beyng therein.

The Event

This text from 1941–1942 attempts to think the themes of the
Contributions even more inceptually than was done there.²⁸¹
Accordingly, it offers profound meditations on the first beginning
and its principal words (*aletheia, idea, hen, ousia, physis, agathon,
tauton, nous, logos, psyche, doxa, peras, apeiron, adikia*); on the end
of metaphysics ("the resonating"); on the other inception and its
principle word: *event*; on the character of and distinctions among
Dasein, Da-sein, Da-Seyn, and human being; and on beyng-historical
saying, including both thinking and poetizing. It is sensible to end at
this point, where we are brought to a thinking that is no longer on
the way toward or on the cusp of the inceptual, but already essentially
transposed. A more comprehensive overview of Heidegger's writings
than has been attempted here would need to include not only the texts
from the forties, but also other texts from the thirties, and indeed the
entire body of his thought, but such an undertaking is beyond the
scope of the current project.

---

280 Heidegger, *Contributions*, 345.

281 Heidegger, *Contributions*, xxiv.

CHAPTER TWO

Strauss

Emil Fackenheim may have been exaggerating when he said that one day Martin Heidegger would be remembered only for making Leo Strauss possible.[1] But that Martin Heidegger somehow did make Leo Strauss possible is not far-fetched. Strauss himself indicates as much. Heidegger, he writes, "made it possible for the first time after many centuries...to see the roots of the tradition [of philosophy] as they are and thus perhaps to know, what so many merely believe, that those roots are the only natural and healthy roots."[2] Strauss is deeply indebted to Heidegger for awakening that possibility.

As Strauss argued in his debate with Kurt Riezler, the search for a "natural frame of reference," rather than a relativistic one, by which to understand societies, may be aided "by recovering the frame of reference used by the classics."[3] This "natural frame of reference" is

---

1 Catherine Zuckert and Michael Zuckert, *The Truth About Leo Strauss: Political Philosophy and American Democracy* (Chicago: University of Chicago Press): 114.

2 Richard L. Velkley, *Heidegger, Strauss, and the Premises of Philosophy: On Original Forgetting* (Chicago: University of Chicago Press, 2011): 7.

3 Colen, José A. and Svetozar Minkov. 2014. "Leo Strauss on Social and Natural Science: Two Previously Unpublished Papers." *The Review of Politics* 76 (4): 619–633.

precisely what Strauss calls "the roots of the tradition." We do no injustice to Strauss by characterizing his lifelong project as the unparalleled endeavor to expose "the roots of the tradition" of philosophy to show that they are "the only natural and healthy roots" or that they constitute the "natural frame of reference," in contrast to both the unnatural and the supernatural frames of reference.[4] Meticulously and intently, Strauss pursued the question of "whether a better understanding of our frame of reference," which is "the outgrowth of the combination of two radically different traditions," Biblical and Greek, "will not liberate us from its limitations,"[5] moving us beyond *our* frame of reference to the *natural* frame of reference, which is not properly speaking "ours" but, as natural, accessible to man as man.

In short, the tension between the universally natural (the philosophical)[6] and the locally unnatural or conventional (the legal); between natural roots (the ancient) and the unnatural tradition that has covered over those roots (the modern); between the claims of the natural (Athens) and the claims of the supernatural (Jerusalem) — these are the well-known themes of Strauss's studies. On his own account, the proper treatment of these themes is indebted to Heidegger.[7]

---

4   Colen and Minkov, "Leo Strauss on Social and Natural Science."

5   Colen and Minkov, "Leo Strauss on Social and Natural Science."

6   Strauss, "Philosophy as Rigorous Science and Political Philosophy," 29: "Almost throughout its whole history political philosophy was universal while politics was particular. Political philosophy was concerned with the best or just order of society which is by nature best or just everywhere or always, while politics is concerned with the being and well-being of this or that particular society...that is in being at a given place for some time."

7   Velkley, *Heidegger, Strauss, and the Premises of Philosophy*, 7. Thus, "[o]ne could almost say that Heidegger is the unnamed presence to whom or against whom all of Strauss's writings are in large part directed." Steven B. Smith, "*Destruktion* or Recovery? Leo Strauss's Critique of Heidegger," *The Review of Metaphysics* 51, No. 2 (1997): 346.

Strauss held Heidegger in the highest esteem as a thinker. In an age when the problem of a "world society" urged itself upon social scientists, Heidegger was "the only man who has an inkling of the dimensions of [that] problem."[8] Heidegger was one of those few thinkers Strauss would characterize as "outstanding," such a man as is one's good fortune if "there is a single one alive in one's time."[9] As with all great thinkers, neither critics nor followers have "understood [him]…adequately."[10] In comparison to Heidegger, "Max Weber, till then regarded by me as the incarnation of the spirit of science and scholarship, was an orphan child,"[11] with respect to "precision, and probing, and competence."[12] Until he heard Heidegger lecture, Strauss "had never before seen such seriousness, profundity, and concentration in the interpretation of philosophical texts."[13] "We saw with our own eyes," Strauss says of him and his generation, "that there had been no such phenomenon in the world since Hegel."[14]

The high regard Strauss had for Heidegger can be seen in the following statement summarizing one of the central problems occupying Strauss: "I am afraid that we shall have to make a very great effort in order to find a solid basis for rational liberalism. Only a great thinker could help us in our intellectual plight. But here is the great trouble, the only great thinker in our time is Heidegger."[15]

However, Strauss also thought that Heidegger had erred severely in matters of great consequence. Strauss did not deny that there is a

---

8   Leo Strauss, "Existentialism," *Interpretation* 22, No. 3 (1995): 317.

9   Leo Strauss, "What is Liberal Education?" in *Liberalism Ancient and Modern* (Ithaca: Cornell University Press): 3.

10 Leo Strauss, "Philosophy as Rigorous Science," in *Studies in Platonic Political Philosophy* (Chicago: University of Chicago Press, 1983): 30.

11 Velkley, *Heidegger, Strauss, and the Premises of Philosophy,* 5.

12 Strauss, "Existentialism," 304.

13 Strauss, "Existentialism," 304.

14 Strauss, "Existentialism," 304.

15 Strauss, "Existentialism," 304.

link between Heidegger the thinker and Heidegger the Nazi: "One is bound to misunderstand Heidegger's thought radically if one does not see" the "intimate connection" of the facts of Heidegger's political life "with the core of his philosophic thought."[16] Yet, these facts "afford too small a basis for the proper understanding of his thought."[17] Thus, most of Strauss's critical engagement with Heidegger proceeds on a different, deeper level than that afforded by his political life alone or primarily. It takes aim at Heidegger's "historicism" as philosophically flawed.

Of particular importance among Strauss's criticisms of Heidegger, given the central role played by Plato and Socrates in Strauss's recovery of the "natural frame of reference," is Strauss's judgment that "what [Heidegger] says about the apriori in Plato and particularly on the idea of the good is simply wrong."[18] As late as 1970, Strauss presented his study of "Socrates" (the quotation marks are his), as part of the study of "classic natural right," (again his) in contradistinction to relativism, the most serious form of which is historicism, whose "hard center" and radical core is Heidegger.[19] Thus, Plato (or Socrates) is in a sense the fulcrum point on which the disagreements Strauss has with Heidegger hinge. As Velkley writes, quoting Strauss on Heidegger, "The central issue for Strauss [was] 'whether he is right in his critique of Plato.'"[20] In the following section, I try to understand and evaluate these disagreements through an examination of Strauss and Heidegger on the idea of the good in Plato.

In the only book in English devoted to the study of Strauss and Heidegger on philosophy, there is no discussion of Heidegger's *Contributions to Philosophy (of the Event)*, which the author expressly does not treat thematically in his work. However, it is in regard to the

16   Strauss, *Platonic Political Philosophy*, 30.

17   Strauss, *Platonic Political Philosophy*, 30.

18   Velkley, *Heidegger, Strauss, and the Premises of Philosophy*, 58.

19   Strauss, *Natural Right and History*, vii; Strauss, *Platonic Political Philosophy*, 30.

20   Velkley, *Heidegger, Strauss, and the Premises of Philosophy*, 55.

principal theme of the *Contributions* and related texts, namely the history of being, that Strauss voices his disagreement with Heidegger over Plato.[21] Moreover, Velkey's book, despite its many merits, does not give sufficient treatment of some of Heidegger's most relevant lectures on Plato.

This is understandable. There is enough material to cover without reference to the *Contributions* and these other texts. In addition, there is no evidence that Strauss read the *Contributions*, which, though they were composed in the thirties, were not published until the late eighties.

Nevertheless, neglect of the *Contributions* and other texts is problematic. We do know that Strauss cites the 1967 *Wegmarken* in his 1971 essay on Heidegger and Husserl. *Wegmarken* is a compilation of fourteen essays, including "Plato's Doctrine of Truth," which contains the main lines of the dispute over the idea of the good. Despite the fact that Strauss probably hadn't read the *Contributions*, he had read other published works upon whose major themes that volume elaborates. Consequently, reconstruction and analysis of Strauss's disagreement with Heidegger over the proper interpretation of the idea of the good should make reference to relevant texts, even if they were unavailable to Strauss, since they elaborate on topics from writings with which he was familiar and which he cited.

This chapter proceeds as follows. It presents what Heidegger says about the idea of the good in Plato, followed by Strauss's account thereof and an attempt to adjudicate the dispute. Then it briefly considers two additional Straussian criticisms of Heidegger: that he shares the vices of modern philosophy as such and is therefore implicated in the arguments against the moderns on behalf of the ancients, and that he is a relativist. Finally, two types of Straussian readings of Heidegger are discussed, an orthodox and revisionist one.

---

21   Velkley, *Heidegger, Strauss, and the Premises of Philosophy*, 36.

Perhaps this analysis will bring us before contrasting accounts about the character of philosophy itself, for according to Heidegger, philosophy "must come to a decision regarding its own essence" precisely "in the transition" beyond "the first beginning," rooted in Athens, "to the other beginning."[22]

Heidegger on The Idea of the Good

Heidegger's discussions of Plato's idea of the good and of the Platonic ideas more generally occur in the broader context of his discussion of the history of Being. Before we turn to the specific argument about Plato, let us briefly review what Heidegger means by "the history of being," so as better to understand what is at stake in the disagreement Heidegger and Strauss have concerning Plato.

According to Heidegger, the term "history of being" does not refer to a mundane historical account of various imperfect or inadequate teachings undertaken by a historian of ideas with an eye to some particular theme, wherein philosophers are praised or criticized for discoveries or errors.[23] The story of being is not an intellectual history. Indeed, Heidegger says of intellectual history that "it amounts to helpless and distracted blather whose unity derives only from the succession of the philosophers and of their writings of 'problems.'"[24]

Rather, what the term "the history of Being" means for Heidegger is that being itself has a history, or "is" as history. *That* history is not the history of a concept or the history of an idea (i.e., it is not the history of the concept of being), because both "concept" and "idea" belong to that history. It is important for Heidegger that we uncover

---

22 Heidegger, *Contributions,* 7.

23 "*The History of Beyng* — meaning: the history whose essence beyng itself 'is.' Not the 'history' that beyng passes through, not the 'history' that can be recorded from it, nor indeed recorded as a sequence of opinions 'about' being." Martin Heidegger, *The History of Beyng* (Bloomington, Indiana University Press 2015): 117.

24 Heidegger, *The History of Beyng,* 168.

what Being "was" before it was taken to be or interpreted as concept or idea. Indeed, it is precisely the interpretation of being as idea that he regards as so fateful for the West and that he tries to overcome inceptually in the transition to another beginning of philosophy.

The history of Being is something essential to Being itself, which is another way of saying that it is not a product of human thought, but as it were the producer of human thought about being. We can signal that shift by speaking not of the history of Being but of Being's own (epochal) history. The distinction in Heidegger's German is between *Historie* — history as a discipline, history as the representation of the past for specific present purposes, history as having taken for granted a vulgar notion of time, etc. — and *Geschichte*, or *Seynsgeschichte* — history as the temporalizing of Being.

We first truly learn about Being's history and play our part in that history as thinkers when we begin to ask questions such as "What is the truth of Being?" "What is the essence of Being?" and "What is the meaning of Being?" Being's history began, as it were, when this questioning occurred in Heraclitus and Parmenides in particular.[25] Their questioning opened up the space for Being to reveal itself in and through thought in a specific configuration that determined the trajectory of what was to come.

Heidegger calls their questioning of Being "the first beginning" (*Anfang*, also translated as "inception" or "commencement" and distinguished from another, more everyday sense of "beginning"). It is "the first *beginning*," because it marks the beginning of philosophy, and determines, in a way, Being's history throughout Western philosophy to its final stage in Nietzsche. It is "the *first* beginning," since a renewed questioning of the truth of Being can, after the more than two thousand year history of the first beginning, make space for a new epochal dispensation of Being, one that twists free from the decisive constraints imposed by the initial inceptive encounters.

---

25   Martin Heidegger, *Parmenides* (Bloomington: Indiana University Press, 1992).

Hitherto, Being's history has been referred to as a history that includes subsequent interpretations of Being and of human being. It is not always easy to speak of these issues clearly. The attempt to "get behind" or overcome not only the main concepts of Western philosophy, but even such things as "the concept of concept" is sure to raise problems regarding how to talk about these things without using terms that contain the thing we are trying to move beyond.[26] Heidegger's language, which can appear frustratingly unclear and full of needless jargon, is inextricably linked to the effort to navigate and resolve this problem. Because Heidegger tries to let Being speak through him, and regards his speaking as not his own, but as Being's speaking in him (language is a sort of special correlation between the speaking being called Da-Sein and the abyssal ground called Sein) he also knows that he needs to help Being find a suitable language in which to express itself, so to speak. Basically, he struggles to hit upon a language that speaks truly and authentically, free from the uprooted conceptuality of the older metaphysics.

The new dispensation of Being cannot be divorced from a new language beyond the familiar talk of "concepts," "rationality," and other terms belonging to the history of the first beginning (which Heidegger calls "metaphysics") and inadequate to the second beginning (which we will call "fundamental ontology"). The new language requires the introduction of new terms or new rendering of old terms to mark the fact that the word is now related not to the history of Being's first beginning, but to Being's second beginning, or, stated differently, that it is taken not primarily from the *tradition of philosophy* but from *genuine exposure to and appropriation by the unique ground of our existence.*

The point is elaborated below. Here, one new term must be introduced. We have taken for granted "Being" in speaking of Being's

---

26 Jacques Derrida has treated this theme beautifully throughout the essays in *Writing and Difference.* Jacques Derrida, *Writing and Difference* (London: Routledge Classics, 2001).

history. In fact, Heidegger invites us to regard "Being" as a partial interpretation of something more fundamental. In that case, "Being," like "concept," already belongs to the history of that more fundamental "thing," which is not a "thing" at all. Specifically, in the sense that Heidegger is trying to think beyond, "Being" answers the question, "What do beings have in common as beings?" It is thus derived from beings. However, we might inquire into Being not as that which beings have in common, i.e., not in a manner derivative of beings, but rather as the clearing that allows beings to be in the first place. To mark this shift, Heidegger speaks, as we shall now do, too, not of Being (*das Sein*), but of Beyng (*das Seyn*). The latter is an archaic spelling of the former. It is used to indicate that "more fundamental non-thing," of which "Being," understood as what is common to beings, is a partial interpretation. It is therefore fitting to speak of Beyng's history, using the German adjective meaning "Beyng-historical," or "Beyng-epochal," *seynsgeschichtlich*.

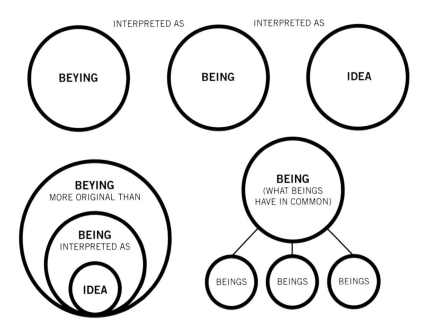

Figure 1. Beyng, Being, Idea, Beings

In the context of Beyng's history, Plato is a central figure. He marks, together with Aristotle, the end of the beginning of the first beginning (whose proper end comes with Nietzsche), the "inceptive end of the great inception," which "remains great, even if we completely discount the greatness of the way it worked itself out in the West."[27] "Platonism dominates" the history of the first beginning.[28]

Plato's principal contribution to the history of Beyng is the thought that the "idea" is the being that most exists and is the highest object of knowledge. Ideas are beings — the highest, yes, and most beingful beings, but nevertheless beings. The problem with this thought is that it turns attention away from Beyng, toward beings. It does not turn thought toward material beings, like rocks and stars, but toward the beings that really and most truly are, namely the ideas. But if beings become meaningful and are what they are on the basis of something other than themselves, that is, something more fundamental, the attention given to them comes only at the expense of the attention given to that "something other." For Heidegger, that "something other" is precisely Beyng.

Plato's emphasis on beings (the ideas) rather than Beyng is also decisive for the question of truth. For Heidegger, in Plato "truth" begins to mean correct speech about the ideas. To know the truth about beauty is to know what beauty is and is not; which is to say that the truth about beauty looks to the idea of beauty, and asserts something about it that is true. But just as Beyng has a history, which can be discussed with reference to the interpretations of Beyng as being, idea, object, and so on, truth, too, has a history, inseparable from the history of Beyng. And just as we followed Heidegger in distinguishing "Being" as a later interpretation from "Beyng" as the original, we must now briefly distinguish between "truth" as the correctness of a

27 Martin Heidegger, *Introduction to Metaphysics* (New Haven: Yale University Press, 2014), 200.

28 Heidegger, *Contributions*, 154.

proposition and truth as a more original phenomenon, one that lies at the basis of our existence.

Heidegger gets at this more original phenomenon through a sustained meditation on the Greek term that is translated into Latin as *veritas* and English as "truth," namely *aletheia*. The word *"aletheia"* has the form of an *alpha*-privative, followed by a root meaning "to conceal," so that *aletheia* can be rendered "unconcealment." On this basis, Heidegger raises the question why the Greeks experienced "truth" as an "unconcealing." It is his argument that this is inseparable from their understanding of Beyng as emergence from concealment (*physis*). What must be noticed is that the Greeks see *concealment* as primary and truth, as well as the emergence of being understood as *physis*, as that which is wrested from, or which arises out of, concealment. Later conceptions of truth as the correctness of a proposition are, he argues, inseparably connected to the interpretation of Beyng as being and beings (ideas) especially.

What is vital is that Heidegger regards *aletheia* in Plato as an unconcealing not of Beyng, but of beings.[29] *Aletheia* illuminates: what does it illuminate? — beings, *"insofar as beings are seen in terms of idea."*[30] By contrast, Heidegger thinks that *aletheia* must "be fathomed and grounded as the openness of beings as a whole," i.e., of that openness which at once opens and closes: Beyng. In the *Contributions* and elsewhere, Heidegger does his best to articulate the structures of Beyng, as it were, including the more original view of *aletheia* and the notion of openness he refers to here. For Heidegger, Plato blocks Beyng with emphasis on the ideas as the beings that most are and accordingly narrows *aletheia* from a fundamental unconcealing of Beyng into a derivative unconcealing not of Beyng, but of beings (the ideas). Roughly, you could see Beyng as an unilluminated light which lights up a room full of intelligible objects. Plato says: look at the

---

29   Heidegger, *Contributions*, 265.

30   Heidegger, *Contributions*, 265.

intelligible objects, and he understands the light as the yoke between the intellect and those objects. Heidegger says: look at the unilluminated light, which as unilluminated remains concealed and as shining has cleared the space for us in which intelligible objects can appear at all.

In this regard, Heidegger sees Plato's allegory of the cave in the *Republic* as especially important and "historically essential."[31] The cave allegory "occupies...a key position" in the history of *aletheia*.[32] Yet, "even the interpretations of the history of the concept of truth, and the interpretations of the cave allegory in particular, are paltry and are dependent on what was itself derived earlier from Platonism and from the doctrine of judgment."[33] "The basic positions are lacking," in short, "for a projection of what is said in the cave allegory and of what is involved in that saying."[34] Heidegger thus notes the necessity for "first of all and for the first time, an interpretation of the cave allegory which is complete and is rooted in the question of truth."[35] He undertook such an interpretation in his 1931–32 course published in English as *The Essence of Truth*.[36]

For the purposes of comparison with Strauss's treatment of the cave, it suffices to isolate two key components of Heidegger's lecture: man as historical and the discussion of the idea of the good. According to Heidegger, the cave allegory properly understood indicates that the act of perceiving the ideas is "an *occurrence* — something that happens 'with *man*.'"[37] This "daring thesis" may suggest that "truth is reduced to something *merely* human and so annihilated," i.e., it might provoke

31   Heidegger, *Contributions*, 284.

32   Heidegger, *Contributions*, 284.

33   Heidegger, *Contributions*, 284.

34   Heidegger, *Contributions*, 284.

35   Heidegger, *Contributions*, 284.

36   Martin Heidegger, *The Essence of Truth: On Plato's Parable of the Cave and the Theatetus* (London: Continuum, 2002).

37   Heidegger, *The Essence of Truth*, 54.

"natural resistance" against "so-called relativism," "bad relativism."[38] "But it must eventually be asked," Heidegger writes, "if this bad relativism is not just the apple from a branch whose roots have long ago become rotten, so that it doesn't mean anything in particular to refer to relativism, but testifies…to a miscomprehension of the problem."[39]

What is the problem, for Heidegger? It is that "when one so naturally struggles against the 'humanization' of the essence of truth, everything depends on what 'human' means here."[40] But the allegory of the cave itself "gives precisely the history in which man comes to himself as a being in the midst of beings."[41] "What man is cannot be established within the cave. It can only be experienced through participation in the whole history of liberation," Heidegger writes. We know what man is only when we know what the philosopher, the man *in truth*, is.[42] "Only by entering into the dangerous region of philosophy," that is, "is it possible for man to realize his nature as transcending himself into the unhiddenness of beings. Man apart from philosophy is something else."[43]

We have already seen that for Heidegger, "history" means something unlike what we normally think of as history. Beyng's history, if you recall, is its essential unfolding or temporalizing. History proper for Heidegger always has meaning only in relation to Beyng. It never concerns mere beings, (just as political philosophy, for Strauss, never concerns mere politics), unless interpreted in light of Beyng and its epochs.

Accordingly, for Heidegger man becomes historical when he raises the question of Beyng. To put it differently, man becomes implicated in Beyng's own history at a fundamental level when he questions

---

38 Heidegger, *The Essence of Truth*, 54–5.

39 Heidegger, *The Essence of Truth*, 55.

40 Heidegger, *The Essence of Truth*, 55.

41 Heidegger, *The Essence of Truth*, 55.

42 Heidegger, *The Essence of Truth*, 56.

43 Heidegger, *The Essence of Truth*, 57.

fundamentally. Heidegger has a specific term for man insofar as he is questioning Beyng: Da-Seyn.[44] The definition of man as "rational animal" does not belong to the questioning of Beyng, but to a later stage in Beyng's history. The definition of man as "Da-Seyn," by contrast, is inceptive.

In short, for Heidegger, "[u]nderstanding the cave allegory means grasping the history of human essence, which means grasping *oneself* in one's ownmost essence."[45] Unlike in Strauss, the distinction within man between the cave-man (non-man) and the man in truth (the philosopher) is *historical*, precisely because it is not merely an analytical distinction, but an event, a movement, an essential occurrence. (We rarely see Strauss discussing the *transformation* of man into philosophical man).[46] A clear sense of what Heidegger means by history and man's place or transformation in that history through questioning will be required when turning to Strauss's critique of Heidegger's "historicism." Strauss's "relativistic" critique of Heidegger amounts to a failure to see the *historical* in the essence of man as presented in the allegory of the cave, according to Heidegger.

Let us return to the idea of the good, "the highest point of [Plato's] philosophy."[47] The idea of the good stands apart from other topics of inquiry. It is unique in that it "must exist *out beyond* being," since, as the highest, it must somehow "become visible *over* all ideas," the beings that most are.[48] It has nothing to do with "sentimental conception[s] of [the] idea of the good" including "all perspectives, conceptions, and definitions belonging to Christian morality and its secularized corruptions (or any kind of ethic), where the good is conceived as the opposite of the bad and the bad conceived as the

---

44   Heidegger, *Contributions*.

45   Heidegger, *The Essence of Truth*, 57.

46   As mentioned in the preface to this study, his essay on Halevi's *Kuzari* is a rare example.

47   Heidegger, *The Essence of Truth*, 70.

48   Heidegger, *The Essence of Truth*, 72.

sinful."[49] Instead, it should be understood in a strictly philosophical sense, Heidegger argues.

Now, the essential philosophical tension Heidegger notices arises from the following consideration. "Idea" signifies the most beingful beings in their aspect as visible to the eye of intellection. Yet, in addition to the ideas as the objects of intellectual vision, there must also be a "yoke" between the objects and the vision, something that "grants unhiddenness to the knowable beings and…lends to the knower the power of knowing."[50] The "good" is what does that. But then, the good must be distinguished from the ideas, since "the ideas are what they are, namely the most beingful beings, and the most unhidden…only by virtue of an empowerment which exceeds them both (the most beingful and the most unhidden) in their unity."[51] In short, the good is not an idea. It "exceeds" the ideas and is therefore beyond being.

Now, Plato fails to heed this distinction. "Plato *equates* the unhidden with what is (beings), in such a way that the question of unhiddenness [i.e. *aletheia*] *as such* does not come to life" for him, or for us.[52] The failure to heed the distinction between the ideas and the good, between the most beingful beings and that which is beyond being and the condition for the comprehensibility of beings, is Plato's fateful error. Plato had an intimation of the clearing-concealing essence of truth, as shown in his talk of the "beyond being." But he did not pursue that intimation. In obstructing the elementary *openness* of beyng with his teaching of *the most beingful beings*, he paved the way to greater and greater emphasis on beings and their objectivity over and against the knower as subject. The history of Western philosophy followed in his wake, culminating at last, in Heidegger's retelling, in Nietzsche's inversion of Platonism. The possibility of another

49 Heidegger, *The Essence of Truth*.

50 Heidegger, *The Essence of Truth*, 75; Heidegger's translation of *Republic* 508e1ff.

51 Heidegger, *The Essence of Truth*, 75.

52 Heidegger, *The Essence of Truth*, 89.

inception of philosophy, however, depends not on inverting Plato but on overcoming him by raising the question he did not raise, the question of the truth of beyng.[53]

Strauss on the Idea of the Good

At the end of his reading of the cave allegory, Heidegger argues that we must turn to study the question of untruth. Why? If truth is *unconcealment*, as Heidegger says it is for Plato and the Greeks, then, inasmuch as it is defined negatively as *not or no longer* concealed, concealment is the fundamental phenomenon. This reasoning leads Heidegger to consider the *Theatetus*, and later also the *Sophist*, in order further to clarify the *aletheia-ic* occurrence in the philosopher.

But whereas Heidegger looks to the *Theatetus* and the *Sophist* to help clarify the essence of truth as discussed in the cave allegory, Strauss refers to the *Theatetus* and the *Sophist* as components of a trilogy that includes the *Statesman*.[54] Our first hint about the disagreement Strauss has with Heidegger concerning Plato, is this question of the theme or figure of the "Statesman" in relation to the themes of truth, sophistry (untruth), and philosophy. Strauss includes what Heidegger does not, that is, the "statesman" as a key part of the question of the relation between truth and untruth, and as a key component of philosophy.

Heidegger's question, "my *unique* question," as he calls it, in which what is at issue is "what is *most unique*," i.e. "the question of *the truth of beyng*," in Strauss becomes the "theological-political question," the theme or highest question for Strauss. Heidegger's question of Being (Strauss never uses the term "beyng," but that is what he means here)

---

53 Heidegger, *Contributions*, 163–176.

54 Leo Strauss, "Plato," in Leo Strauss and Joseph Cropsey, *History of Political Philosophy* (Chicago: Rand McNally and Company): 42.

"evades" Being in its neglect of "the statesman" or the political.[55] Is Strauss's critique of Heidegger, then, the critique of any philosophy that does not attend to the political? If so, does this criticism concern the *essence* of philosophy, or merely its public presentation and political consequences?

What does it mean to say that the "statesman" belongs to the study of philosophy? For Strauss, it would seem to mean that the horizon that opens up the question of Being is fundamentally the political horizon: the question of Being passes through or is raised on the basis of the question of the city, i.e., of law.[56] Richard Velkley, for instance, advances this interpretation of the disagreement between Strauss and Heidegger: Heidegger fails to recognize that "the tension between philosophic inquiry and authoritative custom is at the heart of the articulation of human openness to the whole." We might say that Heidegger regards as the "authoritative custom" the philosophic tradition itself, rather than the political cave.[57]

Socrates "is the founder of the study of politics as offering philosophic access to the character of Being."[58] But what is most important, on this interpretation, is that "the character of Being" and of human being is not uncovered properly if it is not accessed through the study of politics or starting from the political things. Politics is the sole path to ontology. As Velkley writes, "[t]he whole or Being as problem or question can come into human view *only* because humans occupy a part of it that has an imperfect and ordinarily deceptive

---

55 Leo Strauss, *On Tyranny* (Chicago: University of Chicago Press, 1991): 212. Actually, though, Heidegger does not neglect the political, so much as he constitutes it differently than Strauss and his version of the tradition of Platonic political philosophy does. See Michael Gillespie, *Hegel, Heidegger, and the Ground of History* (Chicago: University of Chicago Press, 1984): 139–143.

56 Strauss, *Liberalism Ancient and Modern*, 65–76.

57 Velkley, *Heidegger, Strauss, and the Premises of Philosophy*, 73.

58 Velkley, *Heidegger, Strauss, and the Premises of Philosophy*, 75.

completeness."[59] "One can restate this," he continues, summarizing Strauss, "by saying that there could be no opening to the question of 'What is?' or of Being without the difference (or limit) inherent in politics."[60] The "problem of the true whole," in short, "*cannot come into view unless* one starts with man as political."[61]

We can say more than Velkley does, however, about the point of disagreement between Heidegger and Strauss. We must proceed to interrogate not merely the political aspect of philosophy in Strauss — the importance of the political as potentially pointing man toward the whole — but also the philosophical aspect of philosophy. As the most concrete and important example of the presupposed philosophical aspect of Strauss's political philosophy, we can do no better than to turn to the question of *nature* in Strauss.

The "zetetic" or "skeptical" thrust of Strauss's understanding of philosophy is well known.[62] But something in his presentation of philosophy remains uninterrogated in the scholarship. Philosophy, Strauss writes, "is...the attempt to replace opinions about the whole by knowledge of the whole." We are dealing here with three matters that are thematic for Heidegger (opinion, knowledge, "the whole"), but this third matter ("the whole") at least must be made more precise. Strauss thus adds in explanation that "[i]nstead of 'the whole' the philosophers also say 'all things,'" i.e., the whole is an articulated whole. "Quest for knowledge of 'all things' means quest for knowledge of God, the world, and man — or rather quest for knowledge of the

---

59 Velkley, *Heidegger, Strauss, and the Premises of Philosophy*, 76, emphasis added.

60 Velkley, *Heidegger, Strauss, and the Premises of Philosophy*, 76.

61 Velkley, *Heidegger, Strauss, and the Premises of Philosophy*, 78. Steven Smith agrees. Steven Smith, "*Destruktion* or Recovery?" 363. Compare Martin Heidegger, *Hölderlin's Hymn 'the Ister'* (Bloomington: Indiana University Press, 1996): 118.

62 Crystal Paris, "Leo Strauss: Theology, Politics and Zetetic Philosophy" *European Journal of Political Theory* 93, No. 3 (2010).

natures of all things: the natures in their totality are 'the whole.'"[63] Philosophy is the quest for knowledge of all things, i.e., of the natures of all things.

Recall that for Heidegger the very essence of philosophy is up for decision in the transition to the other beginning. Does Strauss's definition of philosophy accord with or decide for the first beginning or the other beginning? Evidently, it decides for the first beginning, especially in making knowledge of "the natures of all things" the aim of philosophy.[64] For Heidegger, philosophy is not the attempt to acquire knowledge of "the natures of all things." Heidegger *does* ask about world, man, and the divine, to be sure. But he does not ask about them to inquire about their *natures* or *whatness*, which he regards as an inquiry bound to Platonic philosophy, to the interpretation of Beyng as idea (the emphasis on "beings" rather than "Being" or "Beyng" is reflected in the statement by Strauss that philosophy is a quest for knowledge of "all things" or of "all the beings").

Strauss is in agreement with Heidegger that "[g]enuine knowledge of a fundamental question through understanding of it, is better than blindness to it, or indifference to it, be that indifference or blindness accompanied by knowledge of the answers to a vast number of peripheral or ephemeral questions or not."[65] Yet throughout his work Strauss seems *not* to call into question or to treat as a fundamental problem the notion of "nature" that is constitutive of his definition of philosophy, "quest for the knowledge of the natures of all things" and *a fortiori* of his definition of political philosophy, "the attempt to

---

63 Leo Strauss, *What is Political Philosophy* (Chicago: University of Chicago Press, 1959): 11.

64 See Christopher Bruell, "The Question of Nature and the Thought of Leo Strauss," *Klesis — revue philosophique* 19 (2011), available online at: http://www.revue-klesis.org/pdf/Strauss-7-Klesis-Bruell.pdf [Accessed January 2, 2018].

65 Bruell, "The Question of Nature."

replace opinion about the nature of political things by knowledge of the nature of political things."[66]

It is no counterargument that Strauss's most famous book is precisely dedicated to the theme of nature in the guise of natural right. In the introduction Strauss writes that no "adequate solution" to "the problem of natural right" is accessible without solving the problem of the "fundamental, typically modern dualism of a nonteleological natural science and a teleological science of man," which *Natural Right and History* "cannot deal with," limiting itself "to that aspect of the problem of natural right which can be clarified within the confines of the social sciences."[67] To say that the problem of natural right remains within the confines of the social sciences and does not deal with the fundamental problem of nature is to say that Strauss's treatment of nature in his book on natural right does not rise to the level of philosophical analysis and thus remains subject to philosophical critique, such as Heidegger has to offer.

Strauss would hardly have subjected the notion of nature to proper philosophical critique in a book, one of whose aims was to provide a defense for political purposes of "natural right" against the alternatives of positivism and historicism and the "inescapable practical consequence of nihilism," i.e., "fanatical obscurantism."[68] Or should we say that he would not have done so explicitly? Is there evidence in *Natural Right and History* of a potential philosophical critique of the concept of nature? Can we find Strauss's *philosophical* response to Heidegger between the lines?[69]

---

66 Bruell, "The Question of Nature," 11–12.

67 Strauss, *Natural Right and History*, 8.

68 Strauss, *Natural Right and History*, 6.

69 The Zuckerts' call *Natural Right and History* the source of Strauss's primary "philosophical response to 'radical historicism.'" Michael P. Zuckert and Catherine H. Zuckert, *Leo Strauss and the Problem of Political Philosophy* (Chicago: Chicago University Press, 2014): 53. They also write (on page 264) that he "responded most fully and emphatically both to Heidegger's analysis of

Toward the end of the book, Strauss mentions "existentialism" as one of two "faulty extremes" that tried to "recover the possibility of practice" from the thought that "significant human action, History, was completed."[70] In this context, Strauss speaks of "the decisive respect" in which these two extremes are "faulty": "they agree in ignoring prudence, 'the god of this lower world.'"[71] If Strauss were to leave it at that, he would not have been offering a philosophical critique of Heidegger. But he adds the remark that "Prudence and 'this lower world' cannot be seen properly without some knowledge of 'the higher world' — without genuine *theoria*."[72] His critique of those who intend to "recover the possibility of practice" is that they are both atheoretical (i.e. unphilosophical) and imprudent, calling to mind the aforementioned "fanatical obscurantism" of nihilism.

This cannot, however, stand as a critique of Heidegger. It is not possible to regard him as atheoretic and his imprudence or immoderation is no concern for philosophy. As Strauss himself says in a lecture on the *Republic*, "philosophy cannot be moderate. This is impossible. For example, if you call a thinker a moderate thinker you already have an absurdity. You can have a moderate drinker but not a moderate thinker. Philosophy is essentially unlimited and doesn't recognize any limit."[73] Heidegger's imprudence or immoderation is therefore of no philosophical consequence and cannot be the lynchpin of Strauss's critique.[74]

---

human existence and to the history of philosophy on which he later based his radical historicism in *Natural Right and History*."

70 Strauss, *Natural Right and History*, 320.

71 Strauss, *Natural Right and History*, 321.

72 Strauss, *Natural Right and History*, 321.

73 Leo Strauss, "Lecture on Plato's Republic," (University of Chicago, 1957). Available online at The Leo Strauss Center. https://leostrausscenter.uchicago.edu/course/republic [Accessed August 22, 2015].

74 Or is it a mistake to equate the *knowledge* of prudence with the act of moderation?

In *Natural Right and History*, Strauss writes that philosophy "discovers" nature: "The discovery of nature is the work of philosophy."[75] But what is philosophy, and how does it discover nature? It is "primarily the quest for the 'beginnings' of all things or for 'the first things.'"[76] But not inasmuch as the beginnings or the first things are the gods. Instead, philosophy is the quest for the first things understood as *nature*: "Philosophy as distinguished from myth came into being when nature was discovered, or the first philosopher was the first man who discovered nature."[77] What is more, "the whole history of philosophy is nothing but the record of the ever repeated attempts to grasp fully what was implied in that crucial discovery made by some Greek twenty-six hundred years ago or before."[78]

We are now closer to uncovering Strauss' philosophical ground of disagreement with Heidegger, or the decision about the essence of philosophy that separates the two thinkers. What is "nature"? It is not 'the totality of phenomena.'[79] Why not? Because "the discovery of nature consists precisely in the splitting-up of that totality into phenomena which are natural and phenomena which are not natural."[80]

In a footnote, Strauss identifies "the two most important meanings of 'nature'" as the "essential character of a thing or group of things" and "the first things."[81] Strauss derives the quest for the first things from the contradictions that arise about the first things in various

75 Strauss, *Natural Right and History*, 81.

76 Strauss, *Natural Right and History*, 81.

77 Strauss, *Natural Right and History*, 81.

78 Strauss, *Natural Right and History*, 81. Strauss's definition of philosophy is, by his own admission, "provisional" but the provisional character of his definition and of his view of philosophy as open contrasts with the horizon-closing invocation of "nature." In the introduction to *Natural Right and History,* he says he has a "preference" for the teaching of natural right. This "preference" is political, but it cannot be accepted nor is ever established philosophically.

79 Strauss, *Natural Right and History*, 81.

80 Strauss, *Natural Right and History*, 81.

81 Strauss, *Natural Right and History*, 83.

codes of law and calls the quest for the first things also "the quest for the good as distinguished from the ancestral."[82] This "will prove to be the quest for what is good by nature as distinguished from what is good merely by convention."

Strauss writes of "the discovery of nature" that it is "identical with the actualization of a human possibility which, at least according to its own interpretation, is trans-historical, trans-social, trans-moral, and trans-religious."[83] Disregarding all but the first adjective, does Strauss's remark on the discovery of natural right aim at a "refutation" of historicism by showing that at least one human possibility, the birth of philosophy in the quest for the first things, is trans-historical? (Man's *Geschichtlichkeit* is not *historisch*: our historical nature is not "historical," but rather the ground for the possibility of history.)

Velkley thinks so. He writes that for Strauss "the *knowledge* of human dyadic openness to the whole, or the knowledge that access to the fundamental problems…is available only through an erotic ascent from the moral-political realm [i.e. through the discovery of natural right], is the root trans-historical insight."[84] Heidegger would retort, or would have grounds to retort, that the very concept of "nature" is already "historical" or already an interpretation of the more fundamental "event," occurrence, or happening (unfolding, unfurling, temporalizing) of "Beyng."

For Strauss, "nature" is what the philosophers call "the first things, i.e., the oldest things."[85] For Heidegger, "nature" is an epochal interpretation of "the oldest" or most inceptual (the beginnings, Beyng), an interpretation that covers over the oldest things and results in their gradual veiling. For Strauss, "pre-Socratic" philosophy regards "God, or whatever one may call the first cause" as "beyond good and evil

---

82   Strauss, *Natural Right and History*, 86.

83   Strauss, *Natural Right and History*, 89.

84   Velkley, *Heidegger, Strauss, and the Premises of Philosophy*, 161.

85   Strauss, *Natural Right and History*, 91.

and even beyond good and bad."[86] It thus treats right not as natural but as conventional.[87] Socratic political philosophy also orients itself toward knowledge of the natures of things.[88] For Socrates and classic natural right, as for "every other philosopher," wisdom, "the goal of philosophy," is identical to "the science of all the beings."[89]

In Heidegger's light, however, Socrates, together with Strauss, is enmeshed in the "history" of "the first beginning," which aims to know "beings," or "all the beings," through knowledge of their "nature" (by catching sight of the *idea* of the being), rather than to know Beyng or to ask about the truth of Beyng, the clearing-concealing. As Strauss expressly writes in a phrase that seems to draw the starkest contrast with Heidegger's position, "Socrates [identified] the science of the whole, or of everything that is, with the understanding of 'what each of the beings is.'"[90]

If we stopped here, we could fault Socrates and Strauss for the partiality of their orientation toward beings. But Strauss continues that, "'to be' means 'to be something' and hence to be different from things which are 'something else'; 'to be' means therefore 'to be a part.' Hence the whole cannot 'be' in the same sense in which everything that is 'something' 'is'; the whole must be 'beyond being.'"[91] Strauss here seems to agree with the view, or at least he shows evidence of knowing about it, that philosophy is not the study of all the beings but the study also, if not primarily, of the whole as beyond being.[92]

---

86   Strauss, *Natural Right and History*, 93–4.

87   Strauss, *Natural Right and History*, 107–14.

88   Strauss, *Natural Right and History*, 121.

89   Strauss, *Natural Right and History*, 122.

90   Strauss, *Natural Right and History*, 122.

91   Strauss, *Natural Right and History*, 122.

92   Strauss recognizes the ambiguity in the notion of the idea of the good much more explicitly in his University of Chicago lecture course on the *Republic* than he does in *Natural Right and History*. In that lecture, he remarks that "Socrates constantly shifts from speaking of the idea of the good and the good, in the

Immediately after speaking of the "beyond being," however, he writes as follows: "And yet the whole is the totality of the parts. To

latter case omitting the idea," glossing this point as "essential and not simply an accident." However, there, too, he both emphasizes and obscures the meaning of this ambiguity. He obscures it when he says that "you can call this both ways without making an error." He emphasizes it in the following comment:

understand the whole then means to understand all the parts of the whole or the articulation of the whole."⁹³

This quick retreat mirrors the movement from the good *beyond being* to the *idea* of the good. Fittingly, then, Strauss's very next sentence invokes the term "idea": "If 'to be' is 'to be something,'" he writes, "the being of a thing, or the nature of a thing, is primarily its What, its 'shape' or 'form' or 'character,'"⁹⁴ — i.e., as he later finally says explicitly, "the *eidos* of a thing, the shape or form or character or 'idea' of a thing,"⁹⁵ as distinguished in particular from that out of which it has come into being."⁹⁶

> The upshot is that '[t]he whole has a natural articulation,' and that [t]o understand the whole, therefore, means no longer primarily to discover the roots out of which the completed whole, the articulated whole, the whole consisting of distinct groups of things, the intelligible whole, the *cosmos*, has grown, or to discover the cause which has transformed the *chaos* into a *cosmos*, or to perceive the unity which is hidden behind the variety of

---

"The intelligibility of the whole — the premise of philosophy — requires the idea of the good. The question we shall turn to next time remains: what about this promise of philosophy — the intelligibility of the whole? Is this not a dogmatic premise? In view of our understanding should it not be replaced by another and more adequate one? This is a problem. [...] We get one inkling in our assignment (517b-c). Here it is pointed out that the idea of the good is barely seen. Let us assume that this means not merely an accident which happened to Socrates so that his eyes were not good enough but that there was some necessity for that. What would follow from that? If the first idea, the origin of everything, cannot be really seen but only dimly, what follows from that for our whole notion of philosophy?"

Strauss also said in that lecture: "The first idea, as the ground of both ideas and knowledge of ideas, is beyond the ideas." Leo Strauss, Lecture on the Republic, Edited by Peter Ahrensdoft University of Chicago, given Spring 1957, available online https://leostrausscenter.uchicago.edu/course/republic.

93 Strauss, *Natural Right and History*, 122.

94 Strauss, *Natural Right and History*, 122–3.

95 Strauss, *Natural Right and History*, 123.

96 Strauss, *Natural Right and History*, 123.

things or appearances, but to understand the unity that is revealed in the manifest articulation of the completed whole.[97]

No clearer statement of Strauss's repudiation of Heidegger's way can be expected.

In the very paragraph in which Strauss speaks of Socrates's turn to the *idea*, he mentions that "Socrates seems to have regarded the change which he brought about as a return to 'sobriety' and 'moderation.'" "It is," Strauss avers, "no accident that the term *eidos* signifies primarily that which is visible to all without any particular effort or what one might call the 'surface' of the things." This is a veiled critique of Heidegger, whose investigations did not stop at the *eidos* and consequently lacked all political moderation and sobriety.[98] As we have seen, however, Strauss admits that philosophy is *essentially* immoderate.[99]

But Strauss does not stop there, and we cannot help but follow the movement of his argument as he weaves through this most sensitive and consequential issue of the relation of the idea to the "beyond being" in Socratic philosophy, and the meaning of this relation for political philosophy. Strauss now also adds that "the quest for adequate articulation of the whole," which is "unfinishable," "does not entitle one...to limit philosophy to the understanding of a part, however important."[100]

---

97 Strauss, *Natural Right and History*, 123.

98 Strauss, *Natural Right and History*, 123.

99 Admittedly, the theoretical status of political moderation in Strauss is not evident. As Velkley writes: "It is important to add that for Strauss theoretical radicality and political moderation are not merely juxtaposed parts of the philosopher's thought but essentially connected. To recognize that philosophical questioning has a radicality inherently at odds with custom and law is to acknowledge a difference in human life that cannot be overcome. The philosopher's political moderation is a manifestation of a prudence that has a theoretical grounding." Velkley, *Heidegger, Strauss, and the Premises of Philosophy*, 11.

100 Strauss, *Natural Right and History*, 125.

Having previously identified the understanding of the "part" as understanding of the "*eidos*" or idea, look, or character, we are entitled to impute to Strauss the view that Socratic political philosophy has the two-fold character of looking to the whole, i.e., not only to the idea or the part, but also "beyond being," on one hand, yet also to the whole as the articulated totality of parts, or to the idea or ideas, on the other. What is more, the argument shows that emphasis on the part or the idea is inextricably linked to *moderation*.

The conclusion I wish to draw is this: *Strauss regards classic natural right as precisely "political philosophy," not because it deals with a "political" topic, "right," but because in sticking to the idea, i.e., to the look, to "the surface of things," it preserves the politically necessary characteristic of moderation*, lost, with disastrous political consequences, when one's emphasis shifts "beyond being," to the "roots."[101]

The corollary is that Strauss's disagreement with Heidegger over the correct interpretation of the apriori or the idea of the good in Plato amounts to the following: Heidegger regards the idea-interpretation of Beyng as fatefully, philosophically erroneous, whereas Strauss regards it as the correct and prudently deliberate marking of the boundary between the study of the part (being/idea) and the study of the whole

---

101 David Tkatch, *Leo Strauss's Critique of Martin Heidegger* (PhD. diss, University of Ottawa, 2011): 269 — "[I]t is possible to understand Strauss's critique of Heidegger as ultimately merely exoteric. The Straussian philosopher veils the lack of a natural or eternal basis for political life, i.e., the absence of a natural or eternal basis for the life of the ordinary individual, and thus protects politics from philosophy; the Heideggerian philosopher or 'thinker' reveals this absence, and thus permits philosophical speculation to subvert the foundation of political stability."

(beyond being), straddling the boundary between the political or the moderate and the philosophical, which exceeds the moderate.[102]

Let us turn now to Strauss's essay on Plato in the *History of Political Philosophy*, where he treats, however briefly, the allegory of the cave and the "doctrine of ideas."[103] Socrates and his interlocutors are looking for justice itself, the idea of justice:

> Now justice itself... 'is' always without being capable of undergoing any change whatever. Justice is an 'idea' or 'form,' one of many 'ideas.' Ideas are the only things which strictly speaking 'are,' *i.e.* are without any admixture of nonbeing, because they are beyond all becoming, and whatever is becoming is between being and nonbeing. Since the ideas are the only things which are beyond all change, they are in a sense the cause of all change and all changeable things.... They are self-subsisting beings which subsist always... Yet, as is indicated by the facts that there are many ideas and that the mind which perceives the ideas is radically different from the ideas themselves, there must be something higher than the ideas: 'the good' or 'the idea of the good' which is in a sense the cause of all ideas as well as of the mind perceiving them. It is only through perception of 'the good; on

---

See also Gillespie, *Hegel, Heidegger, and the Ground of History*, 167: "Plato's project strikingly resembles Heidegger's own attempt to reawaken a fundamental questioning with the crucial difference that Plato takes extreme care to distinguish politics and philosophy in such a way that he can pose the most extreme and revolutionary theoretical questions without undermining political stability and moderation." If "ontology" or fundamental questioning is subsidiary, it is therefore only because political stability and moderation are the first goal, and they are such as the prerequisite it would seem for the second and true goal of posing the most extreme and revolutionary theoretical questions, i.e. the questions are more important than the politics in the final analysis.

102 That Strauss regarded the doctrine of ideas as "exoteric" is not unknown to the literature on Strauss. But his specific thoughts on the precise ambiguity of the idea of the good as discussed by Heidegger are not usually treated in detail. See for instance Tucker Landy, *After Leo Strauss: New Directions in Platonic Political Philosophy* (Albany: SUNY Press): 65–67.

103 Strauss, "Plato," 7–63.

the part of the human beings who are by nature equipped for perceiving it that the good city can come into being and subsist for a while.[104]

Strauss calls this "doctrine of ideas" "very hard to understand" and remarks that "[n]o one has ever succeeded in giving a satisfactory or clear account" of it.[105] All the same, Strauss believes that it is possible "to define rather precisely the central difficulty":[106]

> 'Idea' means primarily the looks or shape of a thing; it means then a kind or class of things which are united by the fact that they all possess the same 'looks,' i.e., the same character and power, or the same 'nature'; therewith it means the class-character or the nature of the things belonging to the class in question: the 'idea' of a thing is that which we mean by trying to find out the 'what' or the 'nature' of a thing or a class of things… The connection between 'idea' and 'nature' appears in the *Republic* from the facts that 'the idea of justice' is called 'that which is just by nature,' and that the ideas in contradistinction to the things which are not ideas or to the sensibly perceived things are said to be 'in nature.'[107]

There is little here, to be sure, about the "beyond being," and neither "idea" nor "nature" are subjected to the kind of searching inquiry that they receive in Heidegger's treatment. Strauss does little in these passages to highlight the tension between ideas as the "self-subsisting beings which subsist always" and that of "something higher than the ideas," which Plato *also* calls an idea, "the idea of the good." But it is this very tension that constitutes "the central difficulty" for Heidegger.

Unlike in the previously discussed case, Strauss altogether avoids discussing what is philosophically speaking "the central difficulty" in the doctrine of ideas: we find no evidence of a potential refutation or response to Heidegger's interpretation of the apriori of the idea of the good in Plato.

---

104 Strauss, "Plato," 27.

105 Strauss, "Plato," 27.

106 Strauss, "Plato," 27.

107 Strauss, "Plato," 27–8.

Strauss says a little more in his remarks on the *Statesman*. After remarking that the *Statesman* "is more scientific than the *Republic*," Strauss proceeds to an explanation of what "science" means for Plato, referring to a crucial passage from the *Republic*:

> By 'science' Plato understands the highest form of knowledge or rather the only kind of awareness which deserves to be called knowledge. He calls that form of knowledge 'dialectics.' 'Dialectics' means primarily the art of conversation and then the highest form of that art, that art as practiced by Socrates, that art of conversation which is meant to bring to light the 'what's' of things, or the ideas. Dialectics [i.e. science] is then the knowledge of the ideas — a knowledge which makes no use whatever of sense experience: it moves from idea to idea until it has exhausted the whole realm of the ideas, for each idea is a part and therefore points to other ideas. In its completed form dialectics would descend from the highest idea, the idea ruling the realm of ideas, step by step to the lowest ideas. The movement proceeds 'step by step,' *i.e.*, it follows the articulation, the natural division of the ideas.[108]

What is noteworthy about this passage is that it treats Platonic philosophy as dialectic, as movement from the highest idea to the lowest idea through the natural articulation of ideas, which is the presentation of dialectic given by Socrates in the *Republic*, though not remarked on in this manner in the essay on the *Republic*. We see once more that Strauss presents this view of philosophy without any discussion of the tension inherent between the idea (being) and the good (beyond being). Heidegger and Strauss also agree as to these basic features of dialectic in Plato, as indicated by the following line from Heidegger's lectures on Plato's cave: "Beginning from what people commonly (and within certain limits rightly) say and opine about things, knowledge advances to the genuine understanding that seeks beings from the idea (from the perceiving of ideas)."[109]

---

108 Strauss, "Plato," 43.

109 Heidegger, *The Essence of Truth*, 73.

Thus, inquiry into Strauss's understanding of the apriori and the idea of the good in Plato, which has centered on Strauss's understanding of philosophy as the discovery of nature, has shown one potential critique of Heidegger's reading of Plato on those issues: Heidegger is right to regard the idea as partial and the formulation "the idea of the good" as philosophically erroneous, but he fails to recognize the political character of that formulation, which requires for political reasons, rather than philosophical ones, the "moderate" preservation of "the part" (the idea) in the face of the "beyond being."[110]

The foregoing analysis clarifies Strauss's claim that "'political philosophy' means primarily not the philosophic treatment of politics, but the political...treatment of philosophy,"[111] and elucidates the meaning of the following statement by Strauss:

> Historicism...challenges a premise that was common to the whole tradition of political philosophy and apparently never doubted by it. It thus seems to go deeper to the roots, or to be more philosophic, than the political philosophy of the past. It certainly casts a doubt on the very questions

---

110 In his course on the *Republic*, Strauss makes the following two statements about the terms "the idea of the good" and "the good," and hence about what is for Heidegger the decisive act of interpreting the beyond being as idea: (1) "Socrates constantly shifts from speaking of the idea of the good and the good, in the latter case omitting the idea. This is essential and not simply an accident." (2) "You can call this both ways without making an error." Strauss fails, however, to explain how it is not an error to elide the difference, if the difference is "essential." Does he have in mind the need for political philosophy to preserve a link between "truth and goodness" as Rockmore does when he writes as follows: "...unless we merely overlook Nazism and turn away from a central moral problem of our epoch, it is not possible to maintain that great philosophy preserves the link between truth and goodness and to describe Heidegger as a great philosopher"? Rockmore, *Heidegger's Nazism*, 298. See Leo Strauss, *The City and Man* (Chicago: Chicago University Press 1987): 19, "Socrates conceived of his turn to the 'what is' questions as a turn, or a return, to sanity, to 'common sense,'" as refuge from the stupefying study of the mysterious and "hidden" "roots of the whole."

111 Leo Strauss, *What is Political Philosophy?* (Chicago: University of Chicago Press, 1988): 93.

of the nature of political things and of the best, or the just, political order…
The question that it raises is today the most urgent question for political
philosophy.[112]

Is Heidegger Modern?

Strauss cannot have regarded Heidegger as merely or essentially guilty
of the "politicization of philosophy," which Strauss identified as a distinguishing feature of the structurally modern understanding of philosophy.[113] Politicization "consists precisely in this, that the difference
between intellectuals and philosophers," encompassing the distinction
between sophists and philosophers, too, "becomes blurred and finally
disappears."[114] But we have seen that Strauss regards Heidegger as a
philosopher and treats him as such. The question of Heidegger's "modernity" depends on the extent to which Strauss believes (and is able
to show) that in Heidegger there is a fundamental "politicization of
philosophy." It would at any rate be problematic to treat Heidegger as
an exponent of *Weltanschaungsphilosophie*, as Strauss seems to do in
his essay on Husserl, when Heidegger himself averred that "all worldview theories stand completely outside of philosophy, for they can
exist only by denying that" the most fundamental thing "is worthy of
question" and asserted what Strauss does not deny, that "philosophy
possesses its own dignity, one that cannot be derived from elsewhere
and cannot be calculated."[115]

Besides Heidegger's interpretation of Plato, Strauss may have
sought to "refute" Heidegger in the following way: first, by establishing the distinction between the ancients and the moderns; second,
by showing the inadequacy of the moderns or the superiority of the

---

112 Strauss, *What is Political Philosophy,* 57.

113 Strauss, *Natural Right and History*, 34.

114 Strauss, *Natural Right and History*, 34.

115 Heidegger, *Contributions*, 7, 31–4.

ancients; finally, by demonstrating that Heidegger belongs to the moderns.[116]

Strauss does regard Heidegger as a modern, for he regards radical historicism as modern and as formed around the "hard center" of Heidegger's thought — this despite the fact that "[h]istoricism appears in the most varied guises and on the most different levels."[117] Historicism supposedly makes philosophy impossible, because according to historicism "the very idea of philosophy rests on dogmatic, that is arbitrary, premises or, more specifically, on premises that are only 'historical and relative.'"[118] Modern thought assumes the superiority of practice to theory.[119] Regarding modern political philosophy, in particular, Strauss writes that its most "telling" characteristic is that "the philosophic life, or the life of 'the wise,' which was the highest subject of classical political philosophy, has in modern times almost completely ceased to be a subject of political philosophy."[120] Historicism is modern and must be explained "in terms of the specific character of modern thought, or, more precisely, of modern philosophy."[121] In this light,

> we observe that modern political philosophy or science, as distinguished from pre-modern political philosophy or science, is in need of the history of political philosophy or science as an integral part of its own efforts, since…it consists to a considerable extent of inherited knowledge whose basis is no longer contemporaneous or immediately accessible.[122]

Historicism itself "asserts that the fusion of philosophic and historical questions marks in itself a progress beyond 'naïve' non-historical philosophy," but, Strauss avers, "that fusion is…inevitable on the

---

116 Clifford Orwin, personal communication.

117 Strauss, *What is Political Philosophy*, 59.

118 Quoted in Velkley, *Heidegger, Strauss, and the Premises of Philosophy*, 122.

119 Velkley, *Heidegger, Strauss, and the Premises of Philosophy*, 125.

120 Strauss, *What is Political Philosophy*, 91.

121 Strauss, *What is Political Philosophy*, 77.

122 Strauss, *What is Political Philosophy*, 77.

basis of modern philosophy."[123] "An adequate discussion of historicism would be identical with a critical analysis of modern philosophy in general," but "[w]e cannot dare to try to do more than indicate some considerations which should prevent one from taking historicism for granted."[124] Incidentally, Strauss had spoken elsewhere of what we dare not say: "Who can dare to say that Plato's doctrine of ideas as he intimated it, or Aristotle's doctrine of the *nous* that does nothing but think itself and is essentially related to the eternal visible universe, is the true teaching?"[125]

Modern philosophy "reaches its culmination, its highest self-consciousness, in the most radical historicism" — in Heidegger.[126] The most radical historicism allegedly "explicitly condemn[s] to oblivion the notion of eternity," and "oblivion of eternity, or, in other words, estrangement from man's deepest desire and therewith from the primary issues, is the price which modern man had to pay, from the very beginning, for attempting to be absolutely sovereign, to become the master and owner of nature, to conquer chance."[127]

None of this is true of Heidegger. Heidegger does not speak of conquering chance or mastering nature. He does reject the possibility of philosophy as Strauss defines it, but he has dedicated all of his works to true philosophical endeavor and constant meditation on the essence of philosophy. Heidegger is certainly not guilty of any "bad relativism" and his thought avoids the historiological or the mere study of "history" as the passage of time very rigorously, in order to think about philosophical "history," both in the specific case of man's being (as discussed in the passages on the cave allegory) and in the broader sense of *Seynsgeschichte*.[128] It is, moreover, impossible to impute to

---

123 Strauss, *What is Political Philosophy*, 77.

124 Strauss, *What is Political Philosophy*, 77.

125 Velkley, *Heidegger, Strauss, and the Premises of Philosophy*, 163.

126 Strauss, *What is Political Philosophy*, 55.

127 Strauss, *What is Political Philosophy*, 55.

128 Gillespie, *Hegel, Heidegger, and the Ground of History*, 153: "[Heidegger's] understanding of history as the destiny of Being must not, however, be confused

Heidegger's thought "estrangement from man's deepest desire and therewith from the primary issues," for nothing is more important to him than man's being rescued back into being, and all of his writing is in the service of such a return. In short, Strauss has failed to show that the hard core of radical historicism, that is, philosophy as thought by or through Heidegger, is "modern."

Strauss has failed to meet Heidegger on the philosophical plane. At most, his "refutation" of Heidegger is the previously discussed "refutation" on the plane of *political* philosophy. As late as 1971, he himself admits that his own works should not be regarded as refutation in any decisive sense: "As far as I can see," he writes, "[Heidegger] is of the opinion that none of his critics and none of his followers had understood him adequately. I believe that he is right, for is the same not also true, more or less, of all outstanding thinkers?"[129]

This chapter has argued that Strauss's main response to Heidegger's inceptual thinking consists of two primarily rhetorical, sub-philosophical components. The first component is the sub-philosophical identification of philosophy with the discovery of nature and the ideas. That identification is sub-philosophical for two reasons. First, it is motivated by an interest in political moderation, while Strauss himself does not think that moderation is characteristic of philosophy proper, but rather of "political" philosophy, or of the political rhetoric needed to serve philosophy's interests. Second, equating philosophy with the discovery of nature is sub-philosophical in that it fails to respond adequately to Heidegger's movement beyond Plato and the ideas to the truth of beyng.

---

with Historicism. Such thinking is not historical in the ordinary sense of the term...Nor is it a relativism that recognizes itself as fundamentally limited by its own historical context. It is rather thinking according to the history of *Being*, i.e. it thinks what is as the giving and hence the gift of Being, of that which is beyond all historical contexts."

129 Leo Strauss, "Philosophy as Rigorous Science and Political Philosophy," in *Studies in Platonic Political Philosophy*, edited by Thomas L. Pangle (Chicago: Univ. of Chicago Press, 1983): 30.

Strauss's second sub-philosophical response to Heidegger is to accuse him of "historicism" without giving a satisfactory account of Heidegger's own presentation of man's historicity. Strauss uses "historicism" as a rhetorical target at the cost of doing philosophical injustice to Heidegger's thinking. In Kennington's words, "radical historicism…jettison[s] the claim to theoretical truth" and "is opposed to philosophy."[130] But as we have seen, Heidegger neither jettisons claims to truth nor "opposes" philosophy, unless we have decided in advance, without justification, in favor of a contested notion of philosophy.

Orthodox and Revisionist Straussian Approaches to Heidegger

I wish to briefly highlight two sorts of ways in which students of Strauss read Strauss on Heidegger. In an effort to highlight the importance of the question of nature and Heidegger in Strauss, Christopher Bruell, writing with evident sympathy for Strauss, mischaracterizes man's historicity in his own words as follows: "[M]an's finiteness does not necessarily entail that he is also an historical being, in the radical sense that the fundamental problems themselves change from human epoch to human epoch."[131] But as we have seen, man's historicity is not that the fundamental problems change from epoch to epoch, not the relativism of thought to its era. On the contrary, Heidegger is adamant throughout his corpus that the profoundest thought only ever thinks "the same." Bruell has not even tried to say what "the fundamental problems" are for Heidegger. He seems to think that the fundamental problem can be gleaned from "the very philosophy whose recovery is Strauss's lasting glory, Socratic philosophy;" in particular from the recognition that "constitutes" it: "the recognition of the elusiveness of

---

130 Richard Kennington, "Strauss's Natural Right and History," *The Review of Metaphysics* 35, No. 1 (1981): 57–86.

131 Christopher Bruell, "The Question of Nature and the Thought of Leo Strauss," *Klesis, Revue Philosophique* (2011): 19, 100.

that 'necessary and therefore eternal' being" that Strauss mentions in
Natural Right and History.[132]

But does the problem of the elusiveness of being change from
epoch to epoch, for Heidegger? That is not the right way of putting
the question, for epochs themselves are defined or decided by the way
the question of being is raised, rather than the reverse! It is not that
the fundamental problems change from one epoch to another, but
that epochs change according to the form in which philosophers raise
the fundamental problems — a nuance that Strauss seems to have at
least noticed, but fails to treat in a philosophically adequate manner,
having ascribed political reasons, rather than essentially philosophical
ones, for the philosopher's decision to raise fundamental problems in
one form rather than another.

More interestingly, Gregory Bruce Smith offers a "phenomenological" defense of political philosophy as conceived by Strauss.[133] He
argues that "the ethical question" of the best life, individually and
collectively, "takes priority to the ontological question," a question
"regarding the nature of Being as primary."[134] But he himself also states
that the ethical question cannot be answered "until we know what
kind of beings we are," an inquiry that involves us as a matter of priority in the ontological question.[135]

Smith acknowledges "the inevitability of fundamental questioning" and credits Heidegger for demonstrating it.[136] Heidegger's
fundamental questioning provides the resources for philosophy as
"architectonic unity," which Smith calls political philosophy: "[The]
highest unitary or holistic manifestation of philosophy is political
philosophy...[i.e.] the thematic reflection on the questions that every
human being answers either consciously or unconsciously and...

132 Bruell, "The Question of Nature," 101.

133 Gregory Bruce Smith, "What is Political Philosophy? A Phenomenological
     View." Perspectives on Political Science 36, No. 2 (2007): 91–102.

134 Smith, "What is Political Philosophy?" 92.

135 Smith, "What is Political Philosophy?" 93.

136 Smith, "What is Political Philosophy?" 93.

that fashions a persuasive, public articulation and integration of the whole."[137] Although the public context in which the questions are raised varies, "the ensembles of questions themselves remain the same and they are the substance of political philosophy."[138]

Smith and Strauss are of one mind about that. But Smith surprisingly breaks from Strauss over Heidegger's relevance to political philosophy so conceived. Strauss, he notes, asserted "that Heidegger had made traditional political philosophy impossible."[139] Smith agrees, but he adds that "Heidegger also opens a door toward the reestablishment of political philosophy in the future as an architectonic *poiesis*," cautioning against attempts to ignore Heidegger. "After Heidegger's pathbreaking thought," he declares, "no one will be able publicly to present philosophy in any of its past métiers or rhetorical permutations."[140]

But Heidegger was unable "to articulate everyday life in its phenomenological richness in any but formal terms."[141] In his "mature studies of everydayness—found in his works on Xenophon, Thucydides, Aristophanes, Plato, and Aristotle," Strauss, by contrast, "in a precisely Heideggerian vein," "pushed Heidegger's phenomenological insights in a far more concrete and therefore useful and profound direction," using "concrete moral and political categories as a departure."[142] Smith thus recommends Strauss for his phenomenological concreteness. But he also opposes Strauss or the version of him that wants "nature" to be a fixed point of reference: "There is such a thing as nature; but as a phenomena—not as a concept—it clearly is not static."[143] Of the two sorts of "Straussian" response to the challenge of Heidegger, Smith's is the more philosophically satisfying and promising.

---

137 Smith, "What is Political Philosophy?" 93.

138 Smith, "What is Political Philosophy?" 93.

139 Smith, "What is Political Philosophy?" 94.

140 Smith, "What is Political Philosophy?" 93.

141 Smith, "What is Political Philosophy?" 97.

142 Smith, "What is Political Philosophy?" 97.

143 Smith, "What is Political Philosophy?" 100.

CHAPTER THREE

Rorty

Early in the Coen brothers' film *A Serious Man*, young Danny Gopnik listens through his headphones to a song by the band Airplane during his Hebrew lecture: *"When the truth is found to be lies / and all the joy within you dies / don't you want somebody to love? / Don't you need somebody to love? / You'd better find somebody to love."*[1] Catching him unawares, Danny's teacher confiscates his tape player. When the wise old Rabbi Marshak returns the tape player to Danny after the boy's Bar Mitzvah, he does so with these words: "When the truth is found to be lies and all the hope within you dies…what then?" Perhaps the Rabbi thinks that "what then" is a turn to the genuine truth of God and Torah for a meaningful, hopeful life. But Richard Rorty, whose writings this chapter examines, denies that the loss of truth brings the death of hope — to say nothing of joy. Truthlessness and hopefulness are Rorty's bread and butter, setting him apart not only from the Rabbi, to whom we shall return, but also from Heidegger, as we shall now see.

---

1   Ethan Coen, Joel Cohen, Tim Bevan, Eric Fellner, Michael Stuhlbarg, Richard Kind, Fred Melamed, et. al., *A Serious Man* (Universal Studies Home Entertainment, 2010).

Heidegger, Practically Speaking

It is reasonable to approach Rorty's Heidegger by looking at what Rorty calls "the fruits of an abortive, abandoned attempted to write a book about him."[2] According to Rorty, Heidegger ought to be characterized as primarily a "post-Nietzschean philosopher," an epithet that situates him "in a conventional sequence which runs from Descartes through Kant and Hegel to Nietzsche and beyond." For Rorty, no work is "uncontextualizable," but there is no correct context into which a work can be placed. Rorty thus freely elects to put "post-Nietzschean philosophy," including Heidegger, into the context of American pragmatism. Nietzsche and American pragmatism are both "anti-Cartesian, antirepresentationalist, and antiessentialist," though they differ in that unlike the latter, "Nietzsche disliked both his country and his century" and shared nothing of the "sense of a new kind of social freedom" that Rorty finds in writers like Emerson.[3]

Their different moral outlooks notwithstanding, Rorty sees both French and German post-Nietzschean philosophers and American pragmatists as Darwinians, in that they are concerned with improving our ability "to shape the tools needed to help the species survive, multiply, and transform itself." Rorty therefore criticizes Heidegger's inceptual thinking "for succumbing to the urge to make language a quasi-divinity," rather than adopting "a relaxed, naturalistic[4],

---

2   Richard Rorty, *Essays on Heidegger and Others: Philosophical Papers* (Cambridge: Cambridge University Press, 1991): 1. See Martin Woessner, *Heidegger in* America (Cambridge: Cambridge University Press, 2010): 211–230 for a discussion of why Rorty might have abandoned the attempt.

3   Rorty, *Essays*, 2.

4   Counter-intuitively, Rorty defines "naturalism" as "the view that *anything* might have been otherwise, that there can be no conditionless conditions" (Rorty, *Essays*, 55). "Naturalists believe that all explanation is causal explanation of the actual, and that there is no such thing as a noncausal condition of possibility. If we think of philosophy as a quest for apodicticity, for truths whose truth requires no explanation, then we make philosophy inherently antinaturalistic."

Darwinian view of language."[5] Rorty protests against positing anything "mysterious, incapable of being described in the same terms in which we describe tables, trees, and atoms," and he sees in Heidegger's treatment of language precisely such mystification.[6]

When, like Heidegger, we begin to be "enthralled" by descriptions of language as a sort of thing in itself, something that possesses the human rather than something possessed by or employed by him, we "risk losing the advantages gained from appropriating Darwin, Nietzsche, and Dewey." Among these are the insight that it "is never very hard to redescribe anything one likes in terms that are irreducible to, indefinable in terms of, a previous description" and "that there is no such thing as the way the thing is in itself, under description, apart from any use to which human beings might want to put it."[7] We bewitch ourselves into believing that there is a unique description of something that is a certain way, rather than acknowledging that there are no unique descriptions or essences to be described.

There is no way that anything really is, including language: "[It is not the case] that language *really* is *just* strings of marks and noises which organisms use as tools for getting what they want. That...description of language is no more the real truth about language than Heidegger's description of it as 'the house of Being' or Derrida's as 'the play of signifying references.'"[8] For Rorty it is more apt to ask about "how to be useful rather than how to be right."[9] It is useful to think of ourselves as "highly evolved organisms" able to produce "longer and more complicated strings [of marks and noises] which enable [us] to do things [we] had been unable to do with the aid of shorter and simpler strings" — whether those strings include talk of Being, *différance*,

5   Rorty, *Essays*, 3.
6   Rorty, *Essays*, 4.
7   Rorty, *Essays*, 4.
8   Rorty, *Essays*, 4.
9   Rorty, *Essays*, 5.

or whatever.[10] Heidegger's talk of Being tells us nothing about Being. It is not "fundamental," "essential," "inceptual," or "revelatory." Like all other sets of sentences, it is "indefinitely recontextualizable, and so may turn out to be useful in an endless variety of presently unforeseen circumstances."[11]

Hopeful Heideggerianism

"Three answers have been given, in our century," Rorty writes, "to the question of how we should conceive of our relation to the Western philosophical tradition, answers which are paralleled by three conceptions of the aim of philosophizing." These three answers are "the Husserlian (or 'scientistic') answer, the Heideggerian (or 'poetic') answer and the pragmatist (or 'political') answer." Rorty regards the latter two as responses to the former. Heidegger substitutes the poet for the scientist; pragmatists substitute "engineers and the social workers — the people who are trying to make people more comfortable and secure, and [who] use science and philosophy as tools for that purpose." Rorty characterizes Heidegger's approach by saying that it "thinks that the philosophical tradition needs to be reappropriated by being seen as a series of poetic achievements." "The pragmatist," by contrast, "thinks that the tradition needs to be utilized, as one utilizes a bag of tools."[12]

The Heidegger of *Being and Time*, unlike the later Heidegger, however, shares some important features of this pragmatist outlook. "Heidegger and pragmatism belong together" in rejecting the demand for foundations and dissolving "philosophical pseudo-problems through letting social practice be taken as a primary and unquestioned datum." Moreover, both have a "deep distrust of the visual metaphors which linked Husserl to Plato and Descartes." And yet, their

10   Rorty, *Essays*, 5.

11   Rorty, *Essays*, 6.

12   All quotations in paragraph from: Rorty, *Essays*, 9.

"conceptions of philosophy were nevertheless very different." Rorty discusses two components of this difference: "their different treatments of the relationship between the metaphorical and the literal, and their different attitudes toward the relation between philosophy and politics."[13]

In the former discussion, Rorty asks the reader to consider the following two sentences, by Heidegger, which express "Heidegger's 'poetic' answer to the question of our relation to the tradition": (1) "…the ultimate business of philosophy is to preserve the *force of the most elemental words* in which Dasein expresses itself, and to keep the common understanding from leveling them off to that unintelligibility which functions in the end as a source of pseudo-problems"; (2) "It is the authentic function of philosophy to challenge historical being-there (Dasein) and hence, in the last analysis, Being (Sein) pure and simple." This approach is "poetic" because it aims to remind us that our language "is not that of 'human reason' but is the creation of the thinkers of our historical past." On this view, "the *only* aim which philosophy can have at the present time" is to remind us of "the poets of Being, the transcribers of 'Being's poem — man,'" the great "Thinkers," and "to permit us to feel the force of their metaphors in the days before these had been leveled down into literal truths." For Rorty, this means that Heidegger calls for a "rehearing of what can no longer be heard, rather than a speaking of what has not yet been spoken."[14]

Rorty objects to Heidegger's view that it is beneath the dignity of the philosopher to do the mechanical work of "exploring…newly suggested paths of thought." For Heidegger, as Rorty reads him, the philosopher's "metaphors come out of nowhere, lightening bolts which blaze new trails," but it is not the philosopher's task to walk those trails. By contrast, Rorty thinks that, "exploration is the pay-off from the philosopher's work." Thought is "futile unless it is followed

---

13 All quotations in paragraph from: Rorty, *Essays,* 11.
14 All quotations in paragraph from Rorty, *Essays,* 16.

up by a reweaving of the community's web of belief." "The proper honor to pay to new, vibrantly alive metaphors," Rorty exclaims, "is to help them become dead metaphors as quickly as possible, to rapidly reduce them to the status of tools of social progress." "The glory of the philosopher's thought," he concludes, "is not that it initially makes everything more difficult...but that in the end it makes things easier for everybody."[15]

A key difference between Heidegger's poetic and Rorty's pragmatist approaches is that although both "can agree that the poet and the thinker (in Heidegger's special 'elitist' sense of these terms) are the unacknowledged legislators of the social world...Heidegger thinks of the social world as existing for the sake of the poet and the thinker" while for Rorty it is just the opposite.[16]

For the pragmatists (and not only them), "the point of individual human greatness is its contribution to social freedom, where this is conceived of in terms we inherit from the French Revolution."[17] For Heidegger, by contrast, "the political life of both the liberal democracies and the totalitarian states was of a piece with that 'technological frenzy' which seemed to him the essence of the modern age": Heidegger had no more preference for the one than the other, since for him, as we have seen, the principal distinction was between "metaphysics" and inceptual thinking.[18]

Rorty calls the disagreement or "difference in attitude towards recent political history" (the meaning of the French Revolution, of social progress, etc.) "the *crucial difference* between the Heideggerian and the pragmatist attitude towards the philosophical tradition."[19] In contrast to Heidegger, who downplays the difference and elevates the similarity between liberal democratic and totalitarian states, Rorty

---

15   All quotations in paragraph from: Rorty, *Essays,* 17.

16   Rorty, *Essays,* 18.

17   Rorty, *Essays,* 18.

18   Rorty, *Essays,* 19.

19   Rorty, *Essays,* 18, my emphasis.

wants "to suggest that we see the democracy-versus-totalitarianism issue as basic as an intellectual issue can get." For Rorty, that means dropping the idea "that there is a phenomenon called 'modernity' which encompasses both bourgeois democracy and totalitarianism," and a "philosophical grasp of this phenomenon in which the distinction between these two forms of social life is *aufgehoben*."[20]

He defines his political hopes as follows: "that every new metaphor will have its chance for self-sacrifice, a chance to become a dead metaphor by having been literalized into the language," or, in other words, that "the social glue which holds every society together — the language in which we state our shared beliefs and hopes — will be as flexible as possible," that "every human potentiality is given a fair chance."[21] "One can only have such a hope," Rorty writes, "if one thinks that, despite… contemporary critics of political liberalism, a democratic society can get along without the sort of reassurance provided by the thought that it has 'adequate philosophical foundations' or that it is 'grounded' in 'human reason.'"[22] For Rorty, "the most appropriate foundation for a liberal democracy is a conviction by its citizens that things will go better for everybody if every new metaphor is given a hearing, if no belief or desire is held so sacred that a metaphor which endangers it is automatically rejected." This requires that we admit "that the terms in which we state our communal convictions and hopes are doomed to obsolescence, that we shall *always* need new metaphors, new logical spaces, new jargons, that there will never be a final resting-place for thought."[23]

Rorty is explicit about the fact that he tries to use Heidegger's terms in order to accomplish these aims. "It will be apparent," he writes, "that, in formulating the pragmatist view in this way, I am

20 Rorty, *Essays*, 19.

21 Rorty, *Essays*, 18.

22 Rorty, *Essays*, 18–9.

23 Rorty, *Essays*, 19.

trying to turn such Heideggerian notions as 'clearing,' 'opening,' 'authenticity,' and 'historical being-there' to un-Heideggerian purposes." Rorty wants "to yoke them to political movements which Heidegger himself distrusted."[24]

Although Heidegger "was only accidentally a Nazi," he was "essentially anti-democratic," unlike Dewey, whose thought was never "detached from social democratic politics." As Rorty explains, it is not that Dewey has the arguments to support social democratic progressive politics against various challenges to it — Dewey, like Rorty and other pragmatists, "is not scientistic enough to think that there is some neutral philosophical standpoint which would supply premises for such an argument." Instead, like the other pragmatists, including Rorty, Dewey "simply takes his stand within the democratic community and asks what an understanding of the thinkers of the past and of the present can do for such a community."[25]

Non-analytical philosophy ("continental philosophy"), that is, the philosophy that rejects Husserlian scientism, "is, with some exceptions, dominated by a Heideggerian vision of the modern world rather than a Deweyan one, and by despair over the condition of the world rather than by social hope." The result is that when a "typical member" of this approach to the philosophical tradition "turns to politics," he or she rarely does so "in a reformist, pragmatic spirit, but rather in a mood either of deep pessimism or of revolutionary fury." "Except for a few writers such as Habermas," Rorty laments, "'continental' philosophers see no relation between social democratic politics and philosophizing."[26]

---

24 Rorty, *Essays*, 19.

25 Rorty, *Essays*, 20.

26 All quotations in paragraphs from: Rorty, *Essays*, 24. See also Richard Rorty, *Take Care of Freedom and Truth Will Take Care of Itself: Interviews with Richard Rorty*, edited by Eduardo Mendieta (Stanford: Stanford University Press, 2006), 36: "The logical positivists thought that fascism was associated with antiscience, and that respect for science and scientific method was the mark of

But there is no metaphysical reason for this political pessimism. For Rorty, "the difference between Heidegger's and Dewey's ways of rejecting scientism" — pessimistic anti-modernism, on one hand, and optimistic democratic progressivism, on the other — "is *political rather than methodological or metaphysical.*"[27] Rorty thus encourages us to choose in favor of the non-scientistic approach to philosophy and its traditions without adopting the politically pessimistic or reactionary variant thereof.

The latter contributes few or no useful resources to respond to actual, pressing problems. "There are no facts about economic oppression or class struggle or modern technology," Rorty affirms, "which ['the vocabulary of social democratic politics'] cannot describe and a more 'radical' metaphoric can."[28] Since Heidegger's metaphors do not help us deal with such problems as "imminent nuclear holocaust, the permanent drug-riddled black underclass in the U.S., the impossibility of feeding countries like Haiti and Chad except by massive charity which the rich nations are too selfish to provide, the unbreakable grip of the rich or the military on the governments of most of the Third World," we should abandon them in favor of anything that can be put to use in "achieving the greatest happiness of the great number."[29]

---

antifascism in philosophical thought. Heidegger's identification with the Nazis was important for Carnap because he saw Heidegger's 'historicity of Being' and his Nazism as somehow connected. When Carnap came to the United States he imported the belief that philosophy had to be defended from historicism and Nazism by avoiding thinkers like Plato, Hegel, and Nietzsche. Karl Popper presented the same view in his book The Open Society, which was an extremely influential book in America. Popper thought that Plato, Hegel, and Marx were totalitarian thinkers and that we had to avoid their style of thought and embrace a more modern, up-to-date, and scientific way of thinking. This was a very powerful ideological rhetoric, still believed by most American philosophers, who are convinced that political and moral decency is a matter of respect for scientific rationality."

27 Rorty, *Essays*, 25, my emphasis.

28 Rorty, *Essays*, 26.

29 Rorty, *Essays*, 26.

Heidegger can be helpful in overcoming scientism and foundationalism; he is most helpful as a "happy" and "hopeful" Heidegger, read to
serve social-democratic aims.

Against Nostalgia

Rorty introduces the metaphor of the escalator to discuss what he
sees as Heidegger's claim that "if you begin with Plato's motives and
assumptions you will end up with some form of pragmatism."[30] As
Rorty presents it, Heidegger's escalator leads downward from *aletheia*
through such steps and stages as *physis, idea*, and the like, until it hits
the rock bottom of machination. Unlike Heidegger, Rorty wants us to
embrace machination as pragmatism, on the basis of Okrent's pragmatist reading of *Being and Time*.[31] At this point, given a choice between
Plato and pragmatism, bracketing inceptual thinking, "Heidegger
would wryly and ironically opt for pragmatism."[32]

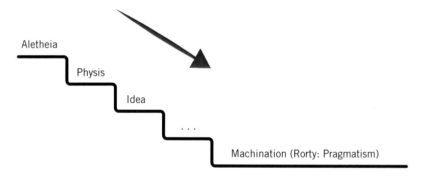

Figure 2. Rorty's Escalator

Unfortunately for Rorty, the later Heidegger abandons the situated pragmatism of being-in-the-world for poetic reflection on the

---

30   Rorty, *Essays*, 27.

31   Rorty, *Essays*, 32.

32   Rorty, *Essays*, 32.

"elemental words" of being.[33] In doing so, Rorty argues, he bewitches himself into fascination with something useless and hence disposable. Heidegger's question of the meaning of being "is a good example of something we have no criteria for answering questions about."[34] It is also "a good example of something we have no handle on, no tools for manipulating — something which resists 'the technical interpretation of thinking.'"[35] Why, then, does Heidegger speak of being? For Rorty, he does so not "to direct our attention to an unfortunately neglected topic of inquiry," but "to direct our attention to the difference between inquiry and poetry, between struggling for power and accepting contingency."[36]

Due to his emphasis on contingency, "one would expect Heidegger to say that no understanding of Being," no "final vocabulary" or founded account of the whole "is more or less an understanding of Being, more or less true (in the sense of truth-as-disclosedness)." But Heidegger wavers here. "Sometimes [he] does say things like this," Rorty observes, but at other times "he seems to be saying the opposite," and "makes all sorts of invidious comparisons" between the Greeks at the top of the escalator and us at the bottom.[37] Rorty wants us to ask whether Heidegger "has any business making such comparisons." Is there or isn't there a measure by which the top of the escalator can be preferred to the bottom? In other words, "does Heidegger have any right to nostalgia?" And "should we read him as telling a story about the contingency of vocabularies or about the belatedness of our age?" Rorty thinks that he is trying unsuccessfully to do both, and that one or the other must give way.[38]

---

33 Rorty, *Essays*, 34–5.

34 Rorty, *Essays*, 36.

35 Rorty, *Essays*, 36.

36 Rorty, *Essays*, 36.

37 All quotes in paragraph from: Rorty, *Essays*, 39.

38 All quotes in paragraph from: Rorty, *Essays*, 39.

Rorty wants nostalgia to go. He thinks that pragmatists can appropriate everything in Heidegger except his nostalgia, which is not an integral part of the story that hopeful social democrats like Rorty want to tell. What lets Rorty reject Heidegger's nostalgia is the "conviction that what Heidegger wanted — something that was not a calculation of means to ends [...] — was under his nose all the time": "the new world which began to emerge with the French Revolution." Heidegger missed this new social reality "because he never really looked outside of philosophy books."[39] If he had maintained a sense of contingency and not succumbed to a narrative of decline and inception, he would have had greater appreciation for what social democratic politics makes possible: "power in the service of love — technocratic manipulation in the service of a Whitmanesque sense that our democratic community is held together by nothing less fragile than social hope."[40] Unlike Heidegger, Dewey "took pragmatism not as a switch from love to power, but as a switch from philosophy to politics as the appropriate vehicle for love."[41] Recognition of contingency gives rise to gratitude "for the existence of *ourselves*, for our ability to disclose the beings we have disclosed, for the embodied languages we are."[42] There is no place in this celebration of human contingency for a narrative of decline, for the sad story of the oblivion of Being, the flight of the gods, and all of that.

According to Rorty, Heidegger needs the despair of decline in order to prop up "the hope that Heidegger himself...will be a decisive event in the History of Being." When reading the tradition of philosophy to listen for the voice of Being, "Heidegger knew what he wanted to hear in advance...something which would make his own historical position decisive, by making his own historical epoch

---

39   Rorty, *Essays*, 49.

40   Rorty, *Essays*, 48.

41   Rorty, *Essays*, 49.

42   Rorty, *Essays*, 48.

terminal."[43] Rorty repeats a similar criticism of Heidegger in the essay "Wittgenstein, Heidegger, and Language," when he writes that "the reification of language in the later Heidegger is simply a stage in the hypostatization of Heidegger himself — in the transfiguration of Martin Heidegger from one more creature of his time, one more self constituted by the social practices of his day, one more reactor to the work of others, into a world-historical figure, the first postmetaphysical thinker."[44] For Rorty, such an attitude stems from the "vain" hope "that the thinker…be capable of rising above his time," of "avoiding immersion in the 'always already disclosed.'" Because Rorty rejects this hope, he concludes that "Heideggerese," e.g. the language of the other beginning, "is only Heidegger's gift to us, not Being's gift to Heidegger."[45]

The Missing Circle

Having considered some of Rorty's basic positions on Heidegger, it is now possible to identify the fundamental axes upon which Rorty's contentions turn.

Rorty rejects Husserlian, scientific, representationalist epistemology and metaphysics because of a set of philosophical arguments concerning language, meaning, and objectivity. He identifies at least two primary ways of being a non-scientistic philosopher, however:

---

43 Rorty, *Essays*, 49.

44 Rorty, *Essays*, 64. Heidegger anticipated and opposed this objection, when he wrote that, "No one understands what 'I' am here *thinking* […] No one grasps this, because others all try to explain 'my' attempt merely historiologically […] As for those who will some day grasp this, they do not need 'my' attempt, for they must have paved their own way to it." In other words, Heidegger knows that some people see the thoughts as "his" and argue that he has merely hypostatized himself into a beyng-historical figure. I think Heidegger is right that the truth of what he says is not a hypostatization of his own thinking, but more akin to genuine revelation, and in that sense a genuine hypo-stasis. Heidegger, *Contributions*, 9.

45 Rorty, *Essays*, 65.

Dewey's optimistic, activistic philosophy in the service of social democracy, and Heidegger's pessimistic, radical nostalgia in the service of lost origins and greater primordiality. Rorty says that the difference between these two responses to the rejection of scientistic philosophy is not a function of philosophical argumentation, but rather of disagreements over the meaning of recent political history (which are by implication independent of philosophical disagreements). It is a political, rather than a philosophical question whether one is to prefer social democratic progressive utopianism to the darker mood of post-Nietzschean, Heideggerian continental thought.

Does Rorty have a philosophical right to his political preference? It would seem that he does, to the extent that he wants to champion social democratic utopianism on the strength of a view of the contingency of languages and the absence of foundations, a view that he expressly develops in the language of philosophy, on the basis of such thinkers as Quine and Davidson, and with reference to specific philosophical positions like naturalism. But if the basis for social democratic utopianism is philosophical anti-essentialism and nonrepresentationalism, developed on the basis of a rigorous inquiry into the philosophy of language, then social democratic utopianism may be said to have a philosophical foundation. And yet, Rorty denies precisely that: the latter is not the ground of the former, because the former rests on convictions independent of the latter. What are we to do with this circle?

James Tartaglia highlights a similar and related inconsistency when he indicates that Rorty holds the contradictory views, on one hand, that there is no way the world is, and, on the other hand, that there is such a thing as a non-linguistic brute force of nature: "Rorty wants to deny that causal pressures have any intrinsic nature, independent of the multiplicity of ways they can be described, but in that case, why does he insist that there are causal pressures that exist however we describe them?"[46] Tartaglia concludes that in order to be consistent, Rorty can only offer a pragmatist or social defense of the metaphor of causal pressures without philosophically admitting their independent existence. Tartaglia points out that Rorty says of his own "strategy for escaping the self-referential difficulties" of his project that it consists of moving "everything over from epistemology and metaphysics to cultural politics, from claims to knowledge and appeals to self-evidence to suggestions about what we should try."[47] "It is not," Tartaglia states correctly, "that Rorty is persuaded by [various philosophical] considerations that the epistemological enterprise is theoretically untenable...but rather that he is persuaded by historical and social considerations that the epistemological enterprise has become an obstacle to progress, and so endorses [those philosophical] descriptions on the grounds that they rule it out."[48]

Rorty, then, does not have a philosophical response to Heidegger, the nostalgic thinker of Being. He has a political response, that is, to highlight and champion the accomplishments of the French Revolution and to take and use only those philosophical positions and tools that further the aims proclaimed by that revolution; to put Heidegger to un-Heideggerian uses. The apparent circularity caused by the impression that Rorty's political commitments arise from his philosophical ones collapses when we are forced to admit that the former are decisive in the sense that they are philosophically unfounded. There is no circle: there's only philosophy in the service of politics.

Indeed, Rorty is *not circular enough*. Although he gives the impression of deriving his social democratic politics from his anti-essentialism, we have seen and will see in greater detail that this is not the case. Rather, his anti-essentialism is adopted in the first place because it can be put to use favorably in the service of his social democratic

---

46 James Tartaglia, "Did Rorty's Pragmatism Have Foundations?" *International Journal of Philosophical Studies* 18:5 (2010): 616.

47 Tartaglia, "Did Rorty's Pragmatism Have Foundations?" 620.

48 Tartaglia, "Did Rorty's Pragmatism Have Foundations?" 622.

commitments, which are derived from elsewhere or are baseless. This view is not circular enough, because it fails to give due recognition to ways in which the non-philosophical terms ("cultural politics," for instance) or events ("French Revolution") are philosophically constituted. It gives just that measure of recognition or non-recognition as is called for by Rorty's apriori political commitment to social democracy.

Rorty is *right* within his horizons not to raise the kinds of questions about the meaning of culture and the meaning of politics and the political that Heidegger asks. He molds his questions, and his answers, to fit neatly together with his political apriori. Accordingly, Bragues writes that "Rorty's nonfoundationalism expresses itself in a historicism that gives way to an overtly politicized conception of philosophy, one which unashamedly descends into the most blatant partisanship."[49] Partisan political thought has its place; but thought should not be completely subservient to a political apriori.

If Rorty's social democratic commitments do not stem from philosophical inquiry but rather co-opt the philosophical inquiries they find congenial, may we not raise the question as to whether those commitments survive or are affected by a philosophical inquiry that has the task of founding, rather than flattering, a regime of political theory?

Grounding Politics Without Philosophy

Rorty believes that there are a-philosophic, self-subsisting domains, such as "cultural politics," for instance, that are sovereign over philosophy or independent of it. Their sovereignty over philosophy means that they are the apriori that should determine the character of philosophical discourse. By contrast, the sovereignty of philosophy means that discourses rooted in philosophical experience should determine the character of the discourses of other domains and even

---

49 George Bragues, "Richard Rorty's Postmodern Case for Liberal Democracy: A Critique" *Humanitas* 19:1–2 (2006): 160.

the contours of those domains. According to the preceding analysis, Rorty has not yet provided a persuasive account of why we should subject philosophy to a social democratic political apriori. What we need to do now is to have a closer look at the grounds, if there are any, other than philosophy, that he adduces for his support of social democratic politics.

As we saw, Rorty's hope is that "every human potentiality is given a fair chance," "every new metaphor is given a hearing."[50] For Rorty, all of language is metaphorical. The different classifications of language uses, for instance, into poetry, philosophy, and fantasy, are a function not of the language itself, all of which is metaphorical, but of its reception, whether or not it "catches on" with people.[51] The implication is that all ways of speaking should be given a "hearing" and "a fair chance." However, Rorty does not seem to give every new metaphor a hearing and a fair chance, but only those metaphors that are consistent with his social-democratic political apriori. One may indeed on Rorty's terms regard Heidegger's "quasi-divinization" of language metaphorically. But Rorty criticizes Heidegger for "succumbing to the urge to make language a quasi-divinity."[52] Why should Heidegger be criticized for what can be re-described in other terms as the free play of metaphorization? Heidegger offers us new metaphors, he strings together words in new ways, and thereby he expresses a human potentiality that ought to be given a hearing and a fair chance. Why does Rorty forestall that potentiality by requiring that it meet social democratic criteria at the outset? Remember, for Rorty, metaphors, and in this context especially those metaphors that comprise what is usually called philosophical discourse, are to be encouraged when they suit social-democratic politics and discouraged when they do not. According to a different notion of "fair chance" and

---

50 Rorty, *Essays,* 18.

51 Günter Leypoldt, "Uses of Metaphor: Rorty's Literary Criticism and the Politics of World-Making," *New Literary History* 39, No. 1 (2008): 148.

52 Rorty, *Essays,* 3.

"hearing," one that seems to me more consistent with Rorty's position on human possibilities, metaphors should not be subject to the bar of political scrutiny, since that bar, the political apriori, by its nature excludes a wide range of human possibilities and metaphors, namely those that constitute, describe, or imagine worlds that are not socially democratic. To subject metaphors, including Heidegger's, to the bar of political utility, which as we have seen Rorty does, is a different matter altogether from giving them a fair hearing.

We can admit with Rorty that Heidegger's metaphors do not necessarily help us deal with problems of impending nuclear war, for example. All the same, a fundamental-ontological, reactionary politics of nostalgia, like a post-metaphysical social democratic politics of hope, is, for Rorty, just another metaphoric language-game. The desire that all metaphors be useful in Rorty's specific sense of contributing to solidarity and cruelty reduction stands, if we follow Rorty, neither above nor below but merely alongside Heidegger's view that what is to be preferred out of its own ground is philosophy as "immediately useless but nevertheless sovereign, knowledge arising from meditation."[53] In other words, given his claims, there must be space for non-democratic metaphors to have their chance, and it hardly seems appropriate to provide them that chance solely within the constraints of a field already constituted in favor of and in opposition to non-democratic options, the field of social-democratic practices.

Recall Rorty's claim that "the most appropriate foundation for a liberal democracy is a conviction by its citizens that things will go better for everybody if every new metaphor is given a hearing, *if no belief or desire is held so sacred that a metaphor which endangers it is automatically rejected.*"[54] Rorty, to be fair, does not *automatically* reject non-social-democratic metaphors, but he does *ultimately* reject them, and he does so, it seems, because of a social-democratic "belief or

---

53 Heidegger, *Contributions*, 35.

54 Rorty, *Essays*, 19, emphasis added.

desire." That belief or desire is "sacredly held" precisely inasmuch as it endangers metaphors that do not meet the criteria of his political apriori.

Indeed, Rorty appears to operate within an artificially constrained notion of "human possibilities." On one hand, "we humans are lords of possibility as well as actuality — for possibility is a function of a descriptive vocabulary, and that vocabulary is as much up for political grabs as anything else."[55] On the other hand, Rorty specifically champions those human possibilities that are disclosed by his actual political decision, ignoring or devaluing others. For example, he devalues what he called the nostalgia of Heidegger's stance concerning the history of beyng. To say that he devalues it is to say (1) that he rejects its usefulness for social-democratic politics and (2) that he rejects its right to constitute a non-social democratic order of any sort. As we shall see, Rorty characterizes positions inconsistent with his own, Heidegger's especially, using such terms of devaluation as "vapid," "sadistic," "resentful, petty, squint-eyed, [and] obsessive." Beyond Heidegger, Rorty would have to regard the entire constellation of right-wing anti-liberalism, for example, as not only incompatible with his own politics, but as therefore worthy of critique. The issue is not whether right-wing anti-liberalism is unworthy of critique, but whether Rorty is consistent in critiquing non-social democratic metaphors as non-social democratic, while at the same time celebrating "human possibilities," the full scope of which must include fundamentally different philosophical-political topographies than his own.

We can further grasp the constrained character of Rorty's thought by referring to it as an expression of "worldview" thinking. For Heidegger, "a 'worldview' sets experience on a definite path and within a determinate range, and this in such a broad way that it does not allow the worldview itself to come into question; the worldview

---

55   Rorty, *Essays,* 186.

thereby narrows and thwarts genuine experience."[56] To submit all thought to the service of social democratic utopianism is precisely to assign it a "definite path" and "determinate range" that "thwarts genuine experience," for instance, the experience that fundamentally calls the worldview into question while simultaneously transforming the questioner. Rorty would not contest this characterization of his thought. What is more, he explicitly states that the only strategies for avoiding the worldview are to "resurrect the early Wittgenstein's doctrine of ineffability…or else hypostatize language in the way in which the older Heidegger does" and he rejects both strategies, embracing worldview and denying the possibility of "rising above [one's time]."[57]

In elevating contingency and immanence to a first principle and denying the merit of all metaphors implying a higher and a lower, or any order of rank, Rorty's position is "founded on the renunciation of essential decisions" and amounts to what Heidegger calls liberal "propaganda" or partisanship.[58] Rorty insists that "the social sciences and the humanities will, unless they become completely moribund, always be politicized, one way or another."[59] The thrust of his politicization of philosophy is clear. The grounds for his preferences, however, are more difficult to discover.

Rorty claims that no "argumentative roads lead from [antiessentialist philosophy] to any particular brand of politics" and that it is not possible to "deduce the truth of antiessentialism from its suitability for democratic societies."[60] That claim is consistent with what we have seen: anti-essentialism is not the "foundation" for social democratic politics, and Rorty is unconcerned with questions of "truth," preferring questions of social utility. For non-philosophical reasons, pragmatists "would prefer to have no high altars," whether dedicated to

---

56   Heidegger, *Contributions*, 31.

57   Rorty, *Essays*, 64–5.

58   Heidegger, *Contributions*, 34.

59   Rorty, *Essays*, 139.

60   Rorty, *Essays*, 132–33.

God, Literature, Being, History, or anything else, "and instead just have lots of picture galleries, book displays, movies, concerns, ethnographic museums, museums of science and technology, and so on — lots of cultural options but no privileged central discipline or practice."[61] Among the reasons for this preference is that pragmatists "see the sort of cultural pluralism which rejects metaphors of centrality and depth as chiming with democratic politics."[62]

Pragmatists prefer social democracy on the basis of their preferences for social democracy, Rorty asserts. And they are willing to embrace a range of "philosophico-literary weapons" in the service of their preference, so long as those weapons are not wrongly limited, as they were by Derrida and de Man, to the analysis of texts.[63] Many injustices are apparent to observant citizens, who do not require philosophical training of any sort to see and to object to those injustices. It takes no "'critical-linguistic analysis' to notice that millions of children in American ghettos grew up without hope while the U.S. government was preoccupied with making the rich richer."[64]

Against Derrida and de Man, Rorty asserts that ideological criticism is "an occasionally useful tactical weapon in social struggles," rather than "somehow central or essential to political thought."[65] Rorty's Heidegger, too, is a "useful tactical weapon," but only to the extent that Heidegger's positions dovetail or are in harmony with social democratic commitments or can be made to be.

Recalling that Heidegger regarded "the imprisonment of his Social Democratic colleagues in 1933" as a matter of "petty details," Rorty urges us to turn away from philosophical indifference toward others and to shift our attention instead to novelists, with their appreciation for human immanence and contingency, in order to develop our

61 Rorty, *Essays*, 132.

62 Rorty, *Essays*, 132–33.

63 Rorty, *Essays*, 129, 136–37.

64 Rorty, *Essays*, 135.

65 Rorty, *Essays*, 135.

abilities to empathize with others, to be comfortable with them, and to leave them alone to self-create.[66] Heidegger tried and failed "to escape from time and chance...into historicity rather than into eternity."[67] For Heidegger, "the West has exhausted its possibilities." But for a novelist, "the novel can no more exhaust its possibilities than human beings can exhaust their hope for happiness."[68] "Because there is no Supreme Judge and no One Right Description," Rorty writes against Heidegger and other philosophers with pretensions of transcending their time and circumstances, "the most important possible job" is for the novelist "to keep us up to date" on the "glory" and "stupidity of the age."[69] This can only be done "by someone untroubled by dreams of an ahistorical framework within which human history is enacted, a universal human nature by reference to which history can be explained, or a far-off divine event toward which history necessarily moves."[70]

We should not have our eyes fixed on Truth or Reality, because "truth and reality exist for the sake of social practices, rather than vice versa."[71] But again, despite this idea that social practices come first and philosophy follows in their wake as a servant, Rorty time and again gives the impression that his preferred social practices are preferred for special reasons, reasons arising from special philosophical training, and not first and foremost from our pre-existing social opinions. For instance, Rorty says that the statement opening this paragraph "can be defended by appealing to the work of a contemporary neo-Hegelian, Robert Brandom."[72] He thus suggests, on one hand, that there is a philosophical (neo-Hegelian) basis for the view that truth

66   Rorty, *Essays*, 80–1.

67   Rorty, *Essays*, 77.

68   Rorty, *Essays*, 77.

69   Rorty, *Essays*, 76–7.

70   Rorty, *Essays*, 77.

71   Richard Rorty, *Philosophy as Cultural Politics: Philosophical Papers, Vol. 4* (Cambridge: Cambridge University Press, 2007): 7.

72   Rorty, *Philosophy as Cultural Politics*, 7.

exists for the sake of social practices, rather than vice versa. On the other hand, he immediately speaks of Bramdon's writings as "the best weapons for defending my version of James' pragmatism," employing the metaphor of the weaponization of philosophy for social purposes that we saw before and that implicitly runs through his work.

As we shall continue to see throughout this chapter, Austin had good reason to tell Rorty: "There's the bit where you say it and the bit where you take it back," a line Geras quotes often.[73] Rorty may say that philosophy provides no foundation for politics, but we don't have to look much further than the initial statement to get to the bit where he takes it back. Consider the following statements, culled from a collection of his interviews:

> I think that philosophical presuppositions are just clothes that you drape over your initial attitude; It is a mistake to think that politics requires a philosophical basis; Let democratic politics be what sets the goals of philosophy, rather than philosophy setting the goals of politics; My bourgeois liberalism does not rest on any philosophical convictions; What pragmatists do say is that our values — the values, for example, of social democrats like myself, or of right-wing opponents of the welfare state — are not capable of being 'grounded' in something like the will of God or Plato's Idea of the Good. Pragmatists think that attempts to back up considered political judgments about what should be done with appeals to religious or philosophical facts are pointless gestures. This is because the appeals are at least as controversial as the original judgments; I think anti-essentialism is the heart of the matter [of pragmatism]. In a culture, either religious or scientistic, that says 'Yes, but this is appearance, what we want is reality,' or 'this is accident, what we want is essence,' you get a kind of authoritarian sadomasochism: the wish to subordinate oneself to something larger. I think of pragmatism, either when applied to democratic practice in politics, or when applied to literary criticism, as precisely debunking the appearance-reality, essence-accident distinctions. Pragmatists say, 'Look, there isn't any authority that we can appeal to settle the quarrels between

---

73 Norman Geras, *Solidarity in the Conversation of Mankind: The Ungroundable Liberalism of Richard Rorty* (New York: Verso, 1995): 49.

us. We're going to have to deal with them ourselves.' That's the kind of change in self-description which could in the end make a difference.[74]

By Rorty's own lights, it is not that it *is* a mistake (i.e., a philosophical mistake) to think politics requires a philosophical basis. Rather, *because* he is a social democrat, he makes this assertion. He "drapes" his philosophical positions over his "initial attitude." But his initial attitude is never called into question.

For Rorty, the conflict between "relativism" and "fundamentalism," where the latter is defined as "the belief that ideals must be grounded in something already real," is "between two visionary poems."[75] Rorty's poem "offers a vision of horizontal progress toward a planetwide cooperative commonwealth." The poem he opposes "offers a vision of vertical ascent toward something greater than the merely human."[76] Although Rorty does his best to make his own poem the more pleasing one, there is no reason to believe that "a vision of vertical ascent towards something greater than the merely human" will not continue to attract its own adherents. Since Rorty's final position is that there is no right answer concerning the choice, which is merely a matter of preference, the preference for Heidegger remains open. Nor does Rorty's *Contingency, Irony, and Solidarity* close the option for Heidegger successfully.

Contingency, Irony, and Solidarity

In this book, too, Rorty giveth and taketh away, often exhibiting "reliance upon what he also simultaneously disclaims."[77] Consistent with the broad positions sketched out above, Rorty writes that "our

74 All passages are from Rorty, *Take Care of Freedom*, from the following pages, in order: 128, 93, 48, 91, 90, 143.

75 Richard Rorty, *An Ethics for Today: Finding Common Ground Between Religion and Philosophy* (New York: Columbia University Press, 2011): 19.

76 Rorty, *An Ethics for Today*, 17.

77 Geras, *Solidarity*, 57.

purposes would be served best by ceasing to see truth as a deep matter, as a topic of philosophical interest, or 'true' as a term which repays
'analysis.'"[78] Our purposes would be better served by repudiating such
talk of truth in favor of elaborating social democratic utopias. But as
elsewhere, Rorty explains the meaning of this repudiation in terms
that render it philosophically interesting and worthy of analysis: "To
say that truth is not out there is simply to say that where there are no
sentences there is no truth, that sentences are elements of human language, and that human languages are human creations. Truth cannot
be out there — cannot exist independently of the human mind — because sentences cannot so exist, or be out there."[79]

But surely it is open to dispute — Heidegger disputed it — that the
sentence is the locus of truth, that language is a human creation, etc.
Yet what Rorty gives with one utterance, namely, a philosophical position liable to philosophical disputation, he takes away with another,
stating such disputations are irrelevant if not harmless and that they
should be omitted or tamed by their social democratic master-trainer.

Rorty writes, inconsistently, that he does not want to offer accounts
of what the world is or of what language is, but merely alternate vocabularies that open new vistas for action: at the same time, he says we
must "face up to the *contingency* of the language we use," by recognizing it — presumably, as a fact about what language is or languages are
and we as language users or speakers and listeners are.[80] Absent a true
account of what these things *are*, it doesn't make much sense to talk
about *facing up* to them. Otherwise, we are as free to face up to them
as we are to turn our backs on them and face up to their alternatives.

Rorty's view of metaphor is unpersuasive.[81] He denies that metaphor can be used to convey a message, since "[i]f one had wanted to

---

78 Richard Rorty, *Contingency, Irony, and Solidarity* (Cambridge: Cambridge
    University Press, 1989): 8.

79 Rorty, *Contingency, Irony, and Solidarity*, 5.

80 Rorty, *Contingency, Irony, and Solidarity*, 9.

81 Rorty, *Contingency, Irony, and Solidarity*, 17–8.

say something — if one had wanted to utter a sentence with a meaning — one would presumably have done so."[82] Metaphors, unlike literal speech, are "the sort [of noises and marks] which makes us get busy developing a new theory [about what people will say under various conditions]."[83] "Once we found out what could be done with a Galilean vocabulary, nobody was much interested in doing the things which used to be done (and which Thomists thought should still be done) with an Aristotelian vocabulary."[84] At a minimum, though, Thomists *were* interested in sticking to an Aristotelian vocabulary, just like Strauss, after modernity, is still interested in exploring what may be done with a vocabulary drawn from Plato, Maimonides and other pre-modern political philosophers.

Rorty stakes too much on our sharing his moral preferences. He offers no arguments for them ("I am not going to offer arguments against the vocabulary I want to replace.") He merely wishes to make his favored vocabulary "look attractive by showing how it may be used to describe a variety of topics."[85] But although it may be useful for various purposes of description and redescription, it may also be less useful than alternative vocabularies in other respects, particularly when it comes to describing and analyzing other moral preferences. Rorty can little account for the usefulness of those alternative vocabularies.

To "fully accept" the argument that "truth is a property of sentences, since sentences are dependent for their existence upon vocabularies, and since vocabularies are made by human beings, so are truths" one must "de-divinize the world" and do away with "reactionary slogan[s]" about truth being out there.[86] Rorty mentions Derrida's term "Heideggerian nostalgia" to describe a reactionary attitude toward old, inherited "intuitions" about truth. They are better

---

82 Rorty, *Contingency, Irony, and Solidarity*, 18.

83 Rorty, *Contingency, Irony, and Solidarity*, 17.

84 Rorty, *Contingency, Irony, and Solidarity*, 19.

85 Rorty, *Contingency, Irony, and Solidarity*, 9.

86 Rorty, *Contingency, Irony, and Solidarity*, 21.

thought of as "platitudes" and "old tools"; not, of course, because they *are* (recall Rorty's claims that he is neither offering a true account of how things are nor advancing arguments against the positions he intends to replace), but because to regard them as tools is to liberate us from the constraints those attitudes place on our actions.[87] We should, Rorty believes, come to "treat *everything* — our language, our conscience, our community — as a product of time and chance."[88] To do otherwise is to speak in a way that does not "serve" the "institutions and culture of liberal society."[89] The vocabularies Rorty wishes to replace, like the vocabularies of morality and rationalism, for instance, "[have] become an impediment to the preservation and progress of democratic societies."[90]

Rorty approvingly cites as a sound liberal principle that "[t]o realize the relative validity of one's convictions and yet stand for them unflinchingly, is what distinguishes a civilized man from a barbarian."[91] Leo Strauss once commented on the same passage by drawing out the implication that according to this view, "every resolute liberal hack or thug would be a civilized man, while Plato and Kant would be barbarians."[92] Thomas Pangle is wrong to characterize Schumpeter's remark as "quasi-Heideggerian": Heidegger could in no manner be thought to place resolute hacks above world-historical thinkers. Unlike Rorty, Heidegger makes a distinction between what is so to speak higher and lower in man: highest is his openness to Being. But distinctions that assume "a self which divides fairly neatly into the part

---

87   Rorty, *Contingency, Irony, and Solidarity*, 22.

88   Rorty, *Contingency, Irony, and Solidarity*, 22.

89   Rorty, *Contingency, Irony, and Solidarity*, 44.

90   Rorty, *Contingency, Irony, and Solidarity*, 44.

91   Rorty, *Contingency, Irony, and Solidarity*, 46.

92   Quoted in Thomas Pangle, *Leo Strauss: An Introduction to His Thought and Intellectual Legacy* (Baltimore: The John Hopkins University Press, 2006): 22.

it shares with the divine and the part it shares with the animals" or
something similar, have, for Rorty, no place in liberal vocabularies.[93]

In Rorty's eyes, liberalism does not need to be justified before its
illiberal critics, like Nazism and Marxism. Those illiberal alternatives
to liberalism are just "one more vocabulary, one more way of describing things."[94] According to Rorty, a liberal culture, so far from seeking
to refute illiberal alternatives or to provide unshakable foundations or
foundations of any sort for itself, should "take as its goal the creation
of ever more various and multicolored" vocabularies: Rorty's liberal
ironism not only does not oppose illiberal alternatives, it also wishes
for one thousand flowers of description and redescription to bloom
alongside liberalism's garden.[95] And yet (the ever-recurring "and yet"
we meet in Rorty's favorite act of giving and taking away, asserting
and denying), Rorty is committed to the principle of reducing harm
and suffering: one thousand flowers had better *not* bloom.[96]

The choice in favor of liberalism and its goals, like the choice of
friends and heroes, does not rest on "reference to criteria."[97] But is it
true that we choose our friends for no good reason, and *a fortiori* our
heroes? And has not Rorty himself called the self-creating person and
the utopian revolutionary "the heroes of liberal society," chosen as
heroes not for nothing?[98] Does he not offer "criteria" of the very kind
he wants us to think he repudiates, when he writes that liberal society:

> is a society whose hero is the strong poet and the revolutionary because it
> recognizes that it is what it is, has the morality it has, speaks the language it

93   Rorty, *Contingency, Irony, and Solidarity*, 47.

94   Rorty, *Contingency, Irony, and Solidarity*, 53.

95   Rorty, *Contingency, Irony, and Solidarity*, 53–4.

96   Rorty, *Contingency, Irony, and Solidarity*, 63.

97   Rorty, *Contingency, Irony, and Solidarity*, 54.

98   Rorty, *Contingency, Irony, and Solidarity*, 60.

does, not because it approximates the will of God or the nature of man but because certain poets and revolutionaries of the past spoke as they did?[99]

Another statement of the relation in Rorty between politics and philosophy is not that philosophy grounds politics, as in Dugin, for instance, but rather that "philosophers help provide a redescription for political liberalism…[and] political liberalism also helps provide a redescription of their activity" as foundationless.[100] This is the apparent circle I commented on earlier. It is circular because there is an interplay between philosophy and politics. But the circularity is merely apparent: the political commitment is sovereign over philosophical redescriptions, which are never permitted to undermine that commitment, but only to restate it more persuasively.

By his own nevertheless frank admission, Rorty's philosophical notions are not "neutral" but are advanced "in the interest of political liberalism."[101] To this extent, his creative language-game is not, as he wants creative language games in general to be, private.[102] Non-liberal philosophers like Heidegger are "at best useless and at worst dangerous" when we transfer their private creations into the public realm.[103] Liberal philosophers like Dewey, Davidson, and Rorty himself are, by contrast, safe for the (liberal) public. Apparently, privatization applies only to undesirable self-creations.

Rorty defines ironism as a capacity for describing things, people, and situations differently. When it comes to people, Rorty acknowledges that they do not necessarily like being described differently from the ways in which they describe themselves. Most people, Rorty thinks, "want to be taken on their own terms — taken seriously just as they are and just as they talk." The position Rorty defends may make

---

99 Rorty, *Contingency, Irony, and Solidarity*, 61.

100 Rorty, *Contingency, Irony, and Solidarity*, 54–5.

101 Rorty, *Contingency, Irony, and Solidarity*, 55.

102 Rorty, *Contingency, Irony, and Solidarity*, 65–8.

103 Rorty, *Contingency, Irony, and Solidarity*, 68.

people uncomfortable, because it shows them that "the language they speak is up for grabs by her and her kind." "There is something potentially very cruel about that claim," Rorty sees; "[f]or the best way to cause people long-lasting pain is to humiliate them by making the things that seemed most important to them look futile, obsolete, and powerless."[104] In short, "[r]edescription often humiliates."[105]

But "redescription and possible humiliation are no more closely connected with ironism than with metaphysics."[106] A metaphysician's redescriptions are likely to be presented as an education in the service of making one free, and hence in the service of authority, power, and freedom. The ironist doesn't share those aims. "She has to say that our chances of freedom depend on historical contingencies which are only occasionally influenced by our self-redescriptions."[107] The ironist cannot offer the same sort of social hope as metaphysicians offer. She cannot claim that adopting her redescription of yourself or your situation makes you better able to conquer the forces which are marshaled against you. On her account, that ability is a matter of weapons and luck, not a matter of having truth on your side, or having detected the 'movement of history.'[108]

Rorty says that those who criticize the ironists' descriptive activity as failing to achieve the right description have misunderstood ironism, which rejects the notion of right description. But Rorty has not responded adequately to the question of whether ironic redescription is not as potentially and actually humiliating as the redescriptive acts he opposes. On Rorty's account a "right-wing" group is not treated better in being described by a liberal ironist in all the ways a liberal ironist might redescribe them than the liberal ironist is treated in being called, for instance, a "liberast," a Russian slang-word used to

104 Rorty, *Contingency, Irony, and Solidarity,* 89.

105 Rorty, *Contingency, Irony, and Solidarity,* 90.

106 Rorty, *Contingency, Irony, and Solidarity,* 90.

107 Rorty, *Contingency, Irony, and Solidarity,* 90.

108 Rorty, *Contingency, Irony, and Solidarity,* 91.

redescribe good old Westernizing liberal reformers as supporters of pederasty and other illicit affairs. In other words, even if the humiliation of redescription does apply to metaphysics, it also still applies to ironism. Rorty could only dispute that with a further act of giving and taking away, i.e., of internal inconsistency.

For Rorty, the critic who claims that ironic redescription fails to get the description right "begs the crucial questions" (since the ironist assumes that there *is* no right description).[109] Now, "to beg the question," means, in logic, to prove an argument by assuming the very thing that is in dispute in the argument as a premise in the proof. That premise cannot be assumed for the proof, since it is the very thing that needs to be proven. There is a method of proof in which a premise is negated by showing that in assuming it one is led to an incorrect conclusion, but that is not what Rorty means.

The metaphysical critic begs the question against the ironist by assuming that there is a standard, criterion, or foundation besides mere creative re-description. But minimally, the ironist *also* begs the question *against the metaphysician* by assuming that there *is not* a standard, criterion, or foundation of that sort. Rorty has already denied that philosophical arguments about contingency provide a basis for that assumption, since that would be to make philosophical arguments about contingency another sort of foundation. Rorty explicitly denies that procedure. On what grounds does he speak disparagingly of the metaphysician's "begging the question" against the ironist, then? Rorty is not offering arguments with premises and conclusions, to which the term "begging the question" might apply. Instead, he is invoking the language of logic and argumentation outside of the domain of logic and argumentation, as a rhetorical move. There is no obligation to accept that move.

Either the standoff between the metaphysician and the ironist is a case of each side "begging the question" against the other, taking up a

---

109 Rorty, *Contingency, Irony, and Solidarity,* 99.

posture that the other side disputes in a language that cannot but have continued recourse to the very terms and perspectives under dispute, in which case a metaphysician could hardly be blamed for begging the question against the ironist, since the same blame would apply to the ironist vis-à-vis the metaphysician, or else there is the possibility of no longer begging the question, i.e. no longer *assuming* for the demonstration what is in dispute, but instead arguing from shared premises or proving the disputed assumption. As the ironist abjures the language of premises, assumptions, demonstrations, and proofs, the dispute between the ironist and the metaphysician can be said to be "decisionistic."

Besides rhetorical invocations of logic for purposes of persuasive redescription, Rorty's decision for ironism appeals to traditions and their accomplishments with no desire to show the inherent goodness of those traditions and accomplishments and with no willingness to see in those traditions their rational aspect. As a result, he has no good response for the metaphysical foundationalist not persuaded by those redescriptions or attracted by those traditions. Rorty's whole aim is to persuade. He seems to have little recourse once he has failed to do so.

Rorty would like us to avoid "factitious and shopworn oppositions like 'art versus morality' or 'style versus substance'" when we talk about what books can do. But Rorty trucks in some oppositions that are hardly less shopworn.[110] He insists on the opposition of public and private. In the private sphere, where the development of one's autonomy is the primary focus, one engages in projects of self-creation, whereas in the public sphere, where solidarity reigns, one acts to minimize cruelty toward others.[111] Intended to negate the notion of public self-creation, this opposition between private self-creation and public concern for others is presented as an accomplished, historical

---

110 Rorty, *Contingency, Irony, and Solidarity*, 146.

111 Leypoldt, "Uses of Metaphor."

fact of Western liberal societies. But it can be disputed or rejected on other grounds.

Rorty is adamant that publicizing private self-creation is a recipe for disaster. The brilliant, private thinker "becomes at best vapid, and at worst sadistic" when publicizing his private fantasies. "As a philosopher of our public life, as a commentator on twentieth-century technology and politics," Heidegger in particular "is resentful, petty, squint-eyed, obsessive — and, at his occasional worst...cruel."[112] The brilliant, private thinker should know his place and remain there. It is thinkers and writers of another sort, those who write books about minimizing cruelty, whose word should carry the day in the public sphere.[113]

Rorty's laudable insistence on minimizing cruelty and maximizing creativity is untenable. The question remains whether there is not something in the nature of radical thought as a result of which, of its own accord, it overflows the vessel of the private person and begins to inundate the realm of the public. Is there not something *inherently constitutional* about certain ways of thinking? And is not the split between public and private constituted not merely by historical processes, as Rorty says, but also and just as importantly by the "private" visions of liberal political philosophers writ large? Rorty denies that *political* (public) philosophy (private) is desirable. But it may be asserted that it is a necessary consequence of a certain kind of thinking. The pinnacle of the public is the private; the peak of the private is the public. The "private creations" of philosophers have, at their peak, a legislative, constitutive, or founding, and hence public, dimension. That need not be a matter of fact. For as Rorty has written in another context,

> [d]eciding between [competing] descriptions...is not a matter of confronting or refusing to confront hard, unpleasant facts. Nor is it a matter of

---

112 Rorty, *Contingency, Irony, and Solidarity*, 120.

113 Rorty, *Contingency, Irony, and Solidarity*, 145.

being blinded, or not being blinded, by ideology. It is a matter of playing
off scenarios against contrasting scenarios, projects against alternative
projects, descriptions against redescriptions.[114]

Moreover, as we have seen, Rorty is not averse to using the language
of logic rhetorically when it suits his purposes to do so. In his chapter
on solidarity, he refers back to his earlier chapter on the contingency
of language, citing the latter as "incompatible with the idea" of a
shared human essence. His position "entails that feelings of solidarity are necessarily a matter of which similiarities and dissimiliarities
strike us as salient," rather than a matter of a shared human essence.[115]
Although he rejects the notion of the compatibility of ideas with one
another, a sort of rational coherence; although he rejects the notion
that philosophical arguments about contingency are a "foundation"
for his political preferences and projects; and although he does not
wish to speak of premises or assumptions entailing conclusions, still
Rorty cannot help but to do those things.[116] He presents his "views
about language and about selfhood" as "only" justified in that they
"[seem] to cohere better with the institutions of a liberal democracy
than the available alternatives do." At the intersection of philosophy
and the political Rorty urges that the philosopher "[subordinate]
sublimity to the [liberal] desire to avoid cruelty and pain." "[T]here is
nothing to back up such a request, nor need there be."[117] "*We*," Rorty
asserts, "have to start from where *we* are," "we liberals."[118] But do "we"?

Let's imagine with Rorty that a person is engaged in private
self-creation. Among her visions is one that envisions that the fruits
of private self-creation should be public. Suppose she envisions in
private self-creation an act of philosophical legislation, where private

---

114 Rorty, *Contingency, Irony, and Solidarity,* 173–74.

115 Rorty, *Contingency, Irony, and Solidarity,* 192.

116 Rorty, *Contingency, Irony, and Solidarity,* 189–92.

117 Rorty, *Contingency, Irony, and Solidarity,* 197.

118 Rorty, *Contingency, Irony, and Solidarity,* 198.

thinking becomes a standard and a measure for some aspect of public life. On Rorty's terms, she is not allowed to pursue that thought any further. It is nipped at the bud by his strict separation between the private and the public, self-creation and cruelty minimization. That means that Rorty unfairly limits the scope of private self-creation to exclude alternatives that do not obey his public-private division.

The fact that Rorty's dichotomy precludes a kind of private self-creation that creates itself as public (i.e. as legislative, constitutional, foundational, etc.) renders his dichotomy suspicious. It seems designed to preclude any link between private and public. It is made to render legislative fantasy, or political philosophy, impossible. But it is not obvious that political philosophy can or should be rendered null and void. Rorty might be closer to the mark when he makes statements that suggest a smaller gap between private and public, for instance in acknowledging that "we're all at the mercy of people of genius."[119]

Questioning Piety

Darren Aronofsky's film *Pi* depicts the unrelenting efforts of mathematician Max Cohen to crack nature's code by understanding the mathematical patterns underlying all things and processes.[120] Cohen is convinced that mathematics is a "final language," as Rorty would put it: not one description among others, but *the* description of the whole. Working obsessively to discover the occult patterns of the stock market, Max happens to meet a nettlesome Chassidic Jew in a café while pouring over the financial section of the daily newspaper. When the Chassid learns that Max is a mathematician, he enthusiastically says that he, too, is occupied with numbers: because every Hebrew letter has a numerical equivalent, the study of the Torah can include the search for numerical codes in the text. Some time later, Max learns that the Chassid and his congregation are seeking a

---

119 Rorty, *Take Care of Freedom*, 145.
120 Darren Aronofsky, Sean Gullette, Eric Watson, *Pi* (Harvest Filmworks, 1998).

special two-hundred-sixteen-digit number in the Torah. Max's former teacher, a secular Jew who once tried to grasp the hidden significance of pi but gave up on that as a fool's errand, had also mentioned to Max a string of two hundred and sixteen numbers he inexplicably encountered when exploring pi. This coincidence encourages Max to pay more attention to a seemingly random string of numbers which his own computer system, Euclid, spat out before crashing.

Eventually, Max is kidnapped by the congregation and asked to give them the number, which he has since committed to memory. The chief Rabbi recounts the tale that the name of God pronounced in the Holy of Holies of the Second Temple in Jerusalem before its destruction was of that length. In his search for a final vocabulary, Max has come into possession of a key word of that vocabulary. The chief Rabbi insists that Max has been sent to carry a message to the Rabbi's community, a message not meant for Max, who cannot understand or safeguard it. But Max does not give them the number. He has found it, he has, he thinks, earned it, and he wants to keep it, to see in light of it, to be transformed by it.

In one scene, Max is pulsing through the city in a maddening daze. We hear the thoughts racing through his mind as he rattles off the mathematical equations that express everything around him, from the mundane to the technically sophisticated. As the madness reaches its apogee, a scene change occurs and Max stands alone in a white light, quietly, reverently uttering the sequence of numbers of God's holiest name. In the following scene, Max is shown smashing Euclid, the computer system occupying the bulk of his small apartment.

If Max was a "metaphysician" when in search of the one true and final vocabulary, he become "post-metaphysical" when he smashed the technological apparatus designed to discover it. After uttering the holiest name of God, the secret word of the entire system of numbers, he was brought to repudiate that very system, or rather the attempt to map it, not in a higher dialectical synthesis but in outright rejection, albeit momentary. Whereas earlier in the film a young girl asks Max to solve mathematical problems she comes up with on the spot — problems like finding the product of two three digit integers — and Max cannot help but perform the operation, in the final scene of the film, when asked, he responds with a smile, stating that he doesn't know the answer. In renouncing the obsessive need to have and to speak a final vocabulary, Max's paranoid psychoses also fall by the wayside, and for once he is depicted as happy.

Rorty would approve of the interpretation that happiness, the highest end of man, on his account, depends on giving up the search for a final vocabulary. But Rorty's story isn't Max's story. Max gives up his search for a final vocabulary as a result of the special act of uttering the numerical sequence of God's Holiest Name. He does *not* give it up, for example, in the way that his teacher did, who had a stroke while working on the study of pi and, according to Max, became soft, having lost his passion (Max eventually brings his teacher to revive his passion, alas: the old man suffers a second, fatal stroke).

Max is *not* Rorty's ironist, abandoning the one true description for a life of free and easy redescription. He has not concluded that there is no true description or final account. Instead, he has abandoned or been liberated from an obsessive, one-sided need to compute that account with an emphasis on the manifest. An interpretation that sticks closer to Heidegger than to Rorty better serves us in understanding what has happened to Max, for when Heidegger comes to linger with the question of the truth of Being, he too is beyond the domain of attempts at a totalizing computation of the whole, which might better characterize the neo-Kantians he opposed. But neither is he merely playing games of redescription like Rorty's ironist, Rorty's reading notwithstanding.

This chapter began with a scene from the film *A Serious Man*. Rabbi Marshak had suggested that when the truth loses its status as truth, or is found to be lies, hope, too, dies, and a turn elsewhere is required. Rorty, we have seen, denies that the loss of truth begets the death of hope. Quite the contrary: hope grows when we topple the false god of truth from the altar, topple the altar itself, and set a liberal utopia in its place.

Rorty and the Rabbi present two different ways of approaching the question of truth. Heidegger is closer to the Rabbi than to Rorty, and closer to Max, too.[121] For Rorty, that is reason enough to reject much of Heidegger, along with the Rabbinate. But he may have his reasons, while we have ours. Let us now take leave of Rorty and follow more appealing roads, as Rorty has done in taking the road paved by Dewey. Rorty followed his heart.[122] We shall follow our question.

Though his son Danny did get to see Rabbi Marshak, Larry Gopnik did not. He therefore never got to ask the wise old Rabbi the question that other Rabbis could give him no help with: "Why does [God] make us feel the questions if he's not going to give us the answers?" Someone who has not "felt the question" doesn't have this problem, nor does someone who is content to declare that the answers are not available. But we must linger a while yet in pondering what it means to feel the question and to lack the answer.[123]

---

121 I shall leave the theme "Max and the Rabbi" for another occasion.

122 Many of Rorty's arguments, as we've seen, are "cardiological," or "psychological," such as when he claims, "I do not think it is *psychologically possible* to give up on political liberalism on the basis of a philosophical view about the nature of man or truth or history"; Rorty, *Contingency*, 182, my emphasis. He also writes that "one would *have to be very odd* to change one's politics because one had become convinced" of a philosophical proposition. Rorty, *Contingency*, 182–83, my emphasis. Anyway, he also admits that "tinkering" with our philosophical notions "might, in the very long run, and in a very indirect way, have a certain amount of political utility." Rorty, *Contingency*, 234. Likewise, he admits that "[h]aving a great imagination and altering the tradition in insensible ways is going to make a difference in public affairs somewhere down the line"; Rorty, *Take Care of Freedom,* 51. Philosophical redescription "may speed up the pace of social change," but only if one already "knows what one wants," and philosophy cannot help us with that; Richard Rorty, *Philosophy and Social Hope* (New York: Penguin, 1999): 232.

123 "Just as there were sixteen different ways of reacting to Hegel in his day," Rorty once said to an interviewer, "there were sixteen different ways of reacting to Heidegger; and I think it's pointless to ask what was the 'true' message of

CHAPTER FOUR

Derrida

Introduction

Let us ask the following question: "Is it possible to move beyond the constraints of logic, rhetoric, and grammar in speaking and in writing? If so, how?" This question about avoiding or surpassing logic, rhetoric, and grammar, which bears resemblance to Heidegger's question whether it is possible to talk about the history of philosophy as completed and in new terms to invoke and articulate the inauguration of another beginning, reproduces the modes about whose avoidance it inquires. It is a question of "possibility," structured according to the logical mode that asks "how" something is possible only once having ascertained "that" it is possible, for instance. Moreover, the question reproduces a rhetorical figure of spatiality when it asks about the possibility of "movement beyond." The question acknowledges that language is always already implicated in constraining structures and

either Hegel or Heidegger — they were just people to bounce one's thoughts off of" — Rorty, *Take Care of Freedom*, 50–1. On Rorty's own terms, he and I, and all the other authors covered in this study, are bouncing our thoughts off Heidegger. Conceived thus, if that exercise does not tell us more about Heidegger, it should at least help us to map out a range of potential approaches to political philosophy, using Heidegger as a sounding board.

unable even to pose the question of its extrication from such structures without reproducing them.

The strange twists and turns of a language that asks about itself
and inquires into the impossible possibility of its liberation from
constraining structures, and perhaps from itself as a self-constraining
structure, abound in Derrida's writings, which track and sometimes
mimic, artificially or by necessity, those twists and turns. His thorough intertwining with language's self-struggle concerning itself
explains why more so than in the case of any other thinker studied
in the present work, it is not possible simply to ask about the place
of Heidegger in Derrida's thought and to move straightforwardly
towards an answer. Derrida's thought proceeds not straightforwardly
but through a labyrinth, as it were, and it has an uneasy relationship
to the question of "the place," not to mention the question of the question. To ask about the place of Heidegger in Derrida's thought is at
least to ask about the place of the place in Derrida's thought.

As Derrida has cautioned against Heidegger's contention that there
is a single spirit of the poem, claiming instead that a poem, rather
than gathering into some unity, will "space itself across multiple undecidable differences," so, too, it is prudent not to regard Derrida's own
texts too hastily as saying one thing or having one stable, homogeneous position on Heidegger and place.[1] Like a poem, Derrida spaces
himself out across undecidable differences. And yet, it is possible to
draw meaningful distinctions about the "space" into which he spaces
himself out as it relates to other "spaces" with their own logics.

One such "limit" or border separating Derrida's space from
Heidegger's space can be inferred from Derrida's remarks on apophatic mysticism. Although there is not one obvious place, one gathering point, to begin the study of the place of Heidegger in Derrida's
thought, it will not be misleading to begin with those remarks, which
treat both anagogic mystical literature — recall the importance of

---

1   David Farrell Krell, "Marginalia to *Geschlecht III*," *The New Centennial Review*
     7, No. 2 (2007): 181.

such mystical literature in the genesis of this study, as discussed in the preface — and the question of the place, in a reflection that explicitly includes a discussion of Heidegger.

Deconstruction and Apophatic Mysticism

Apophatic mysticism refers to a practice of coming closer to God, with the aim of attaining immediate union with God, through a specific form of speech, culminating in silent union. Derrida provisionally characterizes the speech-form appropriate to apophatic mysticism, or to negative theology, as it may also be called, as follows: "Suppose, by a provisional hypothesis, that negative theology consists of considering that every predicative language is inadequate to the essence, in truth to the hyperessentiality (the being beyond Being) of God: consequently, only a negative ('apophatic') attribution can claim to approach God, and to prepare us for a silent intuition of God."[2] God is above being, so all speech ascribing positive attributes to God is inadequate, as indeed is the statement that "God is above being." Because negative speech implicates itself in the twists and turns of a language that cannot be purely negative, apophatic writings, Derrida observes, are full of "apophatic warnings" and disclaimers, insisting that "this, which is called X…'is' neither this nor that, neither sensible nor intelligible, neither positive nor negative, neither inside nor outside, neither superior nor inferior, neither active nor passive, neither present nor absent, not even neutral, not even subject to a dialectic with a third moment, without any possible sublation."[3]

In the essay under consideration, Derrida is responding to the claim that deconstruction resembles or is a form of negative theology. Like those of the apophatic mystics, Derrida's claims often twist

---

2 Jacques Derrida, "How to Avoid Speaking: Denials" in *Derrida and Negative Theology*, edited by Harold Coward and Toby Froshay (Albany: SUNY Press, 1992): 74. (Henceforth cited as Derrida, *Denials*.)

3 Derrida, *Denials*, 74.

and turn until, exhausted and at its limits, language seems to suspend itself. But whereas for the mystics the aim of this spiritual-linguistic exercise is transportation into the silent intuition of God in his hyperessentiality, for Derrida, language is always at its limits, never fully suspended, and he regards such notions as transportation, immediate intuition, and hyperessentiality as problematic.

Acknowledging that his non-mystical alternative could be read as a mystical theology of negation, asking, "Who could prohibit?" such a reading,[4] Derrida nevertheless denies that it is one: "What I write is not 'negative theology.'"[5] An account of the reasons he gives should help us establish distance between a mystically-inclined inceptual thinking and Derridean deconstruction.

One reason Derrida gives for denying that deconstruction is a negative theology concerns what he calls the hyperessentiality of the latter. The hyperessentiality of negative theology means, for Derrida, that it somehow preserves the view that there is *something* beyond Being of which it would make sense to have a direct intuition. This is the notion of "God as *without* Being," or "God as beyond Being."[6] Negative theology must be so thoroughly negative as to place God beyond Being, but not so thoroughly negative as to negate the God beyond Being, union with whom is its *telos*. Derrida criticizes this hyperessentiality as incompatible with deconstructionism, the elements of whose vocabulary are "'before' the concept, the name, the word, 'something' that would be nothing, that no longer arises from Being, from presence or from the presence of the present, nor even from absence, and even less from some hyperessentiality."[7]

Derrida acknowledges that the negative theologian can say that "hyperessentiality is precisely that, a supreme Being who remains

---

4   Derrida, *Denials*, 77.

5   Derrida, *Denials*, 77.

6   Derrida, *Denials*, 77.

7   Derrida, *Denials*, 79.

incommensurate to the being of all that is, which *is* nothing, either present nor absent, and so on."[8] That is, indeed, the argumentative move that one can expect the apophatic mystic to make, for the mystic will deny that the X beyond being toward which he strives is a presence or an absence he intends to make present. Derrida calls that argumentative move "onto-theological reappropriation."[9] It reappropriates the critique of hyperessentiality as part of its negative theology. Reappropriation is "*inevitable* insofar as one speaks, precisely, in the element of logic and of onto-theological grammar." Reappropriation is inevitable, but so is its "ultimate failure," which is due to the failure of logic and onto-theological grammar in the face of its own underlying deconstructive secret (more on that later). All the same, the question of reappropriation "remains a question" and cannot be decided definitively.[10]

If a deconstructive approach to language cannot but be reappropriated onto-theologically, whether or not such reappropriation must ultimately fail, it is unclear to what extent it can be kept rigorously distinct from the mystical approach on that score. It cannot be the case that the deconstructive mode is distinguished by its vigilant attentiveness to the failures of language, for Derrida himself has noted, as we saw, that mystical literature is replete with apophatic warnings about the same thing. Thus, it is important to consider Derrida's other arguments against negative theology as possible indicators of the reasons for his departure from Heidegger's inceptual thinking.

Besides hyperessentiality, Derrida takes issue with the telos of negative theology: intuition of God or union with God. In his critique, Derrida fastens upon the idea that that telos entails "the immediacy of a presence."[11] It is strange that Derrida should regard in those terms

---

8   Derrida, *Denials*, 79.

9   Derrida, *Denials*, 79.

10 Derrida, *Denials*, 79.

11 Derrida, *Denials*, 79.

what he also sympathetically, i.e., with understanding, calls "the vision of a dark light."[12] In other words, it is strange that although he acknowledges the language of non-presence ("*dark* light") as a characteristic feature of negative theology, he nevertheless interprets the mystical experience in terms of immediate presence. Doing so allows him to subject that experience to the general critical deconstruction of a metaphysics of presence, without delving more deeply into the paradox of an encounter or experience with non-presence. On this point, Derrida seems to move too quickly in assimilating the mystical experience to the immediacy of a presence.

In Derrida's telling, however, it is the mystic who moves too quickly. The mystic moves too quickly in the ascent toward the mystical telos, toward "that silent union with that which remains inaccessible to speech."[13] The problem, for Derrida, is that the ascent, to the extent that it passes through language — "this ascent corresponds to a rarefaction of signs, figures, symbols" — must "negatively retraverse all the stages of symbolic theology and positive prediction," an impossible task, which can never reach its limit.[14] When the mystic believes himself to have traversed all such stages, he is in error, for they cannot be traversed. Instead, "the apophatic movement…can only indefinitely defer the encounter with its own limit."[15] Derrida's claim that this movement "cannot contain within itself the principle of its own interruption" distinguishes deconstruction, or as he calls it in this context, "the thinking of differance" from the mode of apophatics, in comparison to which his own mode is "alien, heterogeneous, in any case irreducible to the intuitive *telos*" of "mute vision."[16] Derrida's arrow never hits the tree.

---

12   Derrida, *Denials*, 79.

13   Derrida, *Denials*, 80.

14   Derrida, *Denials*, 80–1.

15   Derrida, *Denials*, 81.

16   Derrida, *Denials*, 81.

Using various figures of speech, Derrida focuses instead on something like a non-present, non-presentable condition of possibility, or, more complexly, "the experience of the (impossible) possibility of the impossible."[17] For instance, the conditions that must be met for a secret to be possible are impossible (secrecy would require perfect non-communication, but the secret must communicate at least itself), so the experience of the secret is the experience of the impossible possibility of the impossible. "Secret" is just one of a few words, figures, markers, or whatever we should call them to be true to the deconstructive attitude, that Derrida analyzes in the deconstructive mode. Another is the "experience of the *khora* which is above all not an experience, if one understands by this word a certain relation to presence."[18] A third example is "the promise," which "as necessary as it is impossible, inscribes us by its trace in language."[19]

In these and other examples, Derrida talks about something that is both necessary and impossible. That duality comprises the main deconstructive aporia. As can be seen from the examples given, in some cases Derrida allows for the (impossible) possibility of an experience that is not an experience because it is not related to presence. But he does not do so in the case of the mystical telos. The reason for the difference, on the previous analysis, is, to repeat, that the mystical telos requires that which the deconstructive mode rejects: a traversal, interruption, or passing of a threshold, the "crossing [of] a frontier."[20]

Another distinction between deconstruction and apophatic mysticism Derrida draws concerns the secret and the place of the secret. In the deconstructive mode, "secret" is one of the terms in the series of terms that draw attention to the aporetic state of being both necessary and impossible. In the mystical literature, by contrast, a "secret"

---

17   "Sauf Le Nom" in Jacques Derrida, *On the Name* (Stanford: Stanford University Press, 1995): 43; Derrida, *Denials*, 84.

18   Derrida, *Denials*, 108.

19   Derrida, *Denials*, 84.

20   Derrida, "Sauf Le Nom," 36.

is rather something vouchsafed to an initiate, who must both guard it from profanation and communicate it to the elect.[21] With the latter view in mind, Derrida raises the question of "the place of the secret" thus conceived: "What is…this place? Between the place and the place of the secret, between the secret place and the topography of the social link which must precede the nondivulgence, there must be a certain homology."[22] This homology "must govern some (secret) relation between the topology of what stands beyond Being, without being — without Being, and the topology, the initiatory politopology which at once organizes the mystical community and makes possible the address to the other."[23] Derrida asks the following questions about this mystical topology: "Where does the speaker stand, and where the one who listens and receives? Where does the one stand who speaks while *receiving* from the Cause which is also the Cause of this community?"[24]

He also emphasizes that the rhetorical "places" in the "topolitology of the secret" are "political strategems" sanctioned by a "divine promise," in the absence of which this "field of rhetoricity" and the "order" it establishes, collapse.[25] Derrida rightly brings into the foreground of his discussion the issue of place in relation to negative theology, for it indeed plays a central role both through "figurative spatialization," such as in the figure of God *beyond* being, and through the idea that the significant event "takes place."[26] Derrida's deconstructive mode seeks to avoid figurative spatializations, though it cannot do so entirely. Indeed, a theme running throughout Derrida's essay, as indicated by the title, "How to Avoid Speaking," concerns the possibility, and impossibility, of course, of avoidance.

---

21 Derrida, *Denials*, 86–90.

22 Derrida, *Denials*, 91.

23 Derrida, *Denials*, 91.

24 Derrida, *Denials*, 91.

25 Derrida, *Denials*, 93.

26 Derrida, *Denials*, 97.

Derrida's remarks on Heidegger in the context of the question of negative theology and place reproduce to an extent the main lines of his departure from negative theology. He indicates the figurative spatialization according to which Heidegger, to mark a different sense of being than that belonging to the history of philosophy, writes the word "being" with an X-like crossing out over the top of it. The X is not primarily a sign of negation, but a sign of spatialization, a pictograph of the fundamental-ontological topography Heidegger called "the fourfold."[27] Derrida also draws attention to the spatialization of Heidegger's statement that "the experience of God…occurs in the dimension of Being," seeing in "the dimension of disclosure" a "place that gives place without being either essence or foundation," a "threshold that gives access to God."[28] Heidegger once said that he would avoid the word being if he were to write a theology. Zeroing in on the place of being, as it were, in Heidegger's statement about the experience of God, Derrida examines the impossibility of avoidance in this case.

The final point he makes about Heidegger distinguishes Heidegger from negative theology, though it brings him no closer to the deconstructive mode. That point is that negative theology is often prefaced by a prayer to the addressee, or to God, or to both, a prayer that "[guides] the apophasis toward excellence, not allowing it to say just anything, and prevent it from manipulating its negations like empty and purely mechanical phrases," whereas Heidegger's remarks on the occasion Derrida examines were not so prefaced, despite sharing with negative theology a "pedagogical or psychological" character.[29] Derrida interprets that absence in Heidegger to indicate the "predominance of the

---

27 See Michael Millerman, "Heidegger, Left and Right: Differential Political Ontology and Fundamental Political Ontology Compared" *Journal of Eurasian Affairs* 2, no. 1 (2014) for an account of the fourfold in right-Heideggerian "topolitology." Derrida, *Denials*, 125–26.

28 Derrida, *Denials*, 127–28.

29 Derrida, *Denials*, 110, 129–30.

theoretical" and the rigorous exclusion of the fideistic in Heidegger's texts.[30] Yet, Derrida also offers an alternative interpretation, according to which the very act of writing would be a sort of prayer, or rather that there is no such thing as "pure prayer," but always only its reduplication, whether in an explicit address to God or to another, or through other forms of "contamination," including "writing, the code, repetition, analogy, or the — at least apparent — multiplicity of addresses, initiation."[31] In this sense, Derrida implies, "prayer," understood in the deconstructive mode, may belong to the set of terms that includes "secret," "promise," and "khora," analyzed above, that is to the domain of necessary impossibilities. Heidegger, therefore, may be thought to be, as all must be, Derrida included, implicated in the logic of prayer, even though not as explicitly as in the case of a traditional apophatic mystic.[32]

Inceptual and Deconstructive Topolitologies

To the extent that Derrida's comments on negative theology also apply to Heidegger, they may be gathered together under three themes: hyperessentiality, spatialization, and presentation. Hyperessentiality refers to the claim that beyond beings and even beyond Being there is still some X that is the telos of the mystic ascent, some X to which the being of the mystic may correspond in mystical union and which may be reached by crossing a threshold or limit. Spatialization concerns discursive figures of place, including height (ascent), distance

---

30 Derrida, *Denials*, 130. Caputo, who has also examined the resonances between Heidegger's thought and the mystical tradition, would agree. John D. Caputo, *The Mystical Element in Heidegger's Thought* (Athens: Ohio University Press, 1978).

31 Derrida, *Denials*, 131.

32 Perhaps Heidegger's statement that "thoughtful speaking is a *directive*" marks the apostrophic moment of inceptual thinking no less than the fact of his writing at all. Heidegger, *Contributions*, 8.

(beyond), and proximity (union). Presentation, finally, means that that which is beyond being and brought near is made present.

It is fair to regard hyperessentiality and spatialization as features of Heidegger's inceptual thought. It is the very nature of inceptual thought as Heidegger describes it to pass beyond the threshold or limit of the history of the first beginning of philosophy to inaugurate another beginning in accordance with a logic of granting and sheltering anchored in the hyperessentiality of "beyng."[33] In describing the "leap" across that threshold, Heidegger has recourse to the figures of a "trans-position," "cleared region," and "playing field," as well as to the transformation of the human "into the builder and steward" of the "site" of truth.[34]

Indeed, Heidegger does not simply deploy figures of place when describing the leap into another beginning. He thinks that the leap into another beginning, "the transporting into that which withholds itself," is essentially correlated with "spatialization."[35] Beyng's self-concealing granting constitutes a space-time, and the "spatializing is grounding and is the site of the moment."[36] Even in *Being and Time*, Dasein's spatiality is regarded as one of its existentials or structural characteristics. So Derrida is surely right to identify spatialization as a characteristic of Heidegger's thought.

It is less fair to regard presentation as a major theme of inceptual thinking. It would seem that something being granted and sheltered must be regarded as present or in terms of its presence. However, what Heidegger says about this matter resembles the sayings of the negative theologians, who, as Derrida acknowledges, deny with all their linguistic capabilities the presence of that which is revealed in the moment of mystical intuition. For instance, Heidegger calls "the

---

33 Martin Heidegger, *Contributions to Philosophy (of the Event)* (Bloomington: Indiana University Press, 2012).

34 Heidegger, *Contributions*, 190–91.

35 Heidegger, *Contributions*, 303.

36 Heidegger, *Contributions*, 303.

openness of the clearing of concealment" an "emptiness," and not "the
mere emptiness of vacancy," but rather "the disposed and disposing
emptiness of the abyssal ground," i.e., an emptiness or nothingness
that is neither simply present nor merely negative.[37]

Since something occurs in the event, Heidegger must speak of
"presencing," but he hastens to add that this presencing, the "presencing of truth" in "the hesitant self-withholding," occurs "not in the way
something objectively present has come to presence" but is rather "the
essential occurrence of what first founds the presence and absence of
beings and not only this."[38] Heidegger's discussion of what happens
in the leap into another beginning does not revolve around or cul-
minate in "the immediacy of a presence," to use Derrida's term, and
his repudiation of the language of objective presence does not amount
to a mere onto-theological reappropriation of negativity, as Derrida
claimed is the case among the apophatic mystics and among anyone
who speaks, as Derrida himself does, at the limits of language.

Heidegger describes the passage beyond the threshold as "transposition into the cleared region," which "ground[s] the clearing itself
as the open realm in which beyng gathers itself into its essence." The
"essential occurrence" of this essence "must be expected to arrive
like a jolt." One cannot force or calculate this arrival. One can only
prepare for it.[39] One may therefore evoke the sense of the leap, which
begins, Heidegger says, not only in the leap but in the run up to the
leap, as preparation for the transposing, transformative arrival of a
hyperessential non-presence in a field-constituting, hence spatializing
trembling of sheltering and granting.

Except for his inaccurate remarks on presence, Derrida's discussion of negative theology can be a fruitful resource for a positive
understanding of Heidegger's inceptual thinking when compared

---

37 Heidegger, *Contributions*, 301.

38 Heidegger, *Contributions*, 301.

39 Heidegger, *Contributions*, 191.

rigorously with Heidegger's own descriptions of the movements of such thinking. That Derrida has drawn a line between the discourses of negative theology and those of deconstruction can help to distinguish a Heideggerian "topolitology," to use Derrida's felicitous term, from a Derridean one, without there necessarily needing to be "critique" or "criticism" of one by the other. There is reason to think that what distinguishes the two positions is an experience, or a set of experiences. Evidently, Heidegger does not write about the leap into another beginning "from the outside," but rather as one to whom what he describes has come "like a jolt." Similarly, mystics who claim to have crossed the threshold of language may be referring to an experience whose possibility Derrida can deny only because he has not undergone it.

There is warrant for this perspective in Derrida's account of one of his own constitutive experiences. Derrida, naked, sees his cat seeing him. This moment forces him to think the absolute alterity of the cat, the relationship between alterity and speech, and the customary philosophical limit drawn between "the human" and "the animal." Derrida suggests that theoreticians and philosophers at least since Descartes are those who have never taken "account of the fact that what they call animal could *look at* them and *address* them from down there, from a wholly other origin."[40] Although their writings may be "sound and profound," they write "as though this troubling experience had not been theoretically registered, supposing that they had experienced it at all."[41] Their disavowal of that experience "institutes what is proper to man, the relation to itself of a humanity that is above all careful to guard, and jealous of, what is proper to it."[42] That is why Derrida regards as "Heidegger's most significant, symptomatic, and seriously dogmatic" sentence, a sentence about a difference between

---

40 Jacques Derrida, "The Animal That I Therefore Am (More to Follow)," *Critical Inquiry* 28, No. 2 (2008): 382.

41 Derrida, "The Animal That I Therefore Am," 383.

42 Derrida, "The Animal That I Therefore Am," 383.

an animal and man: "Apes, for example, have organs that can grasp, but they have no hand." In this sentence, Heidegger denies apes, and through their example all animals, what is proper to man, the ability to manifest the hidden, because he institutes the proper of man through a failure to register the encounter with animals.[43] Unlike theoreticians, poets, Derrida speculates, are those who have both experienced and reflected on the encounter with, not indeed that generality of which Derrida is fiercely critical, namely "the animal" as such, but rather with some specific animal, a cat in his case.[44] He says the following about the experience of seeing his cat see him naked, "Nothing will have ever done more to make me think through this absolute alterity of the neighbor than these moments when I see myself seen naked under the gaze of a cat."[45] And for their part, when "philosophers have always judged and *all* philosophers have judged that limit ['separating man in general from the animal in general'] to be single and indivisible, considering that on the other side of that limit there is an immense group, a single and fundamentally homogeneous set that one has the right, the theoretical or philosophical right, to distinguish and mark as opposite, namely, the set of the Animal in general, the animal spoken of in the general singular," they have seemed to Derrida with this gesture "to constitute philosophy as such."[46]

Derrida, then, has had an experience and registered it theoretically, and this experience more than anything has given him cause to think the fundamental issues of absolute alterity and the proper to man, while the absence or denial of this experience has had a constitutive role, too. Similarly, it is possible that Heidegger has had an experience, an existential conversion (Derrida speaks of a "conversion of existence" in regard to the mystics), which he has both undergone

---

43   Jacques Derrida, *Geschlecht II*, 173.

44   Derrida, "The Animal That I Therefore Am."

45   Derrida, "The Animal That I Therefore Am," 380.

46   Derrida, "The Animal That I Therefore Am," 408–9.

and registered theoretically, an experience that has given him cause to think the fundamental issues of the granting and sheltering of beyng in another inception.[47]

Heidegger may take account of Derrida's experience and incorporate it into the body of his thought, and Derrida may do likewise with Heidegger's experience, as we may do with both their experiences. But on this account it is at least possible that what distinguishes the two modes is not any set of prior commitments but the theoretical registering of a liminal experience that transforms one and constitutes a matter for thought.[48] (Heidegger writes that a "'critique' of the question of being" must be premised on the "experience […] of the plight of the abandonment by being," which would then be one of the transformative liminal experiences of his topolitology).[49]

Moreover, there is an extent to which Derrida is subject to his own criticisms — something he would not deny and would likely regard as inescapable. Although he goes out of his way to distinguish various figures characteristic of the mode of deconstruction from those appropriate to the mode of negative theology, nevertheless the deconstructive figures not only may be thought of as "hyperessential," but must on Derrida's own account necessarily be thought of that way, even as one denies them the status of the hyperessential, for onto-theological reappropriation is inevitable.

Moreover, Derrida is not "beyond" figures of spatialization; he precisely spatializes himself "away" from Heidegger in departing or parting ways with Heidegger. For instance, when arguing that the equality characteristic of his notion of a democracy to come is compatible with heterogeneity, he employs figures of spatialization to distinguish himself from Heidegger, writing that, "A democracy to come should give to be thought an equality that is not incompatible with

---

47 Derrida, "Sauf Le Nom," 38.

48 See also Heidegger, *Contributions*, 13.

49 Heidegger, *Contributions*, 15.

a certain dissymmetry, with hetereogeneity, or absolute singularlity, an equality even requiring them and engaging them *from a place* that remains invisible but that *orients* me here, *from afar*, no doubt *beyond* the Heideggerian aims."[50]

Derrida says he never "criticizes" Heidegger — the quotation marks are his — without showing that some of Heidegger's own statements can be used against other ones: Heidegger is not univocal and not without contradiction.[51] It is no argumentative coup to show that Derrida can also be read against himself, all the more so when the deconstructive mode acknowledges the impossibility of a pure discourse, uncontaminated by metaphysical and onto-theological reappropriations. But then it is also no coup against the Heideggerian mode, no "criticism" of it, to indicate its hyperessentiality and spatialization.

"Being," Derrida writes, "which is nothing, is not a being, cannot be said, cannot say itself, except in the ontic metaphor [that can] only metaphorize, by means of a profound necessity from which one cannot simply decide to escape, the language that it deconstructs."[52] Heidegger's leap into another beginning carries with it a new metaphorization of the language of the first beginning. Concealment, granting, sheltering, leap — these and related terms would all mean something new when employed as metaphors by which to speak beyng or to let beyng speak. For Derrida, "the choice of one or another group of metaphors is necessarily significant."[53] He highlights the selection of metaphors Heidegger makes in order to show that that selection is problematic. Derrida finds in Heidegger "the dominance of an entire metaphorics of proximity, of simple and immediate presence,

50 Jacques Derrida, "Heidegger's Ear: Philopolemology," in *Reading Heidegger: Commemorations*, edited by John Sallis (Bloomington: Indiana University Press, 1993): 183, my emphasis.

51 Jacques Derrida, "*Geschlecht* II: Heidegger's Hand," in *Reading Heidegger*, 189.

52 Derrida, "The Ends of Man," in Jacques Derrida, *Margins of Philosophy* (Chicago: University of Chicago Press, 1972): 131.

53 Derrida, "The Ends of Man," 131.

a metaphorics associating the proximity of Being with the values of neighboring, shelter, house, service, guard, voice, and listening."[54]

The role of "simple and immediate presence" in Heidegger's account of another beginning was disputed above, but it is true that he privileges figures of proximity and associates them, as Derrida says he does, with a significant group of metaphors, a group that may be taken to constitute the axis of the *polit-* in the phrase topolitology. The destabilization of Heidegger's metaphorics that Derrida attempts by examining the "voice of the friend that Dasein carries with it" is more successful than that focusing on hyperessentiality and spatialization.

Philopolemology, or the Philosophical Constitution of the Political

In "Heidegger's Ear," Derrida focuses on a passage in *Being and Time* that mentions "the voice of the friend whom every Dasein carries with it."[55] On the basis of that passage, Derrida launches into an analysis of the place of the "voice," the "friend," the "carry" and the "with" in Heidegger. Does the voice of the friend that Dasein carries with it belong to Dasein's community, speak its language, and share its destiny? "It is not entirely excluded," Derrida notes, "nor is it certain that belonging to the *same* community or to the *same* people, the experience of the *same* tongue, or the participation in the *same* struggle is the requisite condition for a voice of the friend to be carried *bei sich* by Dasein." For in the act of non-sensuous existential hearing, we "prick up our ear toward what is beyond the ear, the open ear, *over there*, in the world, *beside* what is for example usable in the world [and] the enigma of this topics of Dasein's ear and of the *Da* of *Sein* passes through this semantics of the *bei*, of this *beside* [...] whose vicinity is neither the very close nor the infinitely distant."[56] Would

54 Derrida, "The Ends of Man," 130.
55 Derrida, "Heidegger's Ear."
56 Derrida, "Heidegger's Ear," 178.

not a metaphorical topolitology of *Volk*, community, sheltering, and belonging be made to tremble if the voice of the friend that Dasein carries with it is a foreign voice, a voice in another idiom?

Analyzing Heidegger's *Was ist das — die Philosophie,* Derrida shows that Heidegger distinguishes between a philosophical and a pre-philosophical sense of the philosophical. The pre-philosophical sense of the philosophical thinks the philosophical person as the one who *philein to sophon.* Heidegger's task is to understand what those terms mean not in the traditional sense of philosophy but in that original experience that precedes the formalization and encrustation of philosophy as a constituted undertaking. Heidegger wants to know what those terms mean as part of the original experience that gives rise to philosophy. He cannot therefore interpret them using the terms and concepts of the philosophical tradition, Plato and Aristotle especially. He must think them inceptually.[57]

Philein proves to be *homologein,* "to accord oneself," as Derrida puts it, "to the [*legein*] of the [*logos*], to hear and respond to it."[58] This originary accordance precedes "the correspondence called personal, friendly, or loving in general."[59] It is a "harmony" of two beings joined together, and it "supposes the reciprocity of the there-and-back, the going and coming of exchange."[60] Here, Derrida offers the following destabilizing gloss:

> A serious problem [i.e. this reciprocity] when one tries to draw the consequences of the mutuality in the moral and political field of friendship. What would be the political carrying-distance of a thought or an experience of [*philein*] that would no longer respect this law of reciprocity and would appeal to dissemblance, heterogeneity, dissymmetry, disproportion,

---

57   Derrida, "Heidegger's Ear," 180–81.

58   Derrida, "Heidegger's Ear," 182.

59   Derrida, "Heidegger's Ear," 182.

60   Derrida, "Heidegger's Ear," 183.

incommensurability, nonexchange, the excess of every measure and thus of all symmetry?[61]

Does Heidegger's aural metaphorics of harmony and accord construct an otopolitopological field that excludes the items on Derrida's list, privileging instead homogeneity, symmetry, proportion, commensurability, exchange, and measure? It is precisely in this context that Derrida makes his statement quoted earlier, that the equality of a democracy to come "is not incompatible with" and "even [requires] and [engages] them *from a place that remains invisible but that orients me here, from afar, no doubt beyond the Heideggerian aim.*"[62] The metaphorics of harmony, that is, would thus also distinguish the inceptual mode from the deconstructive one, both philosophically and politically.

Derrida shows that in Heidegger the originary harmony is lost through a "scission," and it falls as a task upon the "few" to bring themselves back into originary "correspondence" with "*being,* [*logos,*] and [*philein*]."[63] The origin of philosophy is the nostalgic reaction to the scission that disrupts the harmony.[64] Philosophy as *erotic longing* already comes *after* that event.[65] Yet, is the original *philein* or accord then pre-erotic? "Where then," Derrida asks, "is the voice of the friend placed, the friend that each *Dasein bei sich trägt*? Is this voice pre-erotic or not? What can that mean? What about its *Geschlecht* and its rapport to fraternity?"[66]

---

61 Derrida, "Heidegger's Ear," 183.

62 Derrida, "Heidegger's Ear," 183, emphasis added.

63 Derrida, "Heidegger's Ear," 190.

64 Derrida, "Heidegger's Ear," 190.

65 Derrida, "Heidegger's Ear," 191.

66 Derrida, "Heidegger's Ear," 192.

Geschlecht is a word, or a "mark," as Derrida calls it, with multiple meanings.[67] It can mean "sex, race, species, genus, gender, stock, family, generation or genealogy, community."[68] When Derrida asks about the *Geschlecht* of the voice of the friend and its rapport to fraternity in the context of the notion of a pre-erotic harmony, he is making the point that the voice cannot belong to any fraternal community, to any delimited group, when it is *not yet* marked by the mark of *Geschlecht*. But the idea that Dasein carries with it a voice that is not thus marked threatens to upset a metaphorics of belonging that often is *already* marked by the mark, such as when it speaks of *das Volk,* or indeed when it speaks German and privileges German (or privileges Greek and the act of "hearing with Greek ears").[69] That is why Derrida says that it is not "certain that belonging to the *same* community or to the *same* people, the experience of the *same* tongue, or the participation in the *same* struggle is the requisite condition for a voice of the friend to be carried *bei sich* by Dasein."[70] "Heidegger never escapes from his own idiom," but his statements about the voice of the friend one carries with one taken together with his thoughts on the original harmony seem to suggest that the otherness of another idiom is embedded in one's own existential constitution.[71]

However, Derrida shows that the *philein*, the harmonious accord and perhaps the voice of the friend Dasein carries with it, is elsewhere in Heidegger's writings equivalent also to *eris* and *polemos*, to a *polemos* that is as much before war as originary *philein* is before

67 Derrida, "*Geschlecht*: Sexual Difference, Ontological Difference," *Research in Phenomenology* 13, no. 1 (1983); Derrida, "Heidegger's Ear,"; Derrida, "*Geschlecht II*: Heidegger's Hand," in Jacques Derrida, *Deconstruction and Philosophy: The Texts of Jacques Derrida*, edited by John Sallis (Chicago: University of Chicago Press, 1987).

68 Derrida, "*Geschlecht* II," 162.

69 Derrida, "Heidegger's Ear," 181.

70 Derrida, "Heidegger's Ear," 178.

71 Krell, "Marginalia," 184.

friendship. Although there would be an erotic, questioning discord and struggle that follows the scission of the original harmony, there would seem to have to be as well a *polemos* that precedes the questioning inquiry into the lost harmony.[72] So to the extent that the "voice of the friend" is "pre-erotic," it is also a voice of strife or enmity, as long as the latter is regarded as the originary strife that gathers.[73] If it seemed destabilizing to a metaphorics of belonging to have the voice of the friend untouched by *Geschlecht* (and hence not belonging to one's community or speaking in one's tongue) in such essential proximity to oneself, that is because of the misleading connotations of the term "friend" taken ontically. The voice, though, is not that of an ontic friend. It is the voice of an "enemy-friend that speaks [...] in the heart of [an] originary enmity that forever gathers us for the best and the worst."[74] Unlike the post-scission enmity that may well be "our question as *Gestalt*" (Schmitt), "originary enmity," Derrida writes, is "the originary oneness" of contraries.[75] The voice, then, is apparently that of the holding together in an accord the oneness as strife.

Once we include strife and expand the "friend" to the "enemy-friend," we remove the argumentative force of Derrida's divided line between the deconstructive and inceptual mode as they concern dissonance, dissymmetry and the other items he said Heidegger's metaphorics of harmony privileged. Those items are now contained originarily in the gathering of friendship-enmity.

Derrida's discussion of the pole of *eris*, *polemos*, and *Kampf*, offers a helpful way of thinking about the philosophical constitution of the political, or, in other words, the inceptual constitution, or institution, of a topolitology. "Conflict (*Kampf*)," he writes,

---

72 Derrida, "Heidegger's Ear," 201.
73 Derrida, "Heidegger's Ear," 201–2.
74 Derrida, "Heidegger's Ear," 215–16.
75 Derrida, "Heidegger's Ear," 214.

is [*physis*] inasmuch as it institutes but also inasmuch as it keeps what is instituted. It is institution itself, in the double sense of this word, instituting and instituted. When conflict stops, when one no longer hears what is unheard in conflict, the being does not disappear, but is no longer kept, affirmed, maintained [...], becomes an object [...] *available* there where world has ceased to become world.[76]

Conflict both institutes and preserves the instituted. In its absence, objects become world-deprived, "an object for a gaze [...] or a form or image that faces us, or the object of a calculated production." The society of the spectacle (Debord) is a society devoid of instituting/instituted originary conflict. It is a society of neutralizations (Schmitt). In this lamentable state, "[*polemos*] degenerates into polemics" and "the creators (poets, thinkers, statesmen) then have been removed from the people [and] are regarded as eccentrics or cultural ornaments."[77] As creators, poets, thinkers, and statesman stand under the claim of the instituting "originary upsurging" beyond knowledge and calculation. "The institution or the foundation," Derrida says, providing an account of Heidegger's position, "cannot itself be founded [i.e. is not a matter of production, technique, or calculation]; it inaugurates above an inaudible abyss, and this knowledge [...] [w]hich, by definition, moreover, is not knowledge [...] is the experience of the foundation as the experience of the *Abgrund*."[78]

Derrida has an ear for Heidegger. His presentation of the movement of Heidegger's thought is sympathetic. When he hears dissonances it is because he listens so acutely that ultimately even the dissonances find their proper place in the symphony. Though the pre-erotic voice of the friend threatened to sound a discordant note when played together with the harmonies and harmonics of a metaphoric of belonging, Derrida lovingly re-gathers the dwelling-together of

76 Derrida, "Heidegger's Ear," 212.

77 Derrida, "Heidegger's Ear," 212.

78 Derrida, "Heidegger's Ear," 213.

accordance with discordance and enmity in his reconstruction of Heidegger's "philopolemology." Heidegger's thoughts on that matter hold an important place in Derrida's own self-understanding. "The word that Heidegger privileges," to say this "originary unity of two contraries [...] is *Walten*."[79] In *The Politics of Friendship*, Derrida recalls *Walten* as follows:

> If I am insisting so much on the world *Walten*, and on all the striking occurrences of this verb (sometimes nominalized), throughout Heidegger's corpus after *Sein und Zeit*, this is because, appearing, as we have seen, in our seminar of 1929–30, these occurrences seem without doubt to appeal to a sovereignty of last instance, to a superpower that decides everything in the first or the last instance, and in particular when it comes to the *as such*, the difference between Being and beings, the *Austrag* we were talking about last week, but which appeals to a sovereignty so sovereign that it exceeds the theological and political — and especially onto-theological — figures or determinations of sovereignty. *Walten* seems to be so sovereign, ultra-sovereign, in sum, that it would be stripped of all the anthropological, theological and political, and thus ontic and onto-theological dimensions of sovereignty. It is the point of this excess that matters to me: that of a sovereignty so sovereign that it overruns any historical configuration of an onto-theological and therefore also theologico-political type.[80]

> That is why these last weeks I rather rushed toward [reading *Identity and Difference*,] which both put to work in a decisive place the word and motif of *Walten*, and precisely concerned the limits of onto-theology, of the constitution of the onto-theological [...], and thus the constitution of what is called the theologico-political which can only be *ontic*, by reference to the all-powerful God, cause and ground of beings, *causa sui*. Moreover, that would explain why Heidegger uses so infrequently, if indeed he uses it at all, the word and the political concept of *sovereignty* [...] So the language of sovereignty, in the strictly political or theologico-political sense, would no longer suit him. No longer quite adequately, perhaps, because it would suit him all too well. *Walten* would be too sovereign still to be sovereign, in a sense, within the limits of the theologico-political. And the excess of

79 Derrida, "Heidegger's Ear," 207.
80 Derrida, *Beast II*, 278–89.

> sovereignty would nullify the meaning of sovereignty. [...] As you see, late
> in my life of reading Heidegger, I have just discovered a word that seems to
> oblige me to put everything in a new perspective. And this is what happens
> and ought to be meditated on endlessly.[81]

In this passage, Derrida repeats, to an extent, what he had said about *polemos* in the texts considered above. *Polemos* is "more originary than the human or divine," and hence more originary than the political and the theological.[82] The originary enmity-friend gathering of strife in oneness and named *Walten* is a "point of excess," exceeding in originariness derivative modes, including those Derrida names here, such as the onto-theological. Inasmuch as *Walten* exceeds the theologico-political, Derrida seems to be saying that for Heidegger, it would not implicate, re-implicate, or co-implicate itself in the onto-theological or political-theological. It would be "too sovereign still to be sovereign, in a sense, within the limits of the theologico-political," and its excess of sovereignty "would nullify the [onto-theological-political] meaning of sovereignty."

Derrida thinks that Heidegger does not speak of sovereignty in the political sense because this would imply that there is no final authority above the sovereign, whereas *Walten* names the originary authority above or before both humans and gods. It is not clear to me why the discovery of *Walten* in this sense should force Derrida to "put everything in a new perspective," when he seems already to have described so well in the course of discussing the voice of the silent enemy-friend Dasein carries with it. Nor is it clear to me what the new perspective is into which everything is placed for Derrida as a result of this word, *Walten*. But what is clear is Derrida's sympathetic hearing of the word, *Walten* as that which names "the originary unity of two contraries," of *philein* and *polemos*, of accord and strife, before both gods and humans.

---

81   Derrida, *Beast II*, 279.

82   Derrida, "Heidegger's Ear," 209.

But it is possible to take up for a moment at least the observation concerning "the language of sovereignty." Why does that language no longer suit Heidegger for talking about the theologico-political? Why does Derrida say that it "nullifies" the theologico-politcal meaning of sovereignty? What might the relationship be, if there is one at all, and is there one, in Heidegger, between the sovereignty of philosophy, on one hand, and the philosophical constitution of the political, on the other, or between the two modes and meanings of sovereignty, philosophical and political? Does the sovereignty of philosophy so exceed the theologico-political that it "nullifies" the theologico-political meaning of sovereignty? What is that meaning, and does its nullification mean that the theologico-political is not *reconstituted* or *instituted* inceptually by an excessive sovereignty? The strife gathered in oneness, enmity-friendship, called *Walten* is *instituting* and *instituted*. What, then, is the "interplay," not between the first and the other beginning, as Heidegger uses the term, but rather between the sovereignty that exceeds the onto-theologico-political, on one hand, and the inceptual *institution* of *another* theologico-political domain or axis, on the other?

"Philosophy," Heidegger writes, "is useless, though sovereign, knowledge."[83] Philosophy questions into beyng and grounds the truth of beyng. It is opposed to "worldview," which "claims for itself the determination and regulation of every kind of acting and thinking" and "must ineluctably take everything else that might step forth as necessary and consider it to be hostile and even degrading."[84] As total, worldview "*must close itself off from the opening of its ground and from the fathoming of the ground of its 'creativity,'*" never grasping itself essentially, never "[putting] itself into question."[85] If sovereignty in the theologico-political sense is the claiming of an absolute ground that

---

83   Heidegger, *Contributions*, 30.

84   Heidegger, *Contributions*, 33.

85   Heidegger, *Contributions*, 33–4, italics in original.

is cut off from its essence and never calls itself into question, then theologico-political sovereignty belongs to worldview and is implicated in "bustle," "the gigantism of machination," "propaganda," and "apologetics."

Philosophy, by contrast, is never closed to questioning but is indeed the questioning that "*opens* experience."[86] Yet, that cannot mean that philosophy does not constitute something like an inceptual theologico-political realm. In the next section of the *Contributions*, after the section juxtaposing philosophy to worldview, Heidegger acknowledges that philosophy is "philosophy of a people" (*Volk*). Of course, he requires that we think "people" inceptually, out of the question: "How does a people become a people? Does a people become only that which it *is*? If so, then what *is* it? How can we know: (1) What a people in general is? (2) What this or that people is? (3) What we ourselves are?" Heidegger suggests that we think the category of the people in terms of Dasein and inceptual thought:

> A people first becomes a people when its most unique members appear and when they begin to experience a presentiment. In that way a people first becomes free for its law (to be achieved through struggle) as the last necessity of its highest moment. The philosophy of a people is that which makes people people of a philosophy, grounds them historically in their Da-sein, and destines them to stewardship of the truth of beyng. [...] Thinking about philosophy is genuinely related to a people only if the thinking comprehends the fact that philosophy has to attain through a leap its own most proper origins themselves and that this can succeed only if philosophy still belongs at all to its first, essential beginning. In that way alone can philosophy set the 'people' into the truth of beyng instead of the opposite, namely, being forcibly led into a distorted essence by an alleged people as an existing one.[87]

In this passage, philosophy as inceptual thinking is "politically" constitutive in a few ways. First, it displaces the non-inceptual notion of

---

86 Heidegger, *Contributions*, 34; 31, italics in original.

87 Heidegger, *Contributions*, 35.

the people as already existing with another view that the "people" can only come to be *together with* inceptual thinking. That is already an essential "resistance" of sort to a notion of the people that is either non-philosophical or else "Platonic," i.e. metaphysical.[88] Secondly, the passage suggests that the people understood inceptually are grounded historically as stewards of the truth of beyng, and one form of stewardship is statesmanship or the founding of a *polis*. So inceptual thinking is potentially politically charged in both phases of resistance and institution.

Directly after the section on philosophy as philosophy of a people, Heidegger writes that "philosophy is the immediately useless but nevertheless sovereign knowledge arising from meditation."[89] That modifies his initial definition by changing "useless" to "immediately useless" and expanding "knowledge" to "knowledge arising from meditation." The latter change makes it clear that "knowledge" does not mean the "knowledge" studied by an "epistemology," for instance, but rather that arising from inceptual thinking "into the truth of beyng."[90] The former change, however, suggests that as sovereign knowledge philosophy is only "immediately" useless, but not merely useless. This modification accords with the view that such philosophy carries itself out into a grounding sheltering that cannot but produce "effects," even if it is not pursued for those effects.

Philosophy is a profound meditation that "leaps ahead into the most extreme possible decision, and by opening that decision [is] in advance sovereign over all sheltering of truth in beings and as beings." Heidegger here again calls philosophy *sovereign knowledge.*[91] Philosophy is sovereign because it is the leap that opens the fundamental decision, a decision that "has nothing in common with what

---

88 Heidegger, *Contributions*, 35.

89 Heidegger, *Contributions*, 35–6.

90 Heidegger, *Contributions*, 32.

91 Heidegger, *Contributions*, 36.

we understand as making a choice or the like," but rather "refers to the sundering itself," the sundering of the originary unity called *Walten*.[92] Accordingly, in the next section Heidegger refers to the "self-withholding ground" of a "strife" that is both "compelling" and "propelling" as the "first and most extreme plight," a plight that makes philosophy "necessary."[93]

Because the chain of this meditation is leading increasingly toward the view that philosophy is indeed not simply "useless," the very next section addresses the issue of "the powerlessness of thinking."[94] "The powerlessness of thinking," he writes, "seems to be obvious, especially if what counts as power is the force of immediate effectiveness and achievement." But when he considers whether thinking must be powerless, he notes that it is not thinking but rather the lack of essential thinking, the prevalence of machination, the absence of "a particular level of Dasein" available "to be open to the truth" of "essential thinking," "increasing apathy toward the simplicity of essential meditation," and a "disdaining of every proceeding and path that do not, *with their very first step*, produce 'results' with which we can 'make' and 'experience' something."[95] The claim that thought is powerless "is not so much an objection that applies to 'thinking' as it does to the detractors of thinking." Essential thinking has a "genuine power," and although it "tolerates no *immediate* determination and evaluation," it nevertheless "must *transpose* thinking into beyng and bring into play the whole strangeness of beyng."[96]

Thought, then, is not simply without effect, without use, or without power. It effects a transposition, its power is genuine, and its uselessness is only immediate. And not only is thought neither ultimately useless nor ultimately powerless: it is also not ultimately harmless or

92 Heidegger, *Contributions*, 70–81.

93 Heidegger, *Contributions*, 37–8.

94 Heidegger, *Contributions*, 38.

95 Heidegger, *Contributions*, 38–9, emphasis added.

96 Heidegger, *Contributions*, 39, emphasis added.

without risk. Rather, as Heidegger writes in the next section, thought, thoughtful meditation, and specifically thoughtful meditation on ourselves through the question "Who are we?" is "*dangerous*," and even "*more dangerous* here [i.e. in the context of inceptual thinking] than any other opposition encountered on the same level of certainty about the human being."[97]

Here as elsewhere, far from conceding that inceptual thinking has no political effect, Heidegger again emphasizes that the effects are not immediate: "This question, as a philosophical one, must be prepared for a long time hence and, provided it understands itself, cannot claim to want to replace, or even merely determine, what at the moment is the immediately necessary course."[98]

If meditation on the question of "who are we" prepares the constitution of the people as stewards, custodians, and guardians of beyng; if such meditation displaces and implicitly resists prevailing conceptions of the people as philosophically inadequate; if effects, however late to come, do come, through the "genuine power" of such thinking; and if all this arises in response to the *Walten* of the original gathering of strife and accord; then it would be a mistake to regard the sovereignty of *Walten* and the sovereignty of philosophy *merely* in the negative perspective as nullifications of political sovereignty, for it is not only the nullifying power, but also the *constituting* or *instituting* power, as even Derrida noticed, that comprises the total *political* aspect of inceptual thought.

Conclusion

In one place, Derrida notes that Hitler could have used, and in fact did use, the language of authentic struggle in a way that might implicate Heidegger for furnishing the rhetoric that allows for such appropriation without safeguarding itself against it. "Not only does Heidegger

---

97   Heidegger, *Contributions*, 44, emphasis in original.
98   Heidegger, *Contributions*, 44.

then voice agreement with those that have only the *Kampf* in their mouth, but he can furnish them the most dignified and the most thoughtful justification," Derrida writes, "which can always deepen rather than dissipate the equivocation and the misunderstanding, the mishearing." Derrida raises against Heidegger the objection that Heidegger "had not sufficiently thematized or formalized the essential equivocation of all these strategies"; Heidegger failed to give due regard to the ways in which his rhetoric might be used. He lacked political moderation, in other words. Yet, Derrida's objection is not a simple call for political moderation and rhetorical responsibility. The limits between philosophical discourses and strategies of appropriation, he observes, "are never totally objectifiable, thematizable, and formalizable;

> [t]his limit is even the place of decision, of decision in general, of political decision in particular, its tragic condition of possibility, there where decision cannot finally let itself be guided by a knowledge. And then to say that a *strategy* or the calculus of a *stratagem* is not formalizable, is that not still to situate the project of formalization in what I shall call a war economy?[99]

According to Derrida, then, Heidegger didn't formalize the limit between the philosophical and its political reappropriation, but it can't be done anyway, and the impossible necessity of doing it is the tragic condition of the possibility of a political decision. Perhaps we can say, given Heidegger's musings on the genuine power of thoughtful meditation, the inceptual constitution of the people, and other related themes, that Heidegger at least *thought* the limit between the philosophical and the political — both the limit between inceptual philosophy and metaphysical politics and the limit between inceptual philosophy and inceptual politics — and, moreover, that he thought, or at least indicated the trajectory of a thought, that *crosses the threshold*. If the metaphysical mode is strategic and situated in an economy

---

99 Derrida, "Heidegger's Ear," 211–12.

of war, the inceptual mode is meditative and situated in an economy of originary *polemos* that exceeds and precedes war.

A final thought: When Derrida writes that philosophers and poets can perhaps be distinguished by the fact that the former have not taken account of the experience of the encounter with an animal's gaze, his point is not to deny that there is a "rupture" between man and animal. His comments on the issue of the rupture are not only applicable in that case, however. They apply equally well to the case of the rupture between the deconstructive and the inceptual modes, between Derridean and Heideggerian topolitologies. "The discussion [of the rupture] is worth undertaking," says Derrida,

> once it is a matter of determining the number, form, sense, or structure, the foliated consistency of this abyssal limit, these edges, this plural and repeatedly folded frontier. The discussion becomes interesting once, instead of asking whether or not there is a discontinuous limit, one attempts to think what a limit becomes once it is abyssal, once the frontier no longer forms a single invisible line but more than one internally divided line, once, as a result, it can no longer be traced, objectified, or counted as single and indivisible. What are the edges of a limit that grows and multiplies by feeding on an abyss?[100]

These, perhaps, are the questions that must be left to linger concerning the internally divided line that grows and multiplies and feeds on the abyssal space between "Derrida" and "Heidegger," which not only keeps them apart, but also holds them together.

---

100 Derrida, "The Animal That I Therefore Am," 398–99.

CHAPTER FIVE

Dugin

"The history of the earth of the future is reserved within the essence of the Russian World, an essence that has not yet been set free for itself."

— Martin Heidegger[1]

Since Marlene Laruelle wrote that Alexander Dugin "does not find congenial" the philosophy of Martin Heidegger,[2] he has written no fewer than four books on Heidegger and proclaimed that he provides the deepest foundations for what Dugin calls "the fourth political theory."[3]

Although he did not mention Heidegger in his writings from late 1990s to early 2000s, Dugin openly admits that Heidegger's thought "influenced my intellectual formation in the most direct and

1 Martin Heidegger, *The History of Beyng* (Bloomington: Indiana University Press, 2015): 91.

2 Marlene Laruelle, "Aleksandr Dugin: A Russian Version of the European Radical Right?" Washington, DC: Woodrow Wilson International Center for Scholars; Kennan Institute Occasional Papers Series #294 (2006): 13.

3 Alexander Dugin, *The Fourth Political Theory* (London: Arktos, 2012): 28.

immediate manner." He calls Heidegger a "sine qua non" and declares him "part of our [Russian-Eurasian] worldview, our political theory, our philosophy."[4] By the end of his second book on Heidegger, Dugin makes the astounding statement that to master Heidegger is at present and in the near future "the main strategic task of the Russian people and Russian society," calling Heidegger "the key to the Russian tomorrow."[5]

Having written elsewhere about Dugin's first Heidegger book, here I pick up the thread of Dugin's work on Heidegger starting with volume two of his four-book series.[6] Volume one is notable for its emphasis on inceptual thinking in Heidegger, as indicated in the title itself: *Martin Heidegger: The Philosophy of Another Beginning.* The second volume, *Martin Heidegger: The Possibility of Russian Philosophy* takes up the task, not of presenting an overview of Heidegger to a Russian audience, as does the former, but of thinking with Heidegger about what it means to be Russian. Volume two declares that only through Heidegger's beyng-historical (*seynsgeschichtliche*) narrative will it be possible to grasp what, if anything, Russian philosophy is or could be.

Why does a Russian need Heidegger to access the question of the possibility of Russian philosophy? There is a "gap in cultural context," between Russia and the West that "can give rise among Russians interested in philosophy the illusion that through direct imitation of Western philosophers it is possible to do without 'the whole,'" that is, without some grasp of the entirety of Western philosophy. A Western thinker lives in that whole and can operate in it without necessarily grasping it as such. A Russian thinker lives outside that whole and

4　Alexander Dugin, *Martin Heidegger: The Philosophy of Another Beginning* (Moscow: Academic Project, 2010), note 6.

5　Dugin, *The Possibility of Russian Philosophy*, 455.

6　Michael Millerman, "Heidegger, Left and Right: Differential Political Ontology and Fundamental Political Ontology Compared," *Journal of Eurasian Affairs* 2:1 (2014): 94:104. See also, Michael Millerman, "Alexander Dugin's Heideggerianism," *International Journal of Political Theory* 3, No. 1 (2018).

engenders bizarre monstrosities when trying to insert himself into the Western hermeneutic circle without correctly deciphering its origin, history, and end; its centers, peripheries, and lines of force.

According to Dugin, since at least the Petrine reforms Russian society has structurally consisted of two focal points, the European and the properly Russian. The presence of these two foci in Russian society and Russian thought structures what Dugin calls Russia's "hermeneutic ellipse." The ellipse is the structure of Russia's "archeo-modernity." Concentrated in the Russian focus are Russia's archaic, pre-modern attitudes, emotions, imagination, and points of reference, all of which fall outside the European experience. The European focus, by contrast, grounds what is intellectually "modern" in Russian society.[7]

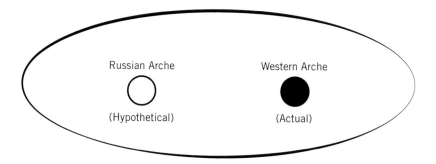

Figure 3. Russia's Archeo-Modern Hermeneutic Ellipse

Taking the European focal point as the center of an actual hermeneutic circle, that of Western European philosophy, Dugin suggests that we examine the history of Russian thought to find out whether any authors have developed the hermeneutic circle whose hypothetical center is Russian, rather than European. To do so, he maps the principal attempts of such authors as Solovyov, Berdyaev, Florensky, Leontiev, Chadaav, and others onto the hermeneutic ellipse, showing that however much interesting and valuable work they might have

---

7   The following figures are adapted from Dugin's book.

done to prepare the ground for Russian philosophy, none of them succeeded in actually developing the Russian hermeneutic circle philosophically. All of them gravitated in varying degrees towards the Russian focal point, but remained centered in the European hermeneutic circle (figure 3).

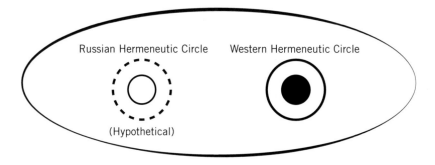

Figure 4. Two Hermeneutic Circles

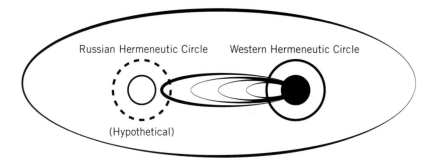

Figure 5. Strange Attractor

Examining the Soviet period, Dugin regards left and right social revolutionaries, and especially the National-Bolsheviks, as those incorporating aspects of the Russian focus into European Marxist philosophy, which, as "anti-Western Westernism" could be taken as "the revenge of the Russian popular spirit against the alienated political elites of the St. Petersburg monarchy," or, in other words, as an expression of the Russian or archaic focus of Russia's hermeneutic, archeo-modern ellipse, embodied also in the split between Trotsky supporters on one extreme, and National-Bolsheviks, on the other.

Following the collapse of the Soviet Union, the two foci of the hermeneutic ellipse were embodied by liberal-reformers, on one hand, and the "red-brown" alliance, on the other.[8] Liberals tried to erase the structure of Archeomodernity, associating it with the Soviet period, rather than acknowledging it as a structure of Russian society. This project amounted to another attempt — not the first in Russian history — to "*place Russian society into the context of Western philosophy* through translation of foreign authors, the introduction of new intellectual paradigms, and the Europeanization of Russian discourse." In opposition to the liberal project, communists (those of them that did not become liberals) and conservatives united with nationalists and traditionalists, as reflected, Dugin notes, in the fact that the platform of the Communist Party of the Russian Federation speaks of "orthodoxy," "empire," "tradition," "geopolitics," and other non-Marxist terms.[9]

As in previous periods of Russian history, the archaic pole of the archeo-modern hermeneutic ellipse — here, the anti-liberal opposition — did not formulate the question of the possibility of Russian philosophy.[10] Instead, the opposition "was limited by its passive opposition to Western reforms" and neither developed an ideological platform nor consolidated its ranks on the ideational level, while political rule was dominated by pro-Western elites. With Putin's ascension, the archeo-modern balance was restored, tipping the scales back toward the archaic and away from the excessively modern tendencies of the Yeltsin period.[11]

---

8   Dugin, *The Possibility of Russian Philosophy*, 122.

9   The program is available online in English at http://cprf.ru/party-program/.

10 Dugin, *The Possibility of Russian Philosophy*, 123.

11 Dugin, *The Possibility of Russian Philosophy*, 125.

For Dugin, structural Archeomodernity is problematic because it *"categorically refuses to recognize itself as an illness"* and *"to recognize itself as that which it is,"* as the Archeomodern. What this means for the question of the possibility of Russian philosophy is that the question cannot be raised, let alone grasped as a question at all.

Russian philosophy is for Dugin neither an established fact, as Russian patriots might think, nor an impossibility, as Russian liberals imply when they state that there is only philosophy as such. Russian philosophy is a possibility. To address the question of the possibility of Russian philosophy properly, it is necessary to penetrate the structure, the composition, and the hermeneutic mechanism of the archeomodern, since it is "the principal obstacle on the path not only to Russian philosophy but to its possibility, and even to the possibility of thinking concretely about this possibility."[12]

The hermeneutic ellipse both hinders and facilitates the task at hand:

> The *structure* of the hermeneutic ellipse [...] is the fundamental, paradigmatic moment that at the outset, in its very first impulse, blocks the very possibility of Russian philosophy. But this same structure is at the same time that which will allow us to map out this possibility preliminarily. At issue is the *existence* of the [archeo-Russian] focus, which reveals itself to us not directly (otherwise we would speak with complete justification of the *actuality* of Russian philosophy, rather than raising the question of its possibility), but indirectly: precisely through the transformation of the potential of the circle of Western European philosophy into an *ellipse*, following the integration of Russian society into its structures.[13]

All "sabotage of Western mechanisms of philosophical thought" is indirect evidence of the influence of the Russian focus of the hermeneutic ellipse.[14] Thus, "the possibility of Russian philosophy reveals

---

12   Dugin, *The Possibility of Russian Philosophy*, 126–7.

13   Dugin, *The Possibility of Russian Philosophy*, 129.

14   Dugin, *The Possibility of Russian Philosophy*, 129.

itself to us through the impossibility of the adequate participation of Russians in the hermeneutic circle of Western European philosophy."[15]

Dugin asks his readers to see in the term "archaic" the surface meaning of "ancient," or "old," but also the sense of "beginning" or principle.[16] He sees the archaic and the modern as fundamentally "*antagonistic* (or at least radically different) beginnings," each at a different stage of development (the modern is developed, whereas the archaic has barely or not yet begun) and the archeomodern as comprised of their clash. In the Russian context, at issue is not the superimposition of the new (modern) and the old (archaic), but that of "a *foreign* (modernized) beginning [or principle] onto *one's own* beginning (less modernized, located *closer to the source*)."[17]

Unlike in some other cases when a conquered nation can find a *modus vivendi* with its conquerors at the level of first principles, establishing new hermeneutic circles or modes of identification, in the Russian case, Dugin asserts, it is a structural fact that there can be no possible adequate compromise between the two poles.[18] At the very least, Russia's hermeneutic ellipse should be considered in the most radical light possible to reveal to the greatest extent the spectrum of fundamental decisions it makes possible.

An attempt must be made to overcome the ellipse. But it can be overcome only through the total articulation of the Western hermeneutic circle, after which it will be possible to subtract what needs to be subtracted so that the Russian "strange attractor" and focal point remains. Heidegger is the most appropriate thinker to help us grasp the Western hermeneutic circle and overcome the structure of the archeomodern.

---

15 Dugin, *The Possibility of Russian Philosophy*, 129.

16 Dugin, *The Possibility of Russian Philosophy*, 131.

17 Dugin, *The Possibility of Russian Philosophy*, 133.

18 Dugin, *The Possibility of Russian Philosophy*, 134.

Besides providing a synoptic overview of Western philosophy as such, Heidegger is a resource for the elaboration of the Russian hermeneutic circle and the possibility of Russian philosophy in other ways. When he introduces the notion of *Dasein* into his discussion of Heidegger's importance for this task, for instance, Dugin raises the "extremely important question" concerning what in Dasein is specifically Western and what is more general. Dasein is discovered in the West and to a certain extent relates to Western philosophy. "In this, its genetic and historical dimension, Dasein is a Western discovery." On the other hand, it is a sort of "remainder," left over "after the bracketing of ontology." It is "that *which remains from the West* if we subtract its deeply *Western* history (and the history of philosophy) from it."[19]

"Can we then," Dugin asks, "strictly regard Dasein as a moment of the Western hermeneutic circle, if its sense consists in *liberation from this very circle*?" Dugin postulates that Heidegger's notions of another beginning and the event emphasize the possibility and in a sense the need for a non-Western beginning, one that is "correlated with the West in a radically opposite way, like truth is correlated with deceit."[20] Since it rethinks the Western tradition, Heidegger's new beginning "can *also* be related *to a non-Western context*." "What is precise and strictly Western," Dugin explains, "is *philosophy* and its corresponding hermeneutic circle…but by itself Dasein is fully thinkable outside the West."[21] Once the history of the first beginning from the pre-Socratics to Nietzsche undergoes *Destruktion*, Dasein, unbounded from the Western context, remains as the possible basis for non-Western Russian philosophy.

Another reason why a turn to Heidegger is justified for elaborating the question of the possibility of Russian philosophy is that unlike the Western beginning, which began and came to an end, the Russian

---

19 Dugin, *The Possibility of Russian Philosophy*, 151.

20 Dugin, *The Possibility of Russian Philosophy*, 151.

21 Dugin, *The Possibility of Russian Philosophy*, 152–3.

beginning has not yet begun and thus cannot simply elaborate itself using its own resources.[22] Heidegger provides the tools and methods that give access to the core of the potential Russian hermeneutic circle, allowing it to come to inception and to speak for itself: "We can study the Russian Beginning, *not yet begun*, with the help of instruments used by Western philosophy (or more accurately 'post-philosophy') for the analysis of the *completed* Beginning or the beginning that can begin *again*."[23]

"*Only in this case*," Dugin writes, "will the appeal to the West (and not to the West as such, but to the concrete complex of ideas, strictly differentiated in time and place in the general structure of Western philosophy) not strengthen Archeomodernity, which blocks the very possibility of Russian philosophy, but rather create the conditions for its destruction and assist in the awakening of the philosophical self-consciousness of *the Russian Beginning*."[24] Thus, Dugin's use of Heidegger doesn't reproduce archeomodernity, does not transpose Russian society into Western philosophy.

Although Dugin encourages drawing on other resources besides Heidegger, he thinks Heidegger provides the deepest foundation for the task at hand. For instance, Wittgenstein's language games, Husserl's noetic thought, Levi-Strauss's structuralism, and Jung's collective unconscious are all useful tools for describing the Russian core (the focal point in the ellipse). They engender notions such as the Russian life-world, the Russian structure, Russian language games, and the Russian collective unconscious.[25]

But all of them are pre-philosophical. Dugin regards Heidegger and the discovery of Dasein as deeper than them all. As he writes, "Dasein is *the core of the Beginning*, the basis of the 'life world,' the

---

22 Dugin, *The Possibility of Russian Philosophy*, 158.

23 Dugin, *The Possibility of Russian Philosophy*, 159–60.

24 Dugin, *The Possibility of Russian Philosophy*, 160–1.

25 Dugin, *The Possibility of Russian Philosophy*, 167.

center of 'noetic thought.'"[26] Dugin admits that Heidegger is less relevant for an account of the collective unconscious, but he thinks that Heidegger's meditations on the sacred and the holy elucidate that domain somewhat. At any rate, Dugin leaves the unconscious out of his account of the possibility of Russian philosophy, having written about it in other works.[27]

The principle reason in this context why Heidegger is the reference point for the discussion of Russian *philosophy* is that he related the discovery of Dasein to the question of *being*, "the highest horizon of philosophy," thereby linking "the domain of the *pre-philosophical* (thought) with the domain of philosophy."[28] Heidegger is alone in doing this and is thus uniquely appropriate for Dugin's task. Whereas Heidegger revealed the possibility of the fundamental, post-metaphysical ontology of the other beginning through the destruction of metaphysics in the West, in the Russian context the task is the destruction of not metaphysics, which Russia never had, but Archeomodernity, in the service of a fundamental ontology of Russia's first beginning.

Heidegger discusses Dasein in terms of its existentials or essential structures, for instance "care" and "being-in-the-world." Dugin asks whether Russian Dasein can be detected by examining Heidegger's existentials in the Russian language and experience to see whether they map over well or not. Dugin begins his discussion of the existentials or fundamental structures of Russian Dasein with "the whole": "Russian Dasein is found *much further* from the individual [than Western Dasein]."[29] "The Russian person is always integrated into a whole and perceives himself as part of a whole" — although which

---

26   Dugin, *The Possibility of Russian Philosophy*, 168.

27   Alexander Dugin, *Sociology of the Imagination* (Moscow: Academic Project, 2010), Alexander Dugin, *Sociology of Russian Society: Russia Between Chaos and Logos* (Moscow: Academic Project, 2010).

28   Dugin, *The Possibility of Russian Philosophy*, 169.

29   Dugin, *The Possibility of Russian Philosophy*, 173.

concrete whole he finds himself a part of varies from case to case.³⁰ "The whole" is thus one of the existentials of Russian Dasein. "The most general word for the determination of this 'integral milieu,'" for Dugin, is "*narod*" (the English equivalent would be "people," in the sense of a people or peoples, somewhat like the German *Volk* or, as Dugin writes elsewhere, the Greek *laos*).³¹ The Russian does not think as an individual. Instead, "something *other* thinks through the Russian person, some kind of thought he himself does not understand"; the Russian "*suffers from thought*"; but in thinking "almost despite himself, the Russian person constitutes the 'narod,' which becomes the general name for the entire *field* of this difficult thought, which neither he nor others understand." In short, "*the Russian person exists not by himself, but through the* narod."³²

Cautioning against relativizing being, Dugin postulates that "Sein (being) manifests itself differently depending on *which* da (place) it is dealing with."³³ On the other hand, he also cautions against essentializing Sein and initially leaves it open whether it is the same Sein or not that manifests itself in various Daseins.³⁴ Instead, he focuses on the more obvious and less contentious claim that the "da" differs in each case (*Abendland, Russland*). In this context, Dugin mentions that the pretensions of the West to universality are evident even in its taking the European Sein as Sein as such, remarking that it is apparently "*the profound destiny* of the West" to be colonial and imperialistic not only in the material, but in the spiritual dimension, too.

30 Dugin, *The Possibility of Russian Philosophy*, 173.

31 Alexander Dugin, *Ethnosociology* (Moscow: Academic Project, 2011).

32 Dugin, *The Possibility of Russian Philosophy*, 174. For a more thorough account of the place of the Volk or narod in Dugin's political theory, see Michael Millerman, "The Ethnosociological and Existential Dimensions of Alexander Dugin's Populism," *Telos* (forthcoming 2020).

33 Dugin, *The Possibility of Russian Philosophy*, 175.

34 Dugin, *The Possibility of Russian Philosophy*, 176.

In order to "finally win back the possibility of actually, freely manifesting the structure of *Russian Dasein*," it is necessary to affirm that
"the [center] of attention of Russian philosophy *can only be Russian
being*— such as it manifests itself in *Russian Dasein*."[35] This transforms
the *narod* into an "*ontological* phenomenon," the "shadow of Russian
being, finding itself in the Russian" *da*, in "*Russian immanence*" or
"Russian phenomenality."[36]

Dugin openly shifts in these passages away from the use of the
Russian word for Sein, *Bytiye*, as a mere equivalent to the German,
toward the elaboration of *Bytiye* as specifically Russian and only
analogous to "Sein" and "being."[37] The Russian word is not simply a
translation of the German. *Bytiye* is phenomenally and ontologically
distinct from Sein.

In a compelling analysis of *Bytiye*, Dugin explains that for the
Russian, unlike for Aristotle and the history of Western philosophy,
being is not principally identified in accordance with a hierarchy of
the senses capped by sight. Rather, being is so close for the Russian
(we see this among other things in that the word *Byt* in Russian refers
to the ordinary, the everyday) that it is more accurate to say that he
tastes it.[38] This lack of distance between the Russian (Slav) and being
explains to a large extent why philosophy did not develop among
Slavs:

> The proximity of Russians to being, our common essence [*yedinosusshch-
> nost'*] with being makes us not a people practicing philosophy, not its 'sub-
> ject,' but rather *a philosophical process* or even the 'object' of philosophy. It
> is not we who must study and strive toward understanding, but rather *we
> are to be studied and attempted to be understood.*[39]

---

35   Dugin, *The Possibility of Russian Philosophy*, 176.

36   Dugin, *The Possibility of Russian Philosophy*, 176–7.

37   Dugin, *The Possibility of Russian Philosophy*, 177.

38   Dugin, *The Possibility of Russian Philosophy*, 180–1.

39   Dugin, *The Possibility of Russian Philosophy*, 181.

In short: "*There is no philosophy among Slavs because we differ princi-pally from other Indo-European peoples in how we regard ourselves in relation to being.*"[40]

Next, Dugin deepens his examination of the Russian relation to being by performing an existential analytic of Russian Dasein. There is not space to reproduce here in detail the existentials Dugin examines. Rather, the discussion can be summarized with the remark that in Russian, many Heideggerian phrases, like "being-in-the-world," which require in German, as in English, unusual, forced formations, can be captured with common Russian words whose root is "being."

After attentively looking for and listening into the Russian terms that might be analogous to the existentials Heidegger mentions, proceeding on the basis of the thesis that what distinguishes the two Daseins is the "da" or localization of the "sein," Dugin comes to the conclusion that the differences are not merely in "the place of loca-tion," but "*in [Dasein's] very structure.*"[41] "Russian Dasein has a struc-ture that differs from the structure of Western Dasein," which means that Russians "differ not only in [their] philosophico-metaphysical *superstructure* (which Europeans have or had...and which we never had) but also in the *basis*, the foundation, the existential soil, the *ground* (*Grund*) of thought and being."[42] The fact that philosophy de-veloped in the West and not in Russia becomes a consequence of the underlying structural differences between the two Daseins.[43]

40 Dugin, *The Possibility of Russian Philosophy*, 182.

41 Dugin, *The Possibility of Russian Philosophy*, 212.

42 Dugin, *The Possibility of Russian Philosophy*, 213.

43 Dugin, *The Possibility of Russian Philosophy*, 214.

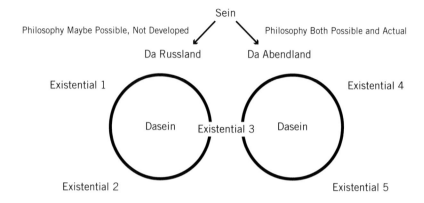

Figure 6. The Existential Multiplicity of Daseins
and the Possibility of Philosophy

Among the fundamental differences distinguishing the two Daseins structurally, Dugin emphasizes that while both are borders or limits that constitute, Western Dasein is much more radically divisive, especially in its division between being and not-being:

> Such Dasein is always tragic, problematic, and asymmetrical. It always hangs over an abyss; it is always finite, it is mortal, seized by anxiety, driven from itself. And it does not matter on what side of the border we place being and in which side non-being. We can place being inside, in the domain of the spirit, of the subject — then it hangs over the abyssal non-being of the external word…or we can recognize being as external…but then non-being (nothing) will arise within the subject and will start to 'nihiliate,' to annihilate the surroundings with the help of technique, Gestell, the will-to-power.[44]

This radical difference between a "radical 'yes' and a radical 'no' is the meaning of the West, its truth," Dugin asserts. It is a consequence of this structural difference between Western and Russian Dasein

----

44 Dugin, *The Possibility of Russian Philosophy*, 214.

that Dugin denies that "care," "thrownness," "projection," and other Western existentials are also existentials of Russian Dasein.[45]

By contrast, Dugin regards the Russian Dasein as a border not between something and its opposite, but between one and the same thing.[46] "It is a border *that doesn't separate anything*," he writes. It is "*auto-referential*."[47] For the Western Dasein, there are strictly speaking "non-Western others," radically distinct from the West. For the Russian Dasein, there is no radical other; for it, "*everything that exists is Russian*," because "*Russian Dasein is entirely inclusive*" — a move that collapses archeo-modernity but might risk becoming colonialist and imperialist itself.[48]

There is an important sense in which auto-reference is more characteristic of the West than of Russia. In his discussion of "being-with," Dugin notes that in the West, society and the individual mirror each other, such that the individual relates to himself when he identifies himself with his society.[49] This is an *auto-referential* relationship. It is a different matter with the Russian person, for whom to identify with the Russian *narod* is to identify with something *other*: "Through identification with the Russian *narod* (i.e. with the Russian Dasein), the Russian individual acquires a quality that always differs from his individual structure, is always something other than himself."[50] Unlike his Western counterpart, he has a "*dual identity*, with himself and with the narod," and he can encounter other individuals as genuinely other, and not as "hell," as Sartre would have it.[51]

---

45 Dugin, *The Possibility of Russian Philosophy*, 218–9.

46 Dugin, *The Possibility of Russian Philosophy*, 215.

47 Dugin, *The Possibility of Russian Philosophy*, 215.

48 Dugin, *The Possibility of Russian Philosophy*, 216. Some have held Dugin's theory to be imperialistic. For further examination, see Millerman, "Alexander Dugin's Neo-Eurasianism."

49 Dugin, *The Possibility of Russian Philosophy*, 222–3.

50 Dugin, *The Possibility of Russian Philosophy*, 223.

51 Dugin, *The Possibility of Russian Philosophy*, 224.

Russians never *are* as individuals or personalities, only as Russians. They are *nothing* otherwise — but a nothing that is *included* in being.[52] Imitating Heidegger's statement that "non-being is," Dugin asserts that "Russian individuality as non-being is, and it is only because it is Russian."[53] These reflections and others here omitted mean to distinguish individual and group identity in the Russian Dasein from Heidegger's account of being-with.

Dugin continues his examination of the relation between the two Daseins by distinguishing the temporality and spatiality appropriate to each of them. His discussion of temporality hinges on the etymology of the German and Russian words for time. The German *Zeit*, unlike its Russian counterparts, has the sense of "a moment of time," rather than "a span or duration of time."[54] Like the difference in their respective temporalities, each Dasein has its own proper spatiality. In the Russian case, time has a spatial character, and this "spatial time," Dugin asserts, just *is* Russian Dasein.[55] Thus, "a book about Russian Dasein could be called 'Being and Space,' so fundamental is space, in all its meanings, to its structure."[56]

Dugin elects to consider the figure of "khōra" from the *Timaeus* — important to Derrida and others — in this connection. The upshot of his analysis of the relevant passages in Plato is that khōra is characterized by a chain of meanings that are "on the utter periphery of the Western European history of philosophy," and that are as it were "its shadow."[57] Khōra is "*a zone of exclusion* in this philosophy and bears the mark of rejection and oblivion."[58] There is a "*deep kinship*

---

52   Dugin, *The Possibility of Russian Philosophy*, 224.

53   Dugin, *The Possibility of Russian Philosophy*, 225.

54   Dugin, *The Possibility of Russian Philosophy*, 245.

55   Dugin, *The Possibility of Russian Philosophy*, 245.

56   Dugin, *The Possibility of Russian Philosophy*, 247.

57   Dugin, *The Possibility of Russian Philosophy*, 273.

58   Dugin, *The Possibility of Russian Philosophy*, 273.

between the Russian and khōra."[59] More strongly stated as a thesis, because of its peripheral status and its spatial characteristics, *"Khōra is Russian."*[60]

In addition to the thesis that khōra is Russia, Dugin explores another interesting reading of khōra, which relates it to its translation in early Slavic bibles as "country." Creatively coupling the translation of khōra as country with Xenophanes' teaching about the importance of "earth" and "horizons" or "places," each with their own elements and their own gods, Dugin posits khōra as the country-horizon through which and in which being and becoming relate. Because there are many country-horizons, being and becoming are and become differently, depending on *where* they do so.[61]

The juxtaposition of khōra and country "brings us to a foundation for a plurality of not only Daseins but also of Seins." The tradition according to which being is singular is *"local…like any* human languages." Being *is* singular — in a certain khōra-context. Being is something else in another khōra.

Thus, Dugin advances from the initial thesis that the "da" of Dasein differs, through the specific difference between Russian and German being, toward the general thesis that the Sein of Dasein *also* differs, not merely in its expression but as such depending on the khōra-context. Dugin does, however, continue to leave open the possibility that "different spatial expressions of being converge" somewhere (his "brave" thesis on this matter is that "they converge *in the earth, in the depths of the earth"*)[62]. In short, khōra is "the field for the unfolding of a logos."[63]

59 Dugin, *The Possibility of Russian Philosophy*, 273.
60 Dugin, *The Possibility of Russian Philosophy*, 273.
61 Dugin, *The Possibility of Russian Philosophy*, 279.
62 Dugin, *The Possibility of Russian Philosophy*, 279.
63 Dugin, *The Possibility of Russian Philosophy*, 280.

Aristotle, Dugin notes, associates khōra with Hesiod's chaos in the *Physics*.[64] Khōra and chaos are etymologically related and both indicate an open space. However, chaos has in addition the meaning of the state of the world before its ordered manifestation as cosmos, wherein all things lie in peace together, despite having contradictory characters.[65] Equating the two, Dugin argues that Plato's introduction of khōra into philosophy "has a deeply *pre-Platonic*, pre-rational (and even pre-pre-Socratic) content."[66] If we elaborate the hidden sense of khōra as chaos, Dugin argues, we get a new picture of the place of spatiality in the Russian Dasein and indeed of the possibility of Russian philosophy.[67]

The upshot of this discussion of chaos is that, whereas from the perspective of logos and order, chaos seems to be ir-rational, dis-order, and the opposite of what is regarded as good, from the perspective of chaos itself, chaos includes logos, rationality, and order in its bosom.[68]

---

64 Dugin, *The Possibility of Russian Philosophy*, 280.

65 Dugin, *The Possibility of Russian Philosophy*, 281.

66 Dugin, *The Possibility of Russian Philosophy*, 282.

67 Two passages on chaos in Heidegger: "Why do the Germans grasp with so much difficulty and so slowly that they lack the *chaos* they would need to arrive at their essence and that 'chaos' is not confusion and blind ferment but is rather the yawning of that abyss which compels a grounding?" Martin Heidegger, *Ponderings VII–XI: Black Notebooks 1938–1939* (Bloomington, Indiana University Press, 2017): 230; "Chaos and χαος are not the same. Chaos mostly refers to the disorder which is a consequence of a loss of order; thus chaos, as the interpenetration and mishmash of all claims, measures, goals, and expedients, is completely dependent on the precedent 'order' which still operates on it as its nonessene [...] In contrast, χαος, chaos in the original sense, is nothing nonessential and 'negative' — instead, it is the gaping open of the abyss of the essential possibilities of grounding an experience of this kind of 'chaos' is reserved for the one who is decided and creative — *this* 'chaos' cannot be brought into order, but 'only' into an unfolding toward an extreme and ever freer opposition. The essentiality — the nearness to being — of a humanity can at times be gauged *by what* it takes, and can take, to be 'chaos.'" Heidegger, *Ponderings VII–XI*, 323.

68 Dugin, *The Possibility of Russian Philosophy*, 282–6; 340.

It is the deep structure that gives rise to order, to being, to becoming. Like the Russian Dasein, it is marked by inclusivity.

The intimacy of Russian Dasein to chaos explains in part the absence of Russian "philosophy," which would require a more strict separation of logos from the khōric-chaotic-mythic than the structure of Russian Dasein would allow.[69] However, if we cease to regard only the Western European philosophical superstructure of Western Dasein as philosophy and admit the possibility of a philosophy of chaos-khōra, then we are able to posit the thesis that "Russian philosophy is possible as the philosophy of chaos."[70]

Having established this possibility, Dugin returns from the discussion of khōra-chaos to a more strictly Heideggerian theme: the Fourfold (das Geviert). He begins by comparing the etymology of the German and Russian words for the force-lines of the Fourfold, especially that line whose two poles are Himmel (Sky), also sometimes called Welt (World), on one hand, and Earth on the other. As in the case of Dasein, he finds that they do not correspond.[71]

The differences are decisive. Dugin points to a passage in Heidegger that speaks of Earth as the not-yet-opened for itself essence of Russianhood (*Wesen des Russentums*).[72] He also indicates another passage, in which Heidegger writes that "we" — which Dugin takes to refer to "Western European Dasein" — should not conquer Russia through technological and cultural means, but rather liberate Russia "for *its own* essence."[73] Dugin's interpretation of these passages rests on the claim that Heidegger is implying that the other beginning can only pass through Earth (Erde) and the Russian, a strange claim nevertheless supported by the etymology of the Russian word for Erde, which,

---

69 Dugin, *The Possibility of Russian Philosophy*, 293.

70 Dugin, *The Possibility of Russian Philosophy*, 292.

71 Dugin, *The Possibility of Russian Philosophy*, 296–301.

72 Dugin, *The Possibility of Russian Philosophy*, 301–2. See Heidegger, *The History of Beyng*, 66.

73 Dugin, *The Possibility of Russian Philosophy*, 302–3.

taken in its broadest sense, links it, Dugin argues, to the themes of khōra and chaos.[74]

Mapping his previous reflections onto the new model of the Fourfold that emerges from his examination of its main structures and etymology, Dugin concludes that Himmel/Welt is the place for Western European Dasein (and its philosophy), whereas Erde, or rather the Russian *Zemlya* is the place for Russian Dasein, with its heart of chaos and its philosophy of chaos.[75] On the heels of his analysis of Heidegger's remarks about Erde/*Zemlya*, Russianness and the future, Dugin adds that the new beginning of chaotic philosophy in the Russian Dasein is not only the liberation of the Russian for itself, but also the salvation of the West from itself.[76] Western European Dasein and its philosophy need Russian Dasein and its philosophy — which they can serve by letting it be — to save themselves from the growing wilderness of their own trajectory.

Next, Dugin draws attention to the other main pair in the Fourfold: gods and people. He undertakes an etymological examination of the corresponding Russian terms, comparing them to the German, Greek, and Latin. Here the main point of the analysis concerns the place of *intentionality*, a crucial notion in the phenomenological tradition. Simply put, the structure of the intentional act in phenomenology runs *from* the person *to* what is intended. Dugin regards the German "Gott" or "God" as an exemplary case of pure intentionality, for instance, since the etymology of the word relates it to a root for "to call": Gott is that to which we call. It is the appeal to another seen from the perspective of the one making the appeal.[77] Intentionality here has a pre-logical, "mythic" character. In the case of the name Deus, something is still intended with the same directionality as before, but

74   Dugin, *The Possibility of Russian Philosophy*, 299, 302.

75   Dugin, *The Possibility of Russian Philosophy*, 303.

76   Dugin, *The Possibility of Russian Philosophy*, 303.

77   Dugin, *The Possibility of Russian Philosophy*, 307.

whereas Gott is etymologically related to the auditory sense, Deus is related to the sense of sight and to the theme of light and illumination. Accordingly, Dugin sees in "Deus" a transposition of the god/man axis onto the axis of Sky/Earth (namely, onto the Sky-pole), just as in the case of the name "homo" for man, there is a transposition onto the Earth-pole of the Sky/Earth axis ("homo" is related to "*humus*," ground).[78]

The result of the comparison with the Russian words for God is that fundamental-ontologically Russian Dasein reverses the arrow of intentionality of Western Dasein. Whereas in the case of God the arrow of intentionality runs from the person to God as that which is intended, Dugin proposes on the basis of his etymological analysis that in the Russian case it is God who intends and the Russian people who are intended. God's intentional act toward the Russian people is one of bestowment or endowment.[79]

Is there one Fourfold with two Daseins (or more?) mapped onto it, or does each Dasein give rise to its own Fourfold? Dugin explores both options. In the former case, the tension between Russia and the West has its fundamental-ontological correlate in the tension between (German) Sky and (Russian) Earth in the single Fourfold. This tension can manifest itself as struggle or love, war or peace. The other beginning, Dugin writes, "would in this case be the clash of two purely existential elements...arranged and related entirely differently...than in the Western European metaphysics of the first beginning."[80] On this account, each Dasein would have its own Ereignis. The Russian Ereignis would, Dugin posits, consist in short-circuiting the archeomodern and bringing the Russian arche to itself.[81] And yet, because Russian Dasein does not, as we saw, have the radically decisive

---

78 Dugin, *The Possibility of Russian Philosophy*, 307–326.

79 Dugin, *The Possibility of Russian Philosophy*, 338.

80 Dugin, *The Possibility of Russian Philosophy*, 330.

81 Dugin, *The Possibility of Russian Philosophy*, 331.

character that Western Dasein has, it also does not have a radically decisive Ereignis appropriate to it.[82]

Indeed, Russian Dasein is so differently constituted from the Dasein of the West that Dugin is forced to correct his previous thesis about the interconnection between two beginnings appropriate to each Dasein. Earlier, Dugin had postulated that even from the Western perspective, (for Heidegger) the new beginning of the West (Sky) depended, as it were, on allowing Russia/Earth to come into its own. Now, he asserts that "the healing of the West from itself and of Russians from Western influence through their own fundamental bases are in no way connected."[83] The initial hypothesis concerning the analogous nature of the terms in Russian and in German finds its limit, and it becomes impossible to liken the German to the Russian Ereignis, the Western to the Russian Anfang.[84]

Accordingly, the next section in Dugin's book considers the possibility of Russian philosophy as founded on the two discoveries of Russian Dasein and the reversed line of intentionality running from God to the Russian people. The introduction of the topic of God and theology to that of Russian Dasein and the philosophy of chaos raises the problem of the relation of Russian philosophy to Russian theology. Dugin now, therefore, turns to the question of the relation of the Russian people to Orthodoxy.[85] But before taking up that question, Dugin expressly *declines* to link God and chaos/khōra directly.[86] "Let it remain an open question," he writes," whether [God] the Bestower is precisely He, Who secures for chaos the possibility of philosophizing or not."[87]

---

82 Dugin, *The Possibility of Russian Philosophy*, 334.

83 Dugin, *The Possibility of Russian Philosophy*, 335.

84 Admittedly, it is not clear how this radical distinction is consistent with the argument concerning Russian Dasein's inclusive nature.

85 Dugin, *The Possibility of Russian Philosophy*, 347.

86 Dugin, *The Possibility of Russian Philosophy*, 344.

87 Dugin, *The Possibility of Russian Philosophy*, 344.

The main observation Dugin makes about the relation between Russian Dasein and Russian Orthodoxy is this: "The Russian people, accepting Christianity, accepted it *in accordance with their inner structure*," embedding it in their chaotic philosophy.[88] The Russian people are, in the religious sense, simply identical to the Russian Orthodox Church. Unlike Jews and Hellenes, for whom the paradoxes of the Gospel are too much to bear, the "Russo-Slavic structure of thought" is perfectly at home with such matters as Christ's dual nature, his death and resurrection, and so on.[89] Moreover, "the [Russian] person is free from the imperative of thinking, because *God thinks for him*, and, what is more, *he is himself a thought of God*, not as a person and all the more so not as individual, but as *the Russian people*, as the *Russian* Church."[90]

Once he completes his detour concerning the role of Orthodoxy in Russian history, which he does by distinguishing the influence of the properly Slavic element in that history from the Greco-Roman, on one hand, and the metalinguistic Christian "Kerygma," on the other, Dugin offers an ingenious reinterpretation of the major themes of the Russian quasi-philosophers of Archeomodernity (Berdyaev, etc.) from the newly gained perspective of the Russian arche (Russian Dasein, Khōra/Chaos, the Russian Fourfold).[91] He derives from such a reading of his predecessors the potential "structural elements" of a proper Russian philosophy.[92] Finally, he does the same for the periods of Soviet history. In this way, after erasing the West, he begins to map out the contours of the strange attractor in Russia's archeomodern structure.

It is interesting to note that, despite how he is sometimes portrayed in the popular media, in this technical work, Dugin expressly

88 Dugin, *The Possibility of Russian Philosophy*, 349.
89 Dugin, *The Possibility of Russian Philosophy*, 357.
90 Dugin, *The Possibility of Russian Philosophy*, 358.
91 Dugin, *The Possibility of Russian Philosophy*, 385.
92 Dugin, *The Possibility of Russian Philosophy*, 387.

rejects the political invocation of any simplistic Russian ideology. As he writes,

> Attempts to advance a 'Russian doctrine,' a 'Project Russia,' a 'National Idea,' and so on…all lack much value, since all initiatives to develop such general systems can under present circumstances give no results and only sow the seeds of an empty and conceited dogmatism. It is much more constructive to honestly admit that there is something we don't know, *that something is missing,* that we need something, and to try to learn about it, to acquire it, to discover it, rather than pretend that everything is in order and that only some purely external factors, 'evil forces' or 'competitors,' hinder the realization of self-evident steps and plans. There are no such steps and plans. There is no Russian *philosophy.* There is no Russian national *idea.* And there won't be until we take upon ourselves the task of beginning by *digging to the fundament,* which we tried to do by studying *Russian Dasein.*[93]

Evidently, despite whatever he may say in other circumstances and for other reasons, Dugin genuinely believes that "the political" — in this case, the question of Russia's national, civilizational identity, its relations with the West, and so on — depends on "the philosophical" — namely, on the methodologically adequate grounding through the most sophisticated philosophical tools available (the existential analytic, for instance) of what it means *to be Russian.* At this level Dugin is so far from championing pedestrian Russian nationalism that he is uniquely harsh on the 19th-century nationalist Russian philosopher contemporary "Kremlinologists" regard as "Putin's philosopher," Ivan Ilyin.[94]

---

93   Dugin, *The Possibility of Russian Philosophy,* 448.

94   Dugin, *The Possibility of Russian Philosophy,* 104–5, Anton Barbashin and Hannah Thoburn, "Putin's Philosopher: Ivan Ilyin and the Ideology of Moscow's Rule," *Foreign Affairs* September 20, 2015.

In Dugin's third Heidegger book, *Experiments in Existential Politics*,[95] the dependence of the political on the philosophical becomes even clearer. Following the Heideggerian Left's operation of mapping the difference between politics and the political onto the ontological difference between beings and being, Dugin takes the additional step — entirely consistent with the unique emphasis he places on *inception*, as opposed to the Left's focus on *destruction* — of introducing beyng into the picture and associating it with something he calls "das Seyn-Politische," the Seyn-Political. The Seyn-Political is "simultaneously meta-politics and even contra-politics, since it does not raise and does not resolve any of the tasks and problems that politics deals with," yet it is the basis for politics. As the basis for politics, Dugin highlights the role of the Seyn-Political (and hence, too, of Dasein) in relation to such themes as citizenship, the referendum, the prince, law and right, borders, revolution, and urbanization.

So, for instance, just as there are three horizons of temporality for Heidegger on the basis of beyng, so Dugin identifies three horizons of political temporality:

> The political past is the politics in the Political, i.e. that which does not participate in the foundational element of the Political. It is ephemeral not only in the past, but also in the present and future. Everything that breaks the connection with the Political and becomes political-technology is the sphere of the political past [...]

> The political present is an open choice between the Political and its technological simulacrum. In this point of open choice, every time the matter is decided in favor of one or the other there is either a projection constituting the political future, or a sudden rupture and fall into the political past. This is a finite moment of freedom: it lasts until a choice is made, but is broken off when a choice can no longer be made. At some point, the freedom dies away.

---

95 Dugin 2014. The translations from this section, when not cited, are from a working draft without citable page numbers, sent by the author.

The political future is a step into the Political as the basis for politics in its immanent presence with its simultaneous abolishment as mere politics. This is the moment of the political Event (Er-Eignis), i.e. the fulfillment of political eschatology.

The political event, in turn, is, as we would expect on the basis of our earlier remarks, embodied in the structure of the Fourfold and concerned with Earth and Sky, Gods and Men. It "consists in preparing a space for [the return of the gods] on a concrete Earth under a concrete Sky."

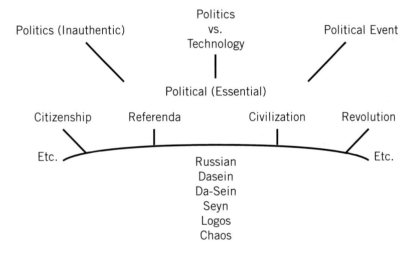

Figure 7. Horizons of Political Temporality and the Political Concepts of Russian Dasein

In a more popular work, the original Russian edition of *The Fourth Political Theory*,[96] Dugin proposes to establish a new "epistéme" or constitution and arrangement of disciplines, on the basis of Heideggerian temporality. Specifically, he argues that "conservatism" should be characterized not as the desire to preserve the past or to

96 Alexander Dugin, *The Rise of the Fourth Political Theory* (London: Arktos, 2017).

return things to the way they were in the past, but rather as "a philo-sophical approach…[that] operates with a specific notion of time." It is not the *period* of time that the conservative emphasizes — the past as opposed to the present or future — but the very *notion* of time. The notion of time that Dugin offers to philosophical conservatives is Heideggerian time, according to which the key issue is not whether something came before, is coming, or will come, but whether it has been, is, and shall be. In other words, properly conservative temporal-ity is not concerned primarily with what has passed and the realm of becoming, but with what is, with the realm of being:

> That which appertains to being surpasses time and does not depend on time. For that reason, that which really was surely is now and will be to-morrow. Moreover, that which will be tomorrow surely was yesterday and is today, inasmuch as time does not rule over being. On the contrary, being rules over time and predetermines its structure, its course, its substance. It is precisely this that makes possible the conservative's position not only in respect to the past and the present, but in respect to what will be. With this, the possibility of the existence of the conservative project is justified.

Because conservatism in this sense is, as it were, (fundamental-) onto-logical rather than temporal, we can discover past-oriented, present-oriented, and future-oriented conservatisms. "The conservative sees the eternal in the past," Dugin writes, "and only for that reason does it stand out for him as a normative for the present and the future." However, "the conservative can also be one who is completely indif-ferent to the past, but who strives to grab hold of being in a direct and actual existential experience" in the present. A future-focused conservatism, for its part, is project-oriented.

From an Orthodox perspective, the future holds both Christ and the anti-Christ: not everything that "comes forth" is or "comes to be." What is more,

> [t]his duality is important for the very structure of the conservative proj-ect. It is necessarily dual, dramatic, at once pessimistic and optimistic.

> The conservative project sees suffering, anxiety, horror, fear, adversity and catastrophes ahead. However, it also sees triumph, victory, the descent to Earth of the Heavenly Jerusalem, the universal revealing of eternity and the abolition of death. The task of the conservative, defending eternity, is to change the coming-forth in favor of the coming-to-be or to fight on the side of the coming-to-be against the coming-forth.

This is another, more popular, yet nevertheless striking characterization of the Seyn-Political, whose event is the existential revolution.

As we saw, in his more rigorously philosophical work, Dugin does not rush to conflate the philosophical domain of fundamental-ontology and the Russian Dasein with Orthodox theology, instead undertaking the patient, methodical operation of trying to correlate the two. Here, however, in a more popular work, he elides the potential structural differences between the two domains to present at once the structural similarities between a fundamental-ontological temporality, on one hand, and the dual eschatology of Orthodoxy.

Dugin argues that, as opposed to the prevailing liberal one, a "conservative episteme" will consist not primarily in economics and jurisprudence, but rather theology, ethnosociology, and geopolitics, regarded as parallels to spirit, soul, and body in man. Having examined some of Dugin's philosophical works, we can see that underlying this popular presentation of a "conservative" constitution of the sciences is a Heideggerian notion of Russian Dasein, Russian Peoplehood, and Russian Spatiality. And just as in the philosophical work Dugin argues that there is no sense invoking a "Russian Doctrine" or "National Idea" without a philosophical grasp of what it means to be Russian, in the more popular *Fourth Political Theory* Dugin states that there is no sense looking around for a "conservative" party in Russia until the groundwork of philosophical conservatism, including the constitution of the conservative episteme, has been accomplished:

> If conservatism establishes itself ontologically, one will be able to raise the question of its political implementation among rulers. But where this becomes possible, society itself will be different. What parties or personalities

will pick it up, how they will popularize it, and, moreover, realize it, is the tenth matter of business. While it doesn't exist, and while it lacks the epistemological prerequisites, it is useless to guess about these things. In this case we sink into simulacra anew.

Earlier, we saw that Dugin, much more so than any of the other main receptions of Heidegger, embraces and elaborates a fundamental-ontological notion of peoplehood. In his third Heidegger book, he moves beyond analysis of Russian peoplehood (Dasein) specifically to the more general issue of peoplehood as such. His thesis is that there is a fundamental-ontological plurality of Daseins. The following discussion briefly summarizes his position.[97]

At heart, Dugin proposes to apply to anthropology the operation that Heidegger applied to questions of being and that his student Eugene Fink applied to the notion of world. In the case of being, the distinction between beings and being can be established variously. It can be done as it was done in the first beginning, according to Heidegger: identifying being with what is common to beings. Likewise, "world" can be regarded as that which is common to or derived from the totality of innerworldly things. The operation here is aggregation of the parts and abstraction from them of the general.

However, this way of performing the operation of distinction is not the only way. It characterizes the first beginning, Dugin says. But just as another beginning is possible in the regard to the question of being (Heidegger) and world (Fink), so another beginning is or may be possible in regard to the anthropological question of man. Dugin introduces the term "*anthropologische Differenz*," the anthropological difference, mirroring Heidegger's "*ontologische Differenz*," or ontological difference, to capture this idea.

The anthropological difference is not between beings and being, but between individuals and humanity. We begin with the

---

97 Alexander Dugin, "Plural Anthropology: The Fundamental-Ontological of Peoples," in *Heidegger in Russia and Eastern Europe,* ed. Jeff Love (Lanham: Rowman and Littlefield, 2017).

given individual. We then aggregate to all individuals past and present. If we abstract what is common to the aggregate, we get the quality that corresponds in this picture to *Seiendheit,* beingness, or essence in the case of the ontological difference. For Dugin, this characterizes "the broadest, most acceptable, well-known, and universal model of anthropological thought." This model allows for "differentiation, taxonomies, and the allocation of segments of humanity on a temporal and spatial scale." Yet, it adheres to the logic of the first beginning. In light of the possibility of another inception, the anthropological difference can be constituted differently.

The "second inception of anthropology," or fundamental-anthropology, as Dugin calls it, differs from the first primarily in that it moves beyond the individual, but not towards what is common in the aggregate. Instead, here

> something unique emerges, the concept of a *Homo Novus* (new man), not identical to humanity; man who does not coincide with the general; a *second man*, who is unique, finite…This is the experience of humanity not as general but as *unique*; not as an aggregate, not as integrated, but rather as differentiating, not in the direction of the individual, but in the opposite direction; in the course of these differentiations, the individual is precisely overcome, not horizontally (through his integration with other individuals and through the elucidating analysis of what they have in common) but *by a path of overcoming the individual in a radically different direction.* Vertically, we can say; transversally in relation to the notion of humanity. Thus, we carry out an *anthropologische Differenz* that overcomes the individual, but *not* through the collective and general. There emerges a kind of *differentiated* human, who becomes man as such.

For Dugin, Heidegger's *Dasein,* as neither individual nor collective, accords with this new anthropology. We have already seen how Dugin attempts to ground the thesis of the plurality of Daseins in the specific case of the difference between the Russian and Western Dasein. In this volume, Dugin explains how he came to postulate the more general thesis on the basis of his initial belief in the universality of Dasein:

In our discussion with Heidegger's student and later secretary Friedrich-Wilhelm von Hermann in Freiburg in 2013, we raised the problematic of the plurality of Dasein. I gave him my book *Martin Heidegger: The Possibility of Russian Philosophy* and I tried, in a few words, in unconfident German, to set out the main thrust of how I honestly came to study Russian philosophy, proceeding from its roots, according to Heidegger's fundamental-ontology, starting from the belief that Dasein is a universal reality. And through coming closer to the Russian Dasein, to Russian Being, I came to the conclusion that a significant part of the Russian existentials does not coincide with the existentials described by Heidegger. That is, Russian Dasein at the level of its inner structure, Russian anthropology as such, proved significantly different from what Heidegger described. Not formally, not on a cultural level, but essentially.

Dugin recounts that von Hermann responded unfavorably to the suggestion of an existential difference among Daseins:

...he answered approximately as follows: 'The difference between the Dasein of a Russian, a German, a Japanese, etc. reduces to the level of the *existentiell*. The existentiell is the structure of a cultural, sociological approach to Dasein. This does not occur on the level of the *existential*, which refers to Dasein's inwardly intrinsic form of existing. Because,' he continued, 'death means the same thing for a Russian, a German, and a Japanese.'

"Herr von Hermann," Dugin replied,

you are likely mistaken, because, studying death in different cultures, I came to the conclusion that death is culturally conditional. And Japanese death, Russian death, and German death certainly represent three fundamentally different phenomena. Only a Russian understands Russian death; it is possible that a Russian does not stand face to face with it, as a European death. Death is behind a Russian's back, and he acts in its name and in its authority [*polnomochie*]. A Japanese is found in some more complex configuration in relation to death. Being-toward-death, the finitude of human Being, is conceived of radically different depending on cultural context. This is precisely the topic of my book, *Martin Heidegger: The Possibility of Russian Philosophy*. In particular, about the fact that even the most grammatical constructions of the Russian language reflect a different *existential*,

precisely *existential* [i.e. not existentiell], i.e. essential, and not only existentiell structure of Dasein.

As Dugin recounts it, the whole exchange ended with these encourag-
ing remarks by von Hermann:

> If you continue this research, it will be grand. Nobody is working on this
> problem. Heidegger was personally convinced of the universality of Dasein.
> And all our constructions reduce to the fact that distinctions among societ-
> ies and peoples are found not on the level of Dasein, but on the level of an
> existentiell, cultural, sociological, if you will, approach to Dasein. If you
> will establish the principle of the plurality of Dasein and demonstrate the
> distinction on the level of Dasein's *existentials*, and not only on the existen-
> tiell level, that will be a very serious accomplishment.

Although he admits and welcomes reflection on the possibility that
Dasein is universal, since reflection at the level of Dasein is still an
improvement over the anthropology of the first beginning, Dugin
nevertheless tentatively holds the thesis that Dasein is existentially
plural. He elucidates this thesis with the help of Heidegger's remarks
on the gods in the *Contributions*.

Heidegger's position is that it is for the gods themselves to decide
whether they are one or many, "whether there is or is not among them
a chief who created them," as Dugin formulates the issue. For Dugin,
the same is true of Dasein. To close the question whether Dasein is
one or many is to close the path to "the experience of discovering
Dasein." It is not for us to say in advance. Accordingly, "the very idea
of the plurality of Dasein can also be false, because too hurried." The
question should remain open. Indeed, we should "take the idea of
the plurality of Dasein not as a final answer, but as an invitation for
an awakened, concrete Dasein to a *ting*, a *veche*," a gathering where
Dasein decides, as do the gods, whether or not there is a chief among
them. This gathering of Daseins can be the basis for a dialogue of

civilizations. Each people has its "Angel," or "national genius," "the authentic, intense, saturated *moment of the people.*"[98]

Everything depends on authentic existence. In a people's authentic existence, the "genuine eidetic King" of the place (Da) exists through Dasein. Russians "need to be with the King, for him to rule over us, for us to be his place, the space of his epiphany, reliably protected from the endless sequence of specters that pass through inauthentically existing people like a corridor." Until that happens, they "do not live; instead of them, das Man lives." According to Dugin, Russians (and other peoples) need to constitute what he calls the "existential City," a project of *Entwurf* of authentic existence. The existential city of the Russians as an expression of authentic being-with is political, among other reasons, because it is discriminatory: "someone is found within the zone of being-with, but someone else remains outside it." Incredibly, however this might be interpreted and elaborated on in his other writings, in this work, Dugin expressly states that *all those who do not philosophize at all or philosophize poorly are excluded from the projection called the existential City*:

> [...] even those who participate in Dasein and are able to climb the ladder with us risk falling out of the Political when they do not exist in the full sense of the world, that is, when they do not philosophize or do so extremely badly.

> Man can 'be-with' only with those who exist. He who exists intensively dwells fully in being-with only with those who exist as intensively. The philosopher lives alone, as though surrounded by animals, until he sees another philosopher; then Mit-Sein begins, then the πολιτεία begins.

---

98 In another series of books, *Noomahia,* Dugin delves further into the open question of the plurality of Daseins through "exploring the existential identities of different civilizations." Michael Millerman, "Alexander Dugin on Martin Heidegger," November 3, 2015. https://www.academia.edu/17674206/Alexander_Dugin_on_Martin_Heidegger_Interview_.

In the "always risky and incomplete" projection that constitutes the existential City, a cosmic order is also constituted, "because the cosmic taxis is created in the same existential process, being-in-the-world." While drawing on Platonic notions, particularly through a reading of Proclus, Dugin demarcates the existential City from the city of the *Republic* in that if the latter is constructed from above through the study of essences (ideas), the former is projected from below through Dasein's authentic existence:

> [T]he divine πολιτεία can be opened through an autonomous decision of Dasein to *exist authentically*. When Dasein decides (entscheidet) in its Da (place) to exist authentically, the project (and hence the projected model of political order and cosmic taxis, cosmic organization, which in extreme exertion it extracts from the Entwurf) receives an astonishing response, coming from the depths of being itself. That is Ereignis.

When the event occurs, the last god appears — or may appear.

The Last God appears on the horizon of authentic existence. Man can create a political system; he is able to organize a cosmos; but by himself he will never be able to replace the Theopolis, θεόπολις, Heavenly City, with himself and his constructs. "The noetic polity is not a matter of human hands," Heidegger lets us understand. "But it is possible...only if we consistently and authentically move upwards from below."

This process describes "a completely unique existential political eschatology... radically different from Platonic politics, where the final horizon of the noetic politeia is given knowingly and it remains for us only to imitate it mimetically." Nothing guarantees the last god's arrival.

In his fourth book on Heidegger, Dugin claims that the Last God has a direct relation to Dionysus, a figure he opposes to Apollo and Cybele. Apollo and Dionysus are intimately related figures. Heidegger errs, as does Nietzsche, in collapsing Platonism into the Apollonian pole and attacking it. Heidegger's error is understandable. He projected scholasticism onto his understanding of Plato. For Dugin, Plato is an apophatic thinker. It is the "titanic," "Cybeline," "semitic," "black logos" that has marred Plato's apophatic teaching and is responsible for various evils. The anti-Platonic logos is the one that engenders modern, metaphysical man, an object of scorn and derision. Reversing Heidegger in this regard, Dugin traces the crisis of European culture to "de-Apollonization and de-Platonization."

We can approach the question of Heideggerian Platonism (or vice versa), Dugin argues, by turning to Henri Corbin. Corbin helps us see that, although Heidegger's strict identification of philosophy with the exclusivist logos was justified in his analysis of Western philosophy, it proceeded by bracketing another philosophical tendency, traceable back to Plato, that Heidegger referred not to philosophy, but to poetry. "What was poetry (the Heilige) for Heidegger," Dugin writes, "was for Corbin and the other neo-Platonists philosophy, *philosophia sacra,* sacred philosophy, which in contrast to logical, exclusive philosophy is sacred precisely because it is not exclusive." Dugin calls these two distinct trajectories "open" and "closed" Platonism.

After an excursus into the *Parmenides* as the *locus classicus* for both variants, Dugin proposes to map the basic idea of Dasein onto the theses of open Platonism. Without reproducing his argument in full, suffice it to say that open Platonism consists of three components: (1) the one, (2) the many, and (3) the one-many. Neither the one nor the many is accessible in itself, which is what gives this structure the character of being open. We dwell in the topos of the one-many. It is when two additional positions are articulated that the system becomes closed, according to Dugin's reconstruction. These positions introduce the coupling of the elements through the word "and": (4) the one and many, (5) the many and one. What is open, inclusive, and out of reach in the first case becomes closed, exclusive, and accessible in the second case. Dugin proposes dropping the "and" formulations and introducing the many-one instead. The many-one, he says, is the formula for Dasein, the angel, and the philosopher, who is neither the one-many (world intellect) nor *not* that.

It is difficult but not impossible, and rather important, when reading Dugin to remember that what he sometimes expresses in terms that do not appear philosophical on the surface, like "angel," for instance, are usually interpreted in comparatively rigorous philosophical terms elsewhere (and vice versa). It is striking to discover when reading the volume under discussion that it answers in detail, with reference to the *Parmenides*, a question posed to Dugin in an interview about the relation between Heidegger and the three-fold distinction of spirit, soul, and body, for instance.[99] Examples like that one no doubt account in part for the exasperation of commentators who are unable to relate with any success what they posit as the "philosophical," the "witch-craft dispensing" and the "ideology-mongering" Dugin.[100]

When even his harshest critics are forced on occasion to concede that he is at least in some measure an interesting philosopher, it becomes incumbent upon us, to the extent that we are admirers of philosophy — not to mention other equally legitimate reasons for reading him — to face our exasperation and see what there is to discover and learn from Dugin. The bulk of his writings are untranslated and so inaccessible. It has been my goal here to contribute to English-language studies of Dugin and Heidegger among political theorists, political philosophers, Russian studies experts, and others. This discussion of Dugin's Heidegger becomes all the more valuable when situated, as done here, in the context of a comparative study of philosophically serious Heidegger receptions by thinkers of relevance to political theorists. Dugin escapes many criticisms made on the basis of inadequate familiarity with his theoretical works. But he is not above all criticism. Let us now sketch some lines of informed criticism.

---

99 Millerman, "Dugin on Heidegger."

100 Ronald Beiner, "Who is Aleksandr Dugin?" *Crooked Timber*, March 10, 2015.

Dugin's approach to Heidegger is to give him the complete submission required by an initial, steadfast (though revocable) assumption of Heidegger's eschatological and prophetic significance. There is something to the argument that only that sort of complete immersion can prepare us in any given case for an adequate critique based on genuine understanding. Even the moderate Heidegger critic Leo Strauss wrote that with thinkers like Heidegger, "refutations are cheap and usually not worth the paper on which they are written," since they do not require that the refuting writer has *understood* the ultimate motives of the adversary."[101] Understanding might require initial submission to an author's claims, using a hermeneutic method that "deepens one's understanding of a text through replicating the perspective of adherence."[102]

But even if complete understanding is desirable, it is difficult here due partly to the scale of Dugin's direct and indirect writings on Heidegger; it may be impossible in all cases due to hermeneutic undecidability and openness. In any event, although the major task of reconstructing Dugin's understanding of Heidegger has barely begun, let alone been completed, we may still benefit from a first pass at adequate criticism of it.

The first criticism is structural. Even before turning to the specific role of Dasein in the fourth political theory, it is possible on the basis of the logic of the fourth political theory to make the structural criticism that this species of Heideggerianism, explicitly a rejection of the three political theories of liberalism, communism, and fascism, risks being deaf from the outset toward resonances of those political theories in Heidegger's thought, perceiving other Heideggerianisms as only a "simulacrum" and "caricature," rather than genuine sensitivity

101 Leo Strauss, "Living Issues of German Postwar Philosophy," in Heinrich Meier, *Leo Strauss and the Theologico-Political Problem* (Chicago: University of Chicago Press, 2006): 133.

102 Anatoli Ignatov, "The Theorist and the Adherent: Godrej's *Cosmopolitan Political Thought*," *Theory & Event* 17:1 (2014).

toward the political-theoretic multivalence of the existential analytic and related themes.

Though in principle a liberal, leftist, or fascistic reading of Heidegger could be a mere weaponization amounting to little more than a caricature, as Dugin thinks, a careful, genuine reading might disclose, not impose, liberal, leftist, and fascistic resonances in the text that are missed by an over-confident initial negation of liberalism, leftism, and fascism, just as first, second, and third-theoretic readings also risk overlooking certain resonances, including those that are not well categorized as either liberal, leftist, or fascistic.[103] The philosophical reading should not proceed according to ideological guidelines.

Dugin is so concerned to present Heidegger beyond the interpretative constraints of the three political theories that he appears to find little merit in such readings, stating that "[Heidegger] cannot be understood by liberals or communists (new leftists). They will criticize him or pervert his thought."[104] Although he is arguably on better ground in this regard in his assessment of Rorty's reading of Heidegger, which he dismisses as "very superficial," "quite idiotic," "[having] no value at all in understanding deep Heideggerian thought," and "ridiculous," he is wrong to claim that "acceptance of some aspects of Heidegger by Sartre, the French New Left, or postmodernists can be valid in nothing if we really want to understand [Heidegger's] own thought."[105] It is fair to wonder what is lost or distorted during the transposition of Heidegger into a leftist political-theoretic context. But it is also fair to grant that new left thinkers who took Heidegger seriously on philosophical grounds could deepen our understanding of Heidegger precisely by fastening onto and developing aspects of his

---

103 Millerman, "Alexander Dugin on Martin Heidegger (Interview)," 5.

104 Millerman, "Alexander Dugin on Martin Heidegger (Interview)," 5.

105 Millerman, "Alexander Dugin on Martin Heidegger (Interview)," 5.

thought that run against the grain of what would call itself a "proper" interpretation or understanding of Heidegger.[106]

A non-structural criticism of the role of Dasein in Dugin's fourth political theory arises upon closer examination of his existential analytic of Russian Dasein. Dugin's tentative, experimental exploration of whether the existentials of *Being and Time* map over onto a Russian-language analytic of Dasein is just that: tentative, experimental, and exploratory. Perhaps for that reason, although it is executed with nuance and ingenuity, the exercise may include false positives. Consider the following example. Discussing the structural differences between Russian Dasein and the Dasein examined by Heidegger, Dugin emphasizes the divisive character of the latter:

> Such Dasein is always tragic, problematic, and asymmetrical. It always hangs over an abyss; it is always finite, it is mortal, seized by anxiety, driven from itself. And it does not matter on what side of the border we place being and in which side non-being. We can place being inside, in the domain of the spirit, of the subject — then it hangs over the abyssal non-being of the external word…or we can recognize being as external…but then non-being (nothing) will arise within the subject and will start to 'nihiliate,' to annihilate the surroundings with the help of technique, Gestell, the will-to-power.[107]

Russian Dasein, by contrast, is not so radically divisive. It is "entirely inclusive," "a border that does not separate anything." Russian Dasein lacks a radical other.[108]

---

106 Rorty had said that Derrida has "too much respect for philosophy" merely to treat philosophy as a handmaiden to politics. In this, Derrida surely distinguishes himself from Rorty's superficiality vis-à-vis Heidegger. Richard Rorty, *Take Care of Freedom and Truth Will Take Care of Itself: Interviews with Richard Rorty*, edited by Eduardo Mendieta (Stanford: Stanford University Press, 2006): 22.

107 Dugin, *The Possibility of Russian Philosophy*, 214.

108 Dugin, *The Possibility of Russian Philosophy*, 214–16.

In this context, Dugin writes that care, throwness, and projection
are not existentials of the Russian Dasein. What are we to make of that
claim? In Heidegger, "care" names Dasein's being-ahead-of-oneself-
already-being-in-the-world. It is related to Dasein's temporal structure. Throwness emphasizes the "always-already" nature of Dasein's
existence, which knows not where it came from. The project-structure
describes how Dasein projects its possibilities of being onto the referential structure called world. Elsewhere, far from rejecting the notion
of Dasein's being-ahead of itself and projecting itself as possibilities,
Dugin explicitly relates the temporality of the fourth political theory
to Heideggerian notions of temporality and to the event as an existential project.[109] When comparing his claim that Russian Dasein lacks
the existentials of care, throwness, and projection to his other works,
an inconsistency arises. Those other writings invoke these existentials
implicitly or explicitly. On its own terms, without comparison to other
texts, the claim likewise is either insufficiently developed, at best, or
impossible.[110]

To be sure, Dugin departs from the emphasis on time in his
second book, noting, as stated above, that a tome about Russian
Dasein could well be called *Being and Space*, given the importance
of existential spatiality for Russian Dasein, an interesting connection
to his geopolitical theories, incidentally.[111] That and other aspects of
his analysis are, to repeat, often compelling and ingenious.[112] But not

---

109 Alexander Dugin, *Martin Heidegger: The Last God* (Moscow: Academic Project,
     2014); Alexander Dugin, *The Rise of the Fourth Political Theory* (London:
     Arktos, 2017, forthcoming).

110 Interestingly, Dugin includes the existential of care in his description of Dasein
     in "The Existential Theory of Society," *Katehon: Geopolitics and Tradition* 4
     (2016): 24–38 [Russian]. Also interesting are Heidegger's statements about
     "Western care," including the statement that "Care is Western care." Heidegger,
     Ponderings VII–XI, 141.

111 Dugin, *The Possibility of Russian Philosophy*, 247.

112 Dugin's general hermeneutic ingenuity has been noted by, for instance, Charles
     Clover. Clover, *Black Wind, White Snow*, part three.

every experimental analysis he undertakes or hypothesis he advances survives philosophical scrutiny. That need not be damning in the end, since for Dugin himself, errors can often be fruitful sources of creative insight.[113]

Another seeming inconsistency concerns the above-mentioned claim that whereas (Western?) Dasein is divisive, Russian Dasein is inclusive, dividing between same and same, rather than same and other. This tentative observation is not tracked consistently. There is comparatively little in Dugin's account of Dasein, not to mention other elements of his political philosophy, that demonstrates Russian Dasein's distinction in this regard. Instead, radical divisions are introduced rhetorically and theoretically between the authentic and inauthentic existence of Russia-Eurasia. The question for Russia is "to be or not to be."[114] Eurasian people are faced with the choice "either to awaken or die."[115] Nor are Eurasia's enemies treated inclusively in Dugin's theories.[116] Dugin does have a plausibly "inclusive" perspective when he states that, "the Eurasia I dream of could one day turn into the existential ground for the meeting of these two families of Dasein — Western and Eastern," but such examples don't change the point.[117] It is not that he never gives any indication of Russian Dasein's distinction in this regard, only that he rather often does not do so.

One of the greatest challenges facing a philosophically adequate reconstruction and critique of the bases of Dugin's thought may well be the experimental character of some of his speculations, which sometimes produces clever but apparently incompatible lines of

---

113 Dugin makes this claim in *The Possibility of Russian Philosophy* when discussing whether Sein is one or many. Wanting to leave the question open, he states that even if it is one (or many) it is fruitful to elaborate the opposite position, too.

114 Dugin, *The Fourth Political Theory*, 11.

115 Millerman, "Alexander Dugin on Martin Heidegger (Interview)," 8.

116 Alexander Dugin, *Foundations of Geopolitics*.

117 Millerman, "Alexander Dugin on Martin Heidegger (Interview)," 7.

thought. What is the status of tentatively advanced hypotheses when many other questions and alternatives are explicitly left open, yet often decided for, to an extent, in practice? It is not easy to say.

Another criticism we can make against Dugin is that his ideas amount to little more than a sophisticated smokescreen concealing cultural relativism. Indeed, when in an interview by Gabriel Gatehouse of the BBC Dugin insists on a "special Russian truth," it sounds like an inadvertent revelation of the sophomoric relativism of his views: you have your truth, we have ours, and there's no fact of the matter about it.[118] But that criticism does not quite hit the mark. The preface, recall, distinguished two senses of historicism that are also two senses of relativism. The first is that "all truth is relative to its time." The second stays closer to Heidegger's analyses of both truth and time and asserts that it is not that truth is relative to a time, but rather that *as* truth (unconcealment), being *is* time. That is imprecise but precise enough to suggest a need for disambiguation. When Dugin refers to a special Russian truth, or to many Daseins, is he speaking in the first, comparatively simple, even sophomoric mode, or in the second, comparative complex, philosophical mode?

Strauss can guide us here. For Strauss, Spenglerian cultural relativism gets the philosophical reconfiguration it needs when we try to find the root source of relativism in human existence.[119] Spengler argued that there is no absolute truth, but only a variety of culturally situated truths.[120] "The only consequence which a theoretical man, a philosopher, could draw from this," Strauss asserts, "was that *the* task of philosophy is to understand the various cultures as expressions

---

118 BBC Newsnight, "Aleksandr Dugin: 'We have our special Russian truth'" Youtube, published October 2016. https://www.youtube.com/watch?v=GGunRKWtWBs.

119 Leo Strauss, "Living Issues of German Postwar Philosophy," in Heinrich Meier, *Leo Strauss and the Theologico-Political Problem* (Chicago: University of Chicago Press, 2006): 117–8, 137–8.

120 Strauss, "Living Issues of German Postwar Philosophy," 118.

of their souls…which are the *roots* of all 'truth.'"[121] Spengler's view therefore "required as its basis an elaborate philosophy of man," which would need to show "that man as *the* historical being is the origin of all meaning," that "truth is essentially relative to human existence."[122] Spengler did not seek to provide that philosophical basis. Heidegger did.[123] Heidegger thus comes to light in Strauss's account as a philosopher engaged in the only task a philosopher could undertake, given the initial thesis about cultural situation.

If we follow Strauss's analysis, then Dugin's thesis of the existential multiplicity of Dasein is not reducible to cultural relativism, for like Heidegger, it aims to root relativity in human existence, in Dasein. Dugin's *may be* a relativism of truth (unconcealment) to peoples (Dasein — *als Volk*), taking the pluralities of "Da" and possibly of "Sein" into account. But if so, the specific character of his relativism differs so drastically from sophomoric relativisms, or comparative sophisticated Spenglerian ones, that it is prudent to withhold judgment until it has been better understood, the more so when Dugin is exploratory, not dogmatic, on the issue of existential plurality.

More than any of the other four thinkers in this study, Dugin believes he draws his inspiration directly from Heidegger's account of the path of inceptual thinking with fidelity in constituting his understanding of the field of political philosophy. That is why when asked in an interview whether he agrees with the characterization of him as a "right-Heideggerian," he responded that he does not, stating instead that, "I am simply Heideggerian, trying to be as close as possible to this greatest thinker in order to understand him better."[124] Yet for that very reason his project is open to the objections that the other three thinkers surveyed in previous chapters had against Heidegger. Despite

121 Strauss, "Living Issues of German Postwar Philosophy," 118.

122 Strauss, "Living Issues of German Postwar Philosophy," 119.

123 Strauss, "Living Issues of German Postwar Philosophy," 119.

124 Millerman, "Alexander Dugin on Heidegger."

its philosophical merits, Dugin's political theory often seems to lack political moderation, contravening a fundamental Straussian dictate and reaffirming Strauss's general critique of Heideggerian thought as politically immoderate.[125] Dugin's fundamental-ontological "nostalgia" contrasts with Rorty's social-democratic hopefulness and commits exactly the sort of political-philosophical errors Rorty cautioned against. Derrida's departures from Heidegger's hyperessentialism, presentism, and topologism must all be departures from Dugin, too, for similar reasons. Straussians, Rortyians, and Derrideans therefore have ready-made grounds for rejecting Dugin.

However, these objections to Dugin's project each suffer in their own way from their inadequacies as criticisms of Heidegger. It is not possible to reject Dugin's political philosophy merely because it seems to or really does lack moderation, at least not if we are going to evaluate it as a competing philosophical account to Strauss's account of the necessary divisions between "the city and man," as a sound Heideggerian existential projection. We are not faithful to Strauss in doing so, unless our rejection is merely exoteric, designed to protect the city from philosophy.

Rorty's laudable commitment to social-democratic politics as opposed to all forms of politically damning nostalgic philosophy, for its part, cannot be sustained once the compelling sovereignty of philosophy has been admitted, or in other words, once we admit that it is legitimate to consider alternatives to social-democracy at the level of thought, as on Rorty's own grounds it is.[126]

---

125 Exceptions: He counsels not to rush into political projects without first having done the necessary philosophical groundwork, and in his writings on geopolitics he examines and warns against scenarios harmful to Russia's national interests, as uniquely defined for instance in *Foundations of Geopolitics*. His immoderation does not extend to acts of national suicide.

126 It is worth comparing Berdyaev's criticism of the atheistic Russian intelligentsia's "need for philosophical sanction of their social sentiments and aspirations" and "hostility to both idealism and religious mysticism" with Rorty's social-democratic weaponization of philosophy. Berdyaev writes of "the almost

Derrida's departures, finally, were not enough to replace or to displace Heidegger, but left the choice between two "topolitologies," the deconstructive and the inceptual, open. It is a question of "places," but not of displacements. Derrida thus takes his place on a level playing field or field of battle, a philopolemological field, with other political philosophers surveyed in this study, including not only Heidegger and Dugin, but even Strauss, concerning the fundamental issues, such as whether deconstruction or inception should guide political philosophy. Without any clear path to his "refutation," and with much in his favor, as the main political theorist to extend Heidegger's inceptual thinking through theses like *Volk als Dasein* and the existential multiplicity of Daseins, Dugin also takes a rightful place among philosophical constitutions of the political.

---

insane tendency to judge philosophical doctrines and truths according to political and utilitarian criteria, and the inability to examine philosophical and cultural achievements in their essence, from the point of view of their absolute value." "The intelligentsia," he continues, partly channeling our critique of Rorty over a hundred years ago, "could not take a disinterested approach to philosophy because it did not have a disinterested approach to truth itself. It demanded instead that truth become an instrument of social upheaval, of the people's prosperity, and of human happiness." *Vekhi=Landmarks: A Collection of Articles about the Russian Intelligentsia*, edited by Marshall Shatz and Judith Zimmerman (Armonk, New York: M.E. Sharpe, 1994): 13.

Conclusion

While we may dispute Heidegger's account of human things, it is absurd to charge him with indifference to them. Heidegger claims to disclose the true horizon for the understanding of human things.

— James F. Ward[1]

How can we consider an author who uses the loftiest words of philosophy to exalt the military power of Nazism and justify the most homicidal discrimination a philosopher? The example of Heidegger shows us that it does not suffice to use philosophical terms or to comment on philosophers to be one. When Heidegger uses the term 'freedom' to mean the possession of the human being by the Fuhrer, or when he defines the word 'spirit' as the equivalent of the word 'storm' (Sturm) to enthuse the students of the SA (Sturmabteilung) present in the classroom, it is not as a philosopher that he is expressing himself but as a being who has agreed to put all his faculties at the service of the supremacy of Nazism.

— Emmanuel Faye[2]

No matter how abominable his politics, no matter how horribly he compromised his philosophy by interweaving it with brutal apologies for fascism,

---

James F. Ward, *Heidegger's Political Thinking* (Amhert: University of Massachusetts Press, 1995): 95.

2 Emmanuel Faye, *Heidegger: The Introduction of Nazism into Philosophy in Light of the Unpublished Seminars of 1933–1935* (New Haven: Yale University Press, 2009): 317.

today his writings remain available to us. We should indeed take comfort
in the fact that we are free to read them in new ways.

— PETER E. GORDON[3]

Access to Heidegger in Political Theory

Heidegger's importance for political theory is immense. But the access to Heidegger required for political theory is not easily obtained. It
requires a destruction, or deconstruction, of both post-Heideggerian-
ism, which lies mainly on the political left, and anti-Heideggerianism,
which characterizes the political liberal right known for invoking
natural right against history. Except for complete indifference to philosophy, perhaps the greatest obstacle blocking access to Heidegger is
the view that his philosophy is Nazism or at the very least abets it.
While thralldom to certain themes in Heidegger can lend itself to
uncritical sympathies for various elements of a Nazistic worldview,
non-Nazi political zealotry concerning Heidegger can also lead to
philosophical blindness or even to war against philosophical inquiry.
Both risks must be avoided, and both the philosophical and the political must receive their due. When they do, political theory can become
more than an academic discipline and can serve as an invitation to

---

Thomas Sheehan has compiled and presented a list of errors in Faye's account
of Heidegger. I am less interested here in whether Faye's radical thesis is correct than I am in exploring what it means for the relationship between philosophical and political commitments. Thomas Sheehan, "Emmanuel Faye: The
Introduction of Fraud into Philosophy?" *Philosophy Today* 59, No. 3 (2015). See
also the brief open letter written in response by various Heidegger scholars:
Anonymous, "An Open Letter to Philosophy Today," *Philosophy Today* 59, No. 4
(Fall 2015).

3   Peter Eli Gordon, review of *Heidegger: The Introduction of Nazism into
     Philosophy in Light of the Unpublished Seminars of 1933–1935* by Emannuel
     Faye, *Notre Dame Philosophical Reviews*, March 12, 2010. http://ndpr.nd.edu/
     news/heidegger-the-introduction-of-nazism-into-philosophy-in-light-of-the-
     unpublished-seminars-of-1933-1935/.

conversions and configurations, transformations and constitutions, turnings and events.

The Politicization of Philosophy

According to Emmanuel Faye, in Heidegger, philosophy becomes handmaiden to Nazism and is thereby discredited as philosophy. Indeed, Faye argues that Heidegger's *Complete Works* do not belong on philosophy shelves, but in the Nazi literature section of our libraries. In response to what he sees as Heidegger's dehumanizing Nazification of philosophy, Faye calls for a humanizing philosophy, consisting of a renewed defense and study of the teachings of Descartes, Montaigne, and others. To Faye, the issue is not that humanistic philosophy is, unlike Heidegger's overly *political* philosophy, so pure and distinct from politics as to maintain its own dignity. For him, too, the political is at "the very heart" of the philosophical.[4] It is precisely because of its political character that humanism is preferred: it is moderate, decent, respectful of the individual and his capacities…in short, it is humane, not cruel; civilized, not barbaric.

The principal issue, then, is not to maintain a distinction between philosophy and politics — as might seem to be the case when a philosopher is criticized for putting his philosophy in the service of politics — but rather to defend the sort of philosophy that provides a basis for decent politics and to discredit the sort that does not.[5]

---

4   Faye, *Heidegger*, 2.

5   Faye himself does not perform this task in this book. As a critical review noted, "Faye leaves the very philosophical ideals with which he wants to oppose Heidegger's Nazism equally ambiguous: Though he appeals incessantly to the 'humanism' operative in his own philosophical approach and to the 'human truths that are the underlying principles of philosophy' he never explains what this means." James Gilbert-Walsh, "Nazism, Philosophy, and Academic Accountability: The Real Controversy Surrounding Emmanuel Faye's Heidegger" *Journal of the History of the Behavioral Sciences* 47, No. 1 (Winter 2011).

"Philosophy," Faye writes, "cannot be constituted except on [the] condition" of "the moral attitude." Once a moral humanism is *assumed*, it is no surprise that a philosophy of a certain sort will be "constituted" thereupon.[6] Faye's, then, is a "political ontology," in that the ontology is in large part, if not exclusively, a function of political commitments whose origin is not itself philosophical.[7]

Although both Heidegger and Faye explicitly or implicitly adopt a political ontology, understood here as an apparently philosophical justification or expression of a prior, underlying political commitment, which modifies that commitment by deepening it in a political-philosophical hermeneutic circle, nevertheless it is not the case that every political ontology opens equally towards the possibility of philosophical activity — at least, one might so object. Not all political ontologies, on this account, are philosophically equal.

"Yes, let's concede," says an imaginary interlocutor, "both Heidegger and his liberal critics are 'political' in their definitions of philosophy — how could they not be? — but there's politics and there's politics: Nazism and anti-Nazism shouldn't be confused, neither in what they mean for politics, nor, indeed, in what they mean for philosophy."

Heidegger's approach, the objection continues, does not allow for the dialectical exchange of arguments that might be thought to define the philosophical enterprise. Thus, as Faye writes, for instance, "[it] is…not surprising that in the tens of thousands of pages left by Heidegger, there is almost no mention of Socrates." Instead, Faye continues, "[t]o the dialectic that, since Plato, has made possible the

---

6   Faye, *Heidegger*, 315.

7   We can thus grant Gordon's softening of Faye, without chasing away the problem. Gordon argues that Faye fails to prove Heidegger's philosophy is "nothing more than an ideological smokescreen for Nazism." Even so, as a political philosophy or political ontology, it may well be inextricably bound up with Nazism, both actual and possible, without being reducible to a smokescreen for it.

vitality of the philosophical dialogue and founded the intellectual requirement of questioning of the level of concepts, [Heidegger] substituted the dictatorial use of the word and exalted combat unto the annihilation of the enemy."[8] A humanistic philosophy, by contrast, though also inherently political, and preferred not only on its own merits but for its consequences, provides for "a better understanding of the human being and the achievement of his own perfection, without confining him within a preconceived doctrine or system." As such it preserves his dignity and freedom, without which philosophy, as dialectic, is not possible.[9]

Stated in these terms, however, each position begs the question — assumes what is in dispute — against the other. When what philosophy is *is itself* up for dispute, one side cannot end that dispute by accusing the other side of destroying philosophy as defined by the side leveling the charge.[10] Faye, for his part, champions "the tradition of philosophy that stands at the service of human evolution," stating expressly — laudably, though contestably — that, "[t]he vocation of philosophy is to serve the evolution of man."[11] In doing so, though, he assumes what he should be concerned to prove, namely, that his definition of the vocation of philosophy is superior to the alternatives.

We could infer from this state of affairs that no resolution of the dispute among competing claims to the essence of philosophy is available on the level of one of those philosophies.

As already suggested, any fundamental philosophical position is, implicitly or explicitly, inextricably bound up with a political position, however broad. A decision concerning the essence of philosophy may not commit one to belonging to one political party or another,

---

8   Faye, *Heidegger,* 317.

9   Faye, *Heidegger*, 320–21.

10 Ward takes this position, quoting Heidegger: "It is not possible to determine 'once and for all what the task of philosophy is,' for 'every stage and every inception of its unfolding bears within it its own law.'" Ward, *Heidegger's Politics*, 87.

11 Faye, *Heidegger,* 321.

but to the extent to which it involves decisions about the essence of man, thought, time, morality, the limits of knowledge, and other issues, it does commit one to one of a number of fundamental political alternatives, whether or not the particular alternative in question is concretely embodied in a political vehicle, such as a party or movement. For instance, the view that philosophy is ultimately zetetic or open, held by Strauss, provides a corrective against totalizing, closed philosophical politics, whether of the left or right (or anywhere else on the topology of actual and possible philosophical politics), while his definition, perhaps exoteric, of philosophy as the discovery of nature provides a corrective against excessive openness tending in the opposite direction.

Perhaps, then, the dispute over the essence of philosophy can be decided, not by begging the question in favor of any one position, but by evaluating the various fruits of the positions and choosing on that basis. Heidegger's philosophy had nothing to say to mitigate the catastrophic destruction of humanity, both the destruction of the "other" to the German and the destruction of the dignity of the German man or woman. Isn't that enough to discredit it, without begging any questions?

It will not do to refer to the dignity of the German, since what constitutes dignity is at stake in the philosophical dispute over what, or who, man is — alas![12]

Cannot the disputants, however, agree that it is the dignity of man to be able to ask after the dignity of man, i.e., to be able to ask, to question into, what man is? On this account, it is in posing the question, not in answering it, that dignity is constituted. Can it be that any answer that removes the possibility of posing the question undermines the condition of the enterprise, however defined by the disputants?

---

12   Among innumerable examples, see e.g. Vattimo, *Farewell to Truth*, xvii.

The condition for philosophizing, *whatever* it means to philosophize, is the existence of the person, however defined;[13] any consequences undermining the existence of the person — such as the annihilation of the person, in the extreme case — discredit, across the board, on the basis of shared assumptions, a definition of the essence of philosophy. Is that not enough? And isn't the annihilation not of a person but of millions of people an argument that stands on its own against a philosophy that allows it, encourages it, and justifies it without compunction?[14]

Faye refers to "human truths that are the underlying principle of philosophy."[15] Yet, the human and his truths are also *determined by* a philosophical inquiry that raises the questions, "Who or what is man? What is truth?" On the other hand, and from the opposite direction, Faye is of course right that philosophical inquiry is determined by the kind of being man is such as to be able in the first place to philosophize, i.e., by "human truths" that *precede* philosophy. Circularity operates here.[16] Man must exist to raise the question of man — "no philosophy can be based on the negation of the existence of man as such"[17] — but the man who exists is (in at least some cases) modified by raising that question. Is he modified to such an extent that the argument is negated that shared initial conditions provide common ground among disputants for rejecting philosophies with supposedly anti-humanistic consequences?

---

13 We might say that it is the existence of the philosopher, more specifically. But because who is to count as a philosopher is itself under dispute, it would beg the question to say that the condition for philosophy is the existence of the philosopher.

14 Tom Rockmore, *On Heidegger's Nazism and Philosophy* (Berkeley: University of California Press, 1992): 187. Rockmore calls Heidegger "chillingly insensitive to the significance of Nazism for human being."

15 Faye, *Heidegger*, 3.

16 Rockmore, *Heidegger's Nazism*, 70.

17 Faye, *Heidegger*, 314.

The Two Risks

Our objective is to access the depths of philosophy. The risk is twofold. The first risk is the one that Faye's book cautions us against: succumbing accidentally to "Nazism and Hitlerism in the domain of thought and ideas" by falling to prey to "Heideggerian hermeneutics," taken, mistakenly, Faye thinks, as philosophy and not as Nazi apologetics.[18] Especially on Faye's strong reading of Heidegger's Nazism, but even on Rockmore's weaker one, to be tricked by Heidegger's philosophy into accepting an unacceptable political outlook that is either its consequence, its bedfellow, or its *raison d'etre* is a real possibility, to be guarded against. Pangle, for his part, speaks of the need to engage with the "sinister," dangerously tempting greatness of Heidegger, but only in order to discover a "non-Heideggerian alternative." We must guard against absorbing dangerous political illiberalisms through the seduction of sinister thoughts.

In another way, Beiner cautions against the kinds of politics that can be smuggled in under the seductive allure of Heideggerianism, particularly in the case of Dugin, the Russian Heideggerian Beiner has called a "fellow philosopher" to Heidegger, yet one "at least as strongly drawn to Heidegger's ideological significance as to his philosophical significance." Using the veneer of "philosophy" and "theory," Beiner writes, Dugin peddles "blatantly totalitarian and ruthlessly imperialistic forms of politics." "We are learning anew," Beiner writes, "that fascism…has a romance that we liberals underestimate at our peril."

---

18   Faye, *Heidegger*, xxiii, 320. Is it that we don't want to smuggle in Nazism under the banner of our philosophy, or that we don't want to smuggle in *any* political –ism? Is that possible not to do? On the left, this is a well-known issue. For instance, Robert Valgenti on Vattimo: "The validity of Vattimo's position is often criticized as an irresolvable dilemma: either his philosophical commitments are politically expedient and thus merely rationalizations of leftist ideology, or those same commitments are based on a descriptive, and hence unavoidably metaphysical, claim about reality." To this "challenge of balancing philosophy and politics," Vattimo himself says he has no "satisfactory solution." Gianni Vattimo, *A Farewell to Truth* (New York: Columbia University Press, 2011): viii.

The first temptation is to fall prey to the "romance" of an anti-liberal philosophy that might have "fascist" political consequences, if not underpinnings.[19] We must not be so naïve as to embrace a *völkisch* and *seynsgeschichtlich* thinking while remaining blind to what are or might be (or have been) its concrete political expressions.

The second risk is to err too excessively in the opposite direction, where there are at least two erroneous paths. On one hand, aversion to Nazi politics of any kind might lead a political philosopher to mount such a zealous defense of liberal political order that philosophy is sacrificed as much to liberalism in the present case as it is sacrificed to Nazism or fascism in the former one.[20] The convenient liberal response that the liberal order is the only political order under which philosophy is protected, or under which it can freely occur is unconvincing,[21] as in the following words of Badiou, linking philosophy to ultrademocratic politics:

---

19 Ronald Beiner, "Who is Alexander Dugin?" *Crooked Timber* March 10, 2015 online. http://crookedtimber.org/2015/03/10/who-is-aleksandr-dugin/. Beiner ends his article very much like Faye ends his book about Heidegger, with a warning to "all responsible citizens in the West" not to be fooled by the external veneer into missing the underlying political danger.

20 Valgenti writes of Vattimo that he aims to "dissolve philosophy into ethics," — precisely the sort of operation or over-compensation in the opposite direction that I wish to oppose. Vattimo, *A Farewell to Truth*, x. It is to be noted that in the case of Vattimo, this operation occurs on the basis of stipulating that "we today" are "Christians" of a certain kind (e.g. not Eastern Orthodox Christians), who regard life in terms of "salvation history" — Vattimo, *A Farewell to Truth*, 48–49. What are Eastern Christians, Jews, or others, to make of the claim that democratization and the end of metaphysics are just the kenosis that is "the very meaning of the incarnation and…thus at the center of the history of salvation"? Vattimo, *A Farewell to Truth*, 54, 71.

21 Thomas A. Sprangens Jr. has argued, for instance, that "the vocation of political theory" has its "natural home" in "liberal democratic regimes" Portis, Gunderland, Shively *Political Theory and Partisan Politics* (New York: SUNY Press, 2012): 91–2.

The key to understanding the obscure knot between politics, democracy and philosophy thus lies in the fact that the independence of politics creates the place in which the democratic condition of philosophy undergoes a metamorphosis. In this sense, all emancipatory politics contains for philosophy, whether visible or invisible, the watchword that brings about the actuality of universality — namely: if all are together, then all are communists! And if all are communists, then all are philosophers![22]

This sort of response recalls Strauss's acerbic remark about the kinship between modern social science and democratic politics.[23] Much worse are attempts to sanitize and liberalize Heidegger, so that, "instead of Heidegger the prophet of extremity, we discover a prophet of sociality and non-deviance; instead of a soothsayer of nihilism and the end of philosophy, we discover a defender of normativity and discursivity."[24]

If the essence of philosophy is up for dispute, and if the dispute itself is not all there is to philosophy; if philosophy configures a space around its heights and its depths; then there will necessarily be a variety of philosophical-political topologies, and not only a liberal one.

If a general restatement of the strong argument against Heidegger is that he put his philosophical work in the service of the prevailing political topology and produced a mutual justification of politics by philosophy and philosophy by politics, the anti-Nazi or non-Nazi risks doing the same, structurally speaking.

---

22   Alain Badiou, "The Enigmatic Relationship Between Philosophy and Politics," in *Philosophy for Militants*, accessed online http://mariborchan.si/text/articles/alain-badiou/enigmatic-relationship-between-philosophy-and-politics/ [Accessed May 6, 2016].

23   Strauss observes that there is "more than a mysterious pre-established harmony between the new political science and a certain version of liberal democracy." Strauss, *An Epilogue*, online, http://contemporarythinkers.org/leo-strauss/essay/an-epilogue/.

24   Eduardo Mendiety, "The Meaning of Being is the Being of Meaning: On Heidegger's Social Pragmatism," *Philosophy and Social Criticism* 33:1 (2007): 102.

It would be insensitive and stupid to fail to see that it is not the structural component of the argument that does the most damage, but rather that it is Nazi thugs on one side and decent liberals on the other, be the structure what it will. Nevertheless, the structural component of the argument matters. A liberal whose politics and philosophy are in bed with each other has no right to criticize any other political philosopher *on that score* under the guise of neutrality, objectivity, etc. We do not, in short, want our anti-Nazism to drive us to become propagandists of a different sort, if we claim to value philosophy over propaganda and ideology.

On the other hand, too excessive a movement away from the philosophical-political topology of Nazism runs the risk of failing to explore the potentially philosophically interesting and politically important spaces that are not Hitlerisms or genocidal racisms, whether biological or spiritual, but that are not for that reason the common anti-Nazi topologies.

For instance, Rockmore, as we saw, is willing to say that Heidegger did not follow official Nazi dogma but developed instead his own form of private National Socialism. That is enough for Rockmore to criticize Heidegger, since *any* form of National Socialism — any concern with the notion of the authentic historical destiny of the people or *Volk* — public or private, official or not, is anathema.[25]

Rockmore goes so far as to implicate not only whatever possible spectrum of ideas might be National Socialist without being genocidal

---

25 For Rockmore, Heidegger's philosophy and official Nazism are slightly distinct. Heidegger perhaps "rejects Nazism as a theory of Being…[y]et he does not object to the political consequences of National Socialism." Although he may have departed from the dogmas of official Nazism, he nevertheless maintained a form of "private" Nationalism Socialism. Faye demurs: "There is…no basis for speaking of a 'Freiburg' National Socialism, or of a 'private' one, as has sometimes been done by authors seeking to mitigate the importance of [Heidegger's] participation [in National Socialism]. Too many texts…reveal to us that he identified himself not only with Nazism but also with Hitlerism." Rockmore, *Heidegger's Nazism*, 147.

and otherwise brutal and bad, but also the philosophical view of politics in general, according to which the philosopher has privileged access to politically relevant knowledge. "Heidegger's pursuit of Being,"
he writes, "...led to Nazism, and could in fact only lead either to this
or another form of antidemocratic, authoritarian political practice,"
since it is like Plato's theory, which "is also antidemocratic...only
the philosopher finally knows, and the philosopher's role is to decide
for everyone."[26] Caputo, too, criticizes Heidegger for his Platonism:
"Derrida was quite right," he says, "...to delimit Heidegger's talk about
'authenticity.' It is Platonic and politically dangerous to go around
dividing people up into the authentic and inauthentic."[27]

Over-zealous and well-intentioned rejections of Nazi political philosophy may thus transform into witch hunts against the supposedly
totalitarian tendencies of Platonic political philosophy — Rockmore
calls it "right-wing Platonism"[28] — or of any claims to privileged access to reality or being, on one hand, as well as to undue disregard
for political ontologies "on the [noetic] right," as it were, that are too
quickly collapsed into shades of Hitlerism (Vattimo: "It is our duty to
resist the temptation to feel ourselves allied with Truth.")[29] We should

---

26 Rockmore, *Heidegger's Nazism*, 72.

27 John D. Caputo, *The Mystical Element in Heidegger's Thought* (New York:
Fordham University Press, 1986): xxiii. Vattimo joins in the ranks of those dis-
paraging Platonic privileged access to politically relevant truths, but he denies
that Heidegger is Platonic in this sense. Vattimo, *Farewell to Truth*, xxxiv.

28 Rockmore, *Heidegger's Nazism,* 54.

29 Vattimo, *Farewell to Truth*, 112. Reviewers have correctly noted the kinds of
important questions that get missed in an overhasty Nazi witch-hunt. For
instance, Grosser: "Faye's insensitivity to the complex, ambiguous, often contradictory relation between Heidegger's thought and Nazism is remarkable. In
his sweeping identification of both, he fails to carve out the unique political
profile of Heidegger's thought and to situate precisely the specific dangerous-
ness of his politics. He neglects to raise questions that are crucial for a differentiated discussion of these politics: What elements of Heidegger's thought can
be legitimately identified as political, politicized or politicizable? What type of
political thinking and what concept of the political emerge if these elements

not let that happen. "[P]hilosophy," writes Beiner, "(or at least political philosophy) thrives when it is a contest of grand visions articulated by grand thinkers."[30] If we run too quickly from the grand visions of the grand thinkers whose visions we must abhor or fear, we do a disservice to the enterprise of political philosophy.

What is Political Philosophy?

For Beiner, "political philosophy means being presented with a range of horizon-encompassing views of life where it is possible or meaningful to ask: which is the comprehensive vision of human existence that, in the face of alternatives or rival views, appears most adequate, most compelling, and least vulnerable to intellectual challenges from equally ambitious visions of the human good?"[31] Political philosophy "*has* to be...the privileged intellectual space wherein human beings reflect, *in the most comprehensive way,* on what it is to be human."[32]

One way, then, to "do" political philosophy is to engage with the comprehensive alternatives. That is, in a sense, what this project has done in the chapters on encounters with Heidegger. In light of their engagement with Heidegger, Strauss, Rorty, Derrida, and Dugin, all present comprehensive, incompatible accounts of man in his philosophical and political life. The account has therefore been "a contest

---

are combined? What is it that is inadequate, risky or even dangerous about this particular political thinking and concept of the political? Finally, how far is the dangerous potential of Heidegger's — philosophically over-determined, fundamentally revolutionary, deeply conflictual, anti-egalitarian, and anti-plural — politics correctly grasped, if it is simply labelled as 'Nazi'?" The same questions can and should be posed about *any* political philosophy that is likely to be dismissed as Nazi or fascist from prevailing liberal and leftist orthodoxies. Florian Grosser, "Reviews," *European Journal of Philosophy* 19, No. 4 (2011): 629.

30   Ronald Beiner, *Political Philosophy: What It Is and Why It Matters* (New York: Cambridge University Press, 2014): 232.

31   Beiner, *Political Philosophy*, xxvii.

32   Beiner, *Political Philosophy*, xxiii.

of grand visions," waged in Heidegger's shadow, to be sure, in order better to understand what is at stake in the various positions taken with respect to him.

There is, though, another way. If the first way stages the contest of grand visions, the second, more fundamental way, is itself the articulation of a grand vision. It enters the battle. It does not just "clarify for ourselves" what "epic political philosophy" is and "why it is necessary" in order to "recognize it when it returns;"[33] it is *itself* epic philosophy, political in the sense discussed earlier, and there is no challenge in recognizing it, because it is as apparent to the philosopher as it was to Heidegger when he wrote the following words in a letter to Father Krebs in 1919:

> It is difficult to live as a philosopher — inner truthfulness regarding oneself and in relation to those for whom one is supposed to be a teacher demands sacrifices, renunciation, and struggles which ever remain unknown to the academic technician. I believe that I have the inner calling to do philosophy and, through my research and teaching, to do what stands in my power for the sake of the eternal vocation of the inner man, and *to do it for this alone*, and so to justify my existence and work ultimately before God.[34]

Let me put it less dramatically. If political philosophy depends, as Beiner thinks it does, on the work of "epic theorists" who articulate a comprehensive vision of the human good, one that is incompatible by assumption with the other comprehensive visions of other epic theorists, then at least one human possibility is to *be* an epic theorist, and thus to be claimed radically by, or to construct, a comprehensive vision of what it is to be human, such as Heidegger and others have done. To be an epic theorist means to put oneself beyond orthodoxies of political philosophy, especially when those orthodoxies doubt the vocation and message of the epic theorist. It is to go against the grain.

---

33 Beiner, *Political Philosophy*, 235.

34 Martin Heidegger, *Supplements from the Earliest Essays to Being and Time and Beyond*, ed. John van Buren (Albany: SUNY Press, 2002), 69–70.

Perversely, given what one has reason to suspect is Beiner's liberal dislike of Heideggerian political philosophy, Beiner, on his account, would have to agree with the sentiment expressed by Heidegger, a sort of mea culpa, as some would have it, for his Nazism, that "he who thinks greatly must err greatly," for the grand horizons Beiner writes of "cannot all be true; nor can they *share* the truth, so to speak, each with their own partial truth."[35] Thus on one hand grand theory is necessary to give expression to the grandest human possibilities, and on the other hand most grand theory must be wrong, and, given its wagers or convictions, we can surely speak of its erring "greatly."

Beiner refers to Heidegger when discussing his own claim that "philosophy and citizenship are defined by radically differ-ent purposes."[36] On this account, "the job of philosophy is to strive unconditionally for truth, and the job of citizenship is to strive for good and prudent judgment about the common purposes of civic life." These are two different tasks, and "each should focus strictly on fulfilling its own appointed end without worrying to much about the other."[37] Thus, "countless of our fellow-citizens in liberal democracy have much sounder judgment and a much better grip on the demands of responsible practice than…Martin Heidegger" and those like him, while "those prudent citizens cannot give us what Heidegger [and others] give us: the capacity in their texts to explode our accustomed categories of experience and thus enable us to see the world afresh."[38]

The challenge for a Beiner-like account of political philosophy is this: what happens when those texts "explode" our commitment to the division of labour between philosophy and citizenship? What happens when our notion of citizenship gets utterly transformed by our inqui-ries into truth? Heidegger in particular poses the challenge when he

35   Beiner, *Political Philosophy*, xxvi.

36   Beiner, *Political Philosophy*, 224.

37   Beiner, *Political Philosophy*, 224.

38   Beiner, *Political Philosophy*, 224.

makes "who are we" into a philosophical question with the potential to upset the model of liberal citizenship.[39]

A two-track model that preserves however much decency, moderation, and good judgment a liberal democratic constitutional monarchy like Canada has at hand, while nevertheless acknowledging the incredible and compelling accomplishments in thought of epic theorists or philosophers, is attractive. To think about the historical destiny of a people and its relationship to beyng is a captivating and satisfying undertaking, even when one knows that it that it does not and should not inform daily political life in a liberal democracy.[40] However, we must also consider the sentiment voiced by Strauss when he wrote the following: "All rationalistic liberal philosophic positions have lost their significance and power. One may deplore this, but *I for one cannot bring myself to cling to philosophic positions which have been shown to be inadequate.*"[41]

One purpose of this study has been to think through what it would mean to accept the philosophical defeat of the position Beiner defends, while nevertheless accepting, if not "clinging to," the political merits of the defeated position. The author whose position most resembles this one is Rorty's. Rorty, as we saw, can agree with Strauss that Heidegger and others have destroyed philosophical liberalism, while also agreeing with Beiner that a two-track approach or something like it is the sensible practice of our democratic community. Beiner writes of Rorty that for the latter "the commitment to truth …is in some fundamental way antithetical to the demands of good citizenship" — which is the position implied by Beiner's division of labor thesis. This is a

---

39 E.g. Heidegger, *Contributions*, 39–44.

40 It may be another matter elsewhere, however. Michael Fagenblat, "The Thing That Scares Me Most: Heidegger's Anti-Semitism and the Return to Zion," *Journal for Cultural and Religious Theory* 14, No. 1 (Fall 2014).

41 Leo Strauss, *The Rebirth of Classical Political Rationalism* (Chicago: University of Chicago Press, 1989): 129, emphasis added.

surprising kinship, to be sure, since Beiner is particularly critical of Rorty's rather dismissive attitude toward epic theory.[42]

Another purpose of this study has been to open inquiry towards the possibility that both the philosophical and the political merits of the two-track position (political liberal citizenship + politically irrelevant epic theory) are mistaken, and especially to supplement the presently available mappings of the resultant philosophical-political topologies, including various leftist political ontologies, with a discussion "from the right" — guided by Dugin's in particular, but not limited in principle to it.

For some, like Vattimo and others, it is self-evident not only that the political ontologies of the right are a problem, but also that they contrast with the spirit of our times and "our" community.[43] Indeed, *all* "ontologies" or philosophies, any concern with truth as something other than consensus, ("we don't reach agreement when we have discovered the truth, we say we have discovered the truth when we reach agreement"), is an issue for such thinkers.

It is surprising, given what's been said above, that Vattimo invokes Heidegger, a "new revolutionary Heidegger," in the service of replacing truth by charity and "[negating]…the violence that is the heritage of metaphysics."[44] But we have already seen in Rorty's reading of Heidegger the "optimistic" and democratic potential in embracing the end of metaphysics, while rejecting the "pessimistic," "nostalgic" being-historical orientation toward another (positive, as it were) inception. Elsewhere, I have called this species of left-Heideggerianism "differential political ontology." Its allegiances are obvious. It does read Heidegger "in new ways," to refer back to the Gordon quotation with which this chapter opens, but those ways are dictated not by "the

---

42 Beiner, *Political Philosophy*, 227.

43 Vattimo, Farewell to Truth.

44 Vattimo, Farewell to Truth, 110. It is surprising only if we haven't learned to spot the trademarks of the Heideggerian Left at a glance. Also, Millerman "Heidegger, Right and Left."

thing itself," so to speak, of Heidegger's thought, but by something else entirely. Heidegger, like Schmitt and Nietzsche, is here "weaponized," against truth, hierarchy, order, rank, and all the other false idols (on this view) of the authoritarian politics of the right, primarily.

The main issue with Vattimo and those like him is that it is *too easy* that they end up where they do, supporting postmodern democracy, *regardless* of what they read.[45] The initial horizon is never at risk from thought, but rather thoughts are, to shift the metaphor, the "yes" men of the ruling presuppositions. Heidegger and others are made to say "yes" to these leftisms, which are free to read the right creatively from a position of dictatorial authority: the dictatorship of the authority of the stipulated confluence between the end of metaphysics and democracy.

Of course, it is also obvious, or it should be, that talk of charity and love *against* the forces of truth and violence masks its own sort of violence against the "others" of this left. Dugin is therefore basically correct when in a work on international relations theory he characterizes postmodernism as its own specific will to power and, hence, as domination against those with the right to *their own* will to power.[46] At any rate, Milan council member Stefano Jesurum should have known better than to "refuse to believe that a well-educated European, a scholar, can see any parallel between Israel," for instance, "and Spain under Franco's regime," a comment he made in response to Vattimo's calling on Europeans to fight Israel, a country "a bit worse than the Nazis," alongside Hamas, as volunteers fought Franco.[47] "Charity" and "love" are some of the verbal Molotov cocktails of this radical leftist theory.

---

45 The same is often true of Dugin, who seems to be able to find ingenious ways of demonstrating Russia's uniqueness using whatever source he happens upon, as a good general might skillfully exploit any omen to bring his men into battle, if the time is right or necessity dictates it.

46 Alexander Dugin, *Theory of a Multipolar World* (London: Arktos, forthcoming).

47 Anna Momigliano, "Well-known Italian philosopher: 'I'd Like to Shoot Those Bastard Zionists'" *Haaretz* July 23, 2014.

It is no longer philosophy — Vattimo is right about that — when the end of metaphysics is invoked to serve specific political aims. Let us beware of every "mysterious pre-established harmony."[48]

Infinitely more satisfying, more philosophical, in the best sense (of essential confrontation) is Thomas Pangle's call, political in its own way, to make the effort to grasp "the relation between civil and dialectical education in the postmodern age."[49]

"We seek serious and thoughtful critics," Pangle writes,

> whose arguments draw us, and are intended to draw us, into a true dialogue, in which the very meaning and purpose of our lives is at stake. We seek critics who challenge us to the core, compelling us to rethink our own foundations [horizons, presuppositions, commitments], and eliciting from us some genuine, if grudging, admiration for the alternative they propose.[50]

Even Pangle is somewhat more hesitant than it is necessary to be, deferring excessively in this discussion to civil education when he writes that "the aim of such a probing, if sympathetic, scrutiny of our treasured beliefs is not, of course, to subvert those beliefs; the aim is to transform our beliefs from mere opinions into such grounded moral knowledge as is available to human beings," through "reenacting for ourselves, accepting or modifying, and therefore making truly our own, the great reasonings, the great choices rooted in argument, that ushered in our modern civilization."[51]

The critique of Beiner is applicable here, too: although Pangle rightly champions a reenactment and encounter like Beiner's contest of grand visions, he underemphasizes the extent to which our beliefs might be subverted in consequence, just as Beiner clings too dearly to his division of labour between citizenship and philosophy. *Yes*, we must stage the content of grand visions, and *yes*, we must make the

---

48 Strauss, "Epilogue."

49 Pangle, *Ennobling of Democracy*, 208.

50 Pangle, *Ennobling of Democracy*, 196.

51 Pangle, *Ennobling of Democracy*, 195.

reasonings our own, but there is *no* guarantee that our opinions not be subverted or our horizons preserved. Any view short of this one *fails* to be sufficiently philosophical.

Pangle is, however, spot on when he observes that "what we suppose to be 'radical' criticisms of the contemporary powers that be are in fact only radicalizations, more extreme versions, of those very powers." "For example," he continues,

> within today's American liberal-democratic cave, the most widely persuasive critiques of democracy will be the ultrademocratic, egalitarian, and the ultraliberal, libertarian critiques. An education that is, in the Socratic sense, truly liberal — that is, truly liberating — must strive to bring into question the seemingly 'necessary givens,' these moral chains, that enslave our souls.[52]

The solution Pangle points toward is "great books education," consisting of readings of,

> on the one hand, those, like the ancient Greek and Roman, or the medieval Muslim, Judaic, or Christian books, which elaborate a rich and philosophically well defended non-liberal and non-democratic conception of law, freedom, virtue, beauty, and love; [and] on the other hand, those books that are the most original, the broadest, and the deepest sources of our own scientific, liberal, and democratic worldview.[53]

Pangle is right, though he omits the relevant category of contemporary "rich and philosophically well defended" non-democratic non-liberalisms, to which this study has contributed by bringing Dugin forward as an interlocutor. Much more work is needed to give an adequate account of the alternatives to our own "moral chains," the better to learn to love and understand them or to replace them with something else.

---

52   Pangle, *Ennobling of Democracy*, 192–93.

53   Pangle, *Ennobling of Democracy*, 196.

Whereas Vattimo opposes charity and love to truth, to which he says "farewell," Pangle finds the loving search "for the truth," undertaken "in the humbling awareness of how short we will inevitably fall in our erotic or needy pursuit of it," to be "the foundation for the firmest attachments and for a truly common humanity...for a sense of the humane and an immunity to the inhumane"[54] — not, then, love *or* truth, but rather the love *of* truth, of the *quest* for it, informs Pangle's broad philosophical humanism.

In response to the "banalizing and belittling effects of the new philosophic elite" and "the ubiquitous mood of doubt [among them] as to the very existence of firm foundations for inquiry into, and judgment of, our gravest political commitments," he aims both to make a case for "modernity, and, above all...its political achievement in American constitutionalism," and to "[gather] our powers for a plunge," as we have seen, "into authentic confrontation with the difficulties in our philosophic origins at their deepest level." The alternative for Pangle, in three words, and most essentially: Heidegger and Socrates, since "it is...especially on Heidegger...that our contemporary 'postmodernists' are, at their best, depending for whatever lasting force their attempted deconstructions of rationalism may have."[55]

The Strauss chapter began to stage the contest between Heidegger and Strauss's Socrates. That effort led mainly to the preliminary conclusion that the issue between them, for Strauss at least, concerns moderation and its philosophical status. Heidegger and Heideggerians may be blameworthy for their immoderation — and perhaps that is not the least of the legitimate criticisms of their "deconstructions of rationalism" — but their philosophical work as such might, despite political immoderation, be better on its merits than the politically preferable political philosophy of moderation, regardless of whether

---

54 Pangle, *Ennobling of Democracy*, 217.

55 Pangle, *Ennobling of Democracy*, 5–6.

their immoderation falls to the left (Derrida) or the right (Dugin) of the center.

Renunciation of the compelling sovereignty of the inceptual, it sometimes seems, is the price one must pay for political moderation and sanity. And yet that sovereign grace, as Heidegger calls it, tames, orders, and ennobles.[56] What does the properly ennobled and splendor-crowned fruit of philosophy have in it of the rabid and sick?

Recapitulation

This study was about the philosophical constitution of the political. Beginning with Heidegger, that is, beginning with Heidegger's inceptual thinking, with his thought of the other beginning, with his reception by important interlocutors for whom he is in many ways the fulcrum point of their reflections, and with the case of the Heidegger affair, the task was to come to a better understanding of the meaning of philosophy for the political, and vice versa, of their points of origin and departure.

Rorty was left behind because unlike Strauss, Derrida, Dugin, and Heidegger, he put philosophy too completely in the service of politics for reasons that were not ultimately persuasive and that failed to account adequately for the phenomenon of philosophy, as we have apparently experienced it. Strauss fell short in his philosophical criticisms of Heidegger, despite the attractive political (though not sufficiently philosophical) tenor of his criticisms. Derrida, as Rorty lamented, has "too much respect for philosophy" to treat it so slavishly, and thus cannot be read as putting philosophy in the service of a preconceived political commitment. But there is a dividing and divided line between inceptual, deconstructive, and other "topolitologies," and it would seem that vital liminal experiences akin to mystical transport

---

56 Heidegger, *The History of Beyng*, 59: "Sovereignty is the Χάρις of beyng as beyng, quiet worthiness of the gentle binding that never needs to calcify into the need for power."

are best represented outside Derrida's domain. Still, Derridean political philosophy is a legitimate contender on the polemical plain, but
that means that it is secondary to that plain itself, and that it cannot
unfold or decide the question of the constitution of that field as comprehensively, it seems, as Heidegger does.

Of the authors studied, Dugin's Heidegger is the closest to
Heidegger himself. Dugin does not make Heidegger into a tool, like
Rorty does. He does not worry about or make Heidegger's immoderation his primary theme, like Strauss does. He does not feel driven to
depart from Heidegger's more "reactionary" philosophical notions at
the very outset, like Derrida admittedly does.[57] He is the only thinker
who does not need to *avoid* Heidegger's inceptual thinking. He is the
most consistently Heideggerian thinker of the lot. And because this
study is premised on the experience of Heidegger's philosophy as
genuinely inceptual, these facts recommend Dugin over the others.
Heidegger's critics are right, though, to worry about what Heidegger
means for liberal democracy: Dugin is no friend of liberal democracy,
and that fact emphatically does not recommend him. But Strauss,
Pangle, and other friends of liberal democracy have observed that
amica liberalis democratia, sed magis amica veritas (aletheia).

It is, however, not enough to leave it at that. "Dugin" names the
project of carrying inceptual thinking through into new experimental
domains. It cannot suffice for us to collapse that project into the version of it that the man Dugin has been engaged in. "As for those who

---

57 …I have marked quite explicitly, in *all* the essays I have published, as can be
verified, a *departure* from the Heideggerian problematic. This departure is related particularly to the concepts of *origin* and *fall* of which we were just speaking…This departure also, and correlatively, intervenes as concerns the value
proper (propriety, propriate, appropriation, the entire family of *Eigentlichkeit,
Eigen, Ereignis*) which is perhaps the most continuous and most difficult thread
of Heidegger's thought. (I will take this occasion to specify, in passing, that I
have also explicitly criticized this value of propriety and of original authenticity, and that I even, if it can be put thus, started there.[…]). Derrida, *Positions*,
54–5.

will some day grasp [what I am thinking]," Heidegger once wrote, "they do not need 'my' attempt, for they must have paved their own way to it."[58] We philosophers do not need "Dugin's" attempt either, for our task, to which we are paving our own way, is to continue to bear, withstand, shelter, and project in and out of our Dasein, through lingering questioning, whatever the graciousness of the inceptive grants us, and there is no guarantee that our "to-come" will have anything to do with Dugin's talk of the Russian inception (different Da, different Sein, "perhaps"). In fact, that outcome is rather unlikely.

The man Dugin cannot answer the question "who are we" with the answer "liberal democrats." But neither can we answer that question without admitting that we are liberal democrats, for even those among us who are opponents of liberal democracy oppose, to an extent, something that determines our identities today. Among supporters, it will not do to put our philosophical thought in the service of the search for a philosophical foundation for liberal democracy, for it is not the proper task of philosophy to provide foundations for a preconceived project, which is also why it will not do among critics to put our philosophical thought into the service of a critique of liberal democracy. And we are dedicated, for better or worse (better, we hope) to living up to philosophy's proper task.

That task, in sum, is to search and explore the meaning of being for us, neither sacrificing politics to philosophy nor philosophy to politics, not wandering astray down foreign paths, but keeping to our way, step by step, questioning and following our questions where they lead. If they once moved us "beyond being," towards Dasein and even Da-Seyn, and if we yet find ourselves in a forest dark, can we say now where they shall yet lead, or whether something else shall move us?

---

58   Heidegger, *Contributions*, 9.

A Way Forward

Must we remain in the dark after all?

A prejudice in favor of Heidegger's inceptual thinking meets the worry that it exposes us to sympathy for Nazism. Yet, burdened by that worry at the outset, do we not risk depriving ourselves of Heidegger's contributions to philosophy? Too passionate a love for philosophy may entail too high a political price to pay. Conversely, excessive political solidarity may deprive us of a light that either belongs to us or to which we belong, as humans.

There are ways out of this impasse. Dugin's extension of Heidegger's thought shows what Polt, Dallmayr and others have argued. However reprehensible his acts as a representative member of the Nazi party, Heidegger had in addition his own "private" National Socialism, which earned him rebuke from the party. He mounted a "secret resistance" to the movement.[59] His opposition to liberal and communist metaphysics does not imply support for Nazi metaphysics. There can be authentic "thrown projections" from the depths of fundamental ontology that are not reducible to Nazism. Even if his errors in supporting Hitler's regime are unforgiveable, his attempts to move past its metaphysical attitudes are undeniable.

Dallmayr has argued that Heidegger sought to overcome the dominant ideologies of liberalism, communism, and nationalism (Nazism and Fascism) and thereby to clear "a space for innovative thinking and for that basic questioning that [for Heidegger] is the lifeblood of philosophy and also the genuine sine qua non of humanity."[60] But that is precisely the stated aim of Dugin's fourth political theory. If certain acts of thinking characterize us as human, and if the horizons for such acts have been artificially, or "being-historically" constrained, should

---

59 Richard Polt, "Beyond Struggle and Power: Heidegger's Secret Resistance," *Interpretation* 35, No. 1 (2007): 11–40.

60 Fred Dallmayr, "Heidegger's *Notebooks*: A Smoking Gun?" in *Reading Heidegger's Black Notebooks 1931–1941* edited by Farin and Malpas (Cambridge: MIT Press, 2016): 25.

not any expansion of those horizons, such as Heidegger and Dugin provide, be met with gratitude? Dugin thinks so: "I really do not understand," he writes, "why certain people, when confronted with the concept of the Fourth Political Theory, do not immediately rush to open a bottle of champagne, and do not start dancing and rejoicing, celebrating the discovery of new possibilities."[61]

Nothing guarantees that prudence will characterize the political dimension of those newly disclosed possibilities. Nothing guarantees that it won't. If the details can be devilish, they can also be humane and even angelic. Much depends not only on the details, but also on us.

Is it possible to combine an extended Heideggerianism with liberal democracy such that both the philosophical merits of the former and the political merits of the latter are preserved? Emphatically, this question is not equivalent to the liberal *fides quarens intellectum*, in which liberal democratic theorists seek to construct a foundation or justification for a given set of political commitments. However, although one might repudiate the servility of philosophy implied by such aims, philosophy can after all "serve" without being merely servile. From the perspective of inceptual thought, it shouldn't fall into subservience. But that does not mean it must be a-servient. The combination question avoids both extremes.

If "neo-Eurasianism" is in part the name of the Russian political project of the Fourth Political Theory, there are as yet unnamed programs for its enactment elsewhere. That follows from Dugin's models. The interaction between Da and Sein differs at least as a function of Da, even holding Sein constant. And Sein may hypothetically be held variable.

The cutting edge of Dugin's extended Heideggerianism is his twenty-plus volume *Noomahia* series of books.[62] There, not Sein, to

---

61 Dugin, *The Fourth Political Theory*, 35.

62 Alexander Dugin, *Noomahia: Wars of the Intellect: Volume One — Three Logoi: Apollo, Dionysus, Cybele* [Russian] (Moscow: Academic Project, 2014).

be sure, but Logos is held variable. Dugin identifies three logoi — the Apollonian, the Dionysian, and the Cybelene — and posits their structural universality. Each comprises a spectrum, with the Apollonian merging into the Dionysian and the Dionysian blending with the Cybelene at the transition points. In his culturological analysis, the three logoi are treated as ideal types: in reality, all three tend to coexist, but in different proportions, which change in time. This "vertical" dimension interpenetrates a horizontal one, the methodological principles of the study of which are outlined in the second volume.[63] The spatialities interpenetrated by the multiplicity of logoi are diverse, complex, and variable; their planar angle may vary. If we slightly misleadingly but still illustratively identify the vertical dimension with Sein and the horizontal one with Da, then Dugin's series gives us both the method for the study of political plurality based on extended Heideggerianism and some of its results (most volumes study particular civilizational logoi, e.g. the Iranian logos, the Serbian logos, etc.).

It is probable that at least some building blocks for a philosophically extended liberal democracy can be discovered in the methodological texts and relevant case studies of that series. At a simpler level, Dugin's suggestion that a Heideggerian deepening of liberal individualism could proceed through a renewal of the mystical traditions of Eckhart and others also tends in that direction.[64] The point is that the project of a combination of the two commitments — to inceptual philosophy and to liberal democracy — need not produce either the artificial servility of philosophy or the unwanted destruction of liberal democracy. The positive experiment of "liberalism and the Fourth Political Theory" can be justified and is promising. In admittedly different political circumstances, Dugin's antipathies towards Zionism

---

63 Alexander Dugin, *Noomahia: Wars of the Intellect: Volume Two — Geosophy: Horizons and Civilizations* [Russian] (Moscow: Academic Project, 2017).

64 Lauren Southern, "Aleksandr Dugin on Millenials, Modernity and Religion," Filmed 2018. Youtube video, 1:12:57. Posted June 2018. https://www.youtube.com/watch?v=sl2--OHvxK4.

have not been an obstacle for the positive experiment of "Zionism and the Fourth Political Theory."[65] I therefore suggest that the first way out of the impasse is precisely to attend to the possibilities of a fourth-political-theoretic liberalism.

At least two other options should be considered. First, it may be worthwhile to consider the question of whether more significant adjustments to liberal democracy must be made to bring it into greater consistency with the discoveries of inceptual thought and extended Heideggerianism. Second, incompatibilities between the political and the philosophical in our case, and the inability of extended Heideggerianism to speak constructively to our political situation, may be taken as a *reductio ad absurdum* of the initial prejudices and presuppositions of this project.

In the most extreme case, the profoundest "significant adjustment" to liberal democracy that could be undertaken is its upending through a political revolution based on a philosophical one. If Burke could criticize the French revolutionaries for their lack of good sense in rejecting the past *in toto* and desiring to inaugurate their own new beginning from year zero, the conservative revolution of an extended Heideggerianism, given its fundamental ontology of time, could not but ground itself—indeed it must do so—at least in part, in the "heritage" of the "Volk" effecting the revolution. This heritage must be not horizontal, stemming from the temporal past, but "vertical," arising as it were from proximity to the primordial.

It is impossible to describe this option as a plausible alternative. Not only is its desirability absolutely unclear, its preconditions are unreachably remote. Both Heidegger and Dugin are highly critical—Heidegger more consistently than Dugin—of the attempt to

---

65 Michael Millerman, "An Experiment in Jewish Heideggerianism: Zionism and the Fourth Political Theory," presented at the 2018 Center for Jewish Studies Graduate Conference at the University of Toronto. Available at https://www.academia.edu/36170072/An_Experiment_in_Jewish_Heideggerianism_Zionism_and_the_Fourth_Political_Theory.

operationalize philosophical inquiry politically.[66] Heidegger, as we saw, recognizes that whatever effect inceptual thinking might have is an incalculable matter resting with "the future ones" who "ground" the new beginning. His failed attempt to reconfigure the university inceptually caused him great consternation and redoubled his doubts about the prospects of a philosophico-political revolution.[67]

To call for the political overthrow of liberal democracy, as a liberal democrat, within a liberal democracy, is, on Heideggerian grounds, woefully ridiculous. It is pure machination to try to operationalize and institute philosophical discoveries at this stage. Such "discoveries" are far from won or absorbed. Nowhere near enough time has passed for us to catch a glimpse of what the authentic interplay of Da and Sein portends in our circumstances even if we do assume that basic insights have been gained — and they haven't been. For us, any notion of a fundamental ontological anti-liberal revolution is a preposterous fraud.

Dugin has written that, lacking extended Heideggerianism's attitude towards time, Russia's conservative parties are nothing but simulacra.[68] Moreover, he argues, it is senseless to imagine what the political implementation of that attitude might be, because once it has become so prominent as to make its implementation feasible, everything will have transformed to such an extent that the projections of the thought experiment will have long since ceased to apply.

Though it is not obvious how to square them with his political activities or politicized interpretation of Heidegger, these reflections apply *a fortiori* in the liberal democratic case. It is at least an old tradition in Russia to speculate in a philosophical theology about Russia's

---

66 Dugin, *The Rise of the Fourth Political Theory*, 13.

67 Heidgger, *Ponderings II–VI: Black Notebooks 1931–1938* (Bloomington: Indiana University Press, 2014): 86, 92–8, 102, 108, 109, 112–20. "It is time to call off the semblant revolution of the university" (108).

68 Dugin, *The Rise of the Fourth Political Theory*, 13.

unique identity and its place in the world.[69] If *there* the institution-alization of an extended Heideggerianism at best proceeds haltingly with caution, *here* it is best to remain silent about it and thus to spare ourselves the removal of all doubt concerning our foolishness. What can be ventured is a modest hope that a space can still be found in the constituted space of the regime for a philosophical inquiry that refuses to sell its conscience for silver.

Perhaps the greater risk to liberal democracy, when seen from within, comes not from too much but from too little philosophy. Can inquiry lead us astray? Can it lead us into error? Into confusion? Can it turn good people off the path of noble action toward contemplation and embolden dangerous minds to become politically active in undesirable ways? Yes, it can do all of that, and it should therefore be handled responsibly. But what is the alternative? When a citizen travels abroad, he may find political orders there more desirable to himself than his domestic ones, and he may agitate for reform or revolution upon return. Should we forbid travel? Who can travel more easily and see more comprehensively than the reader of a good book? Should we banish literature? No one is arguing for a total Heidegger ban. Yet hostility grows in some quarters, indifference in others. Ultimately, however, liberal democracy cannot be a humanizing regime if its hostility or indifference to philosophy dulls the human to the call of being.

But to *promote* philosophical reflection, is that not machination? Is it the fate of fundamental questioning to face hostility or indifference? Is it its destiny to win ground only imperceptibly and by ages?

It was said above that the enterprise of starting with a prejudice for inceptual thought and failing to arrive at any constructive political conclusions may be read as *reductio ad absurdum*. This project did not fail to produce a positive result. It showed how Strauss, Rorty, and Derrida, as well as Dugin, may all profitably be read as responding

---

69   Alyssa Deblasio, *The End of Russian Philosophy: Tradition and Transition at the Turn of the 21st Century* (New York: Palgrave Macmillan, 2014).

to Heidegger, and that their responses are often politically constitutive. The insight that Strauss's project of political moderation is in part dialectically related to Heidegger's musings on the status of the idea of the good in Plato is not a meaningless discovery. It amounts to a demonstration of why the defense of natural right is incompatible with open philosophizing about nature, about the ideas: natural right stands on the shaky ground of a "history" that many Straussians hardly fathom. The project also showed that Heidegger can be reinterpreted and redeployed optimistically, as Rorty has done, but at a cost. So the claim that it amounts to a *reductio ad absurdum* is not applicable to its positive result in sorting out a range of politically relevant, philosophically informed responses to Heidegger by a group of political theorists.

But is it applicable to the prejudice in favor of inceptual thinking and its political dimensions, whatever they might be? Heideggerian political philosophy does not address many issues that it would seem political thought should address. It does not suggest how tax dollars should be spent or what tax rates should be. It doesn't take a position on school choice. It is uncomfortably aloof from the general topic of law. It speaks much more of "being" than of human rights, but not so much about it that it includes basic human "well-being" in its purview. Is it absurd after all to argue that inceptual thought carries with it something like a constitution of the political even though *responses and objections* to it might do so? Does not the paucity of its *political* content and its apparent indifference to *politics* render the approach absurd and recommend that its presuppositions be dropped or at least supplemented?

Yes and no. A prejudice in favor of inceptual thought and the idea of the philosophical constitution of the political are surely not enough for an adequate account of political things. This project has suggested a few ways of supplementing Heidegger without rejecting him. In the Strauss chapter, I mentioned the work of Gregory Bruce Smith. Unlike some Straussians, Smith acknowledged that Straussianism cannot return to a philosophically naïve, pre-Heideggerian attitude, but must rather find ways to read Strauss with Heidegger, not against him. He proposes approaching Strauss's late studies of Socrates and Xenophon as a political phenomenology. Those studies are not laden with philosophical jargon. They do not speak of the "existential" of "everydayness" but they do illuminate commonly recurring themes and attitudes of political life as expressed in the lives and reflections of those historical characters. In short, Smith's Heideggerianized Strauss may offer a political supplement to Heidegger that need not be inconsistent with Heidegger.

We can also extend Heidegger using Rorty, so long as we bracket Rorty's groundless commitment to social democracy. There is room to combine what Rorty called Heidegger's nostalgia for lost origins with a rich literature that depicts a great range of human political potentialities and conveys a political education. Given Russia's long tradition of regarding philosophy as literature and vice versa, we can surely turn to Russian authors for a literary extension of Heideggerianism, which can consist of either new literature or the philosophically informed study of existing classics.[70]

Although we only scratched the inexhaustible surface of a select handful of Derrida's writings, doing so showed that we can experiment with extensions of Heidegger in the direction of mystical political theology. Although such extensions are further from everyday political things than Strauss's Socratic studies or Russian philosophical literature, they at least have the benefit of bringing us closer to such themes as "the heart," treated by mystic theologians though not by Heidegger. The theme of "the heart" is undoubtedly of tremendous significance for political reflection, so an extension in its direction is welcome.[71] And we also saw the richness of Derrida's approach in his sympathetic writing on "Heidegger's ear," as well, in a reflection that touched upon

---

70 Deblasio, *The End of Russian Philosophy.*

71 Dietrich von Hildebrand, *The Heart: An Analysis of Human and Divine Affectivity* (South Bend, Ind.: St. Augustine's Press, 2007).

friendship and enmity, the harmony of belonging and the dissonance of the foreign, and the useful notion of the "topolitological."

Finally, while Dugin's own work in political theory remains deeply indebted to Heidegger, his broad Russian *razmakh* embraces a myriad of other fields, approaches, and thinkers, and then works to see where and how coordination with Heidegger's philosophy is possible.

It is absurd to expect a comprehensive political philosophy from Heidegger if we do nothing to bring him closer to political reflections of a Socratic or Xenophonic type, to the richness of the human experience as expressed in great literature, to our religious depths as plumbed by mystics of every tradition, and to everything that other fields of inquiry into human affairs have to offer. The task is to undertake these enriching extensions without rushing to extend what has hardly been gained, and, when we do venture forth, without losing ourselves and again forgetting the fundamental, constitutive dimension of human existence disclosed by Heidegger.

OTHER BOOKS PUBLISHED BY ARKTOS

OTHER BOOKS PUBLISHED BY ARKTOS

OTHER BOOKS PUBLISHED BY ARKTOS

OTHER BOOKS PUBLISHED BY ARKTOS

Made in United States
North Haven, CT
25 March 2024

50495919R00181